THREE MEN IN A GARDEN

STEFAN BUCZACKI · CLAY JONES · GEOFFREY SMITH

THREE MEN
IN A GARDEN
A PERSONAL GUIDE TO GARDENING

BBC PUBLICATIONS

Published by BBC Publications
A division of BBC Enterprises Ltd
35 Marylebone High Street, London W1M 4AA

First published 1986
© Dr Stefan Buczacki, Clay Jones, Geoffrey Smith 1986

ISBN 0 563 20491 5

Typeset in 9/11pt Century Schoolbook by Ace Filmsetting Ltd, Frome
Printed in England by W. S. Cowells Ltd, Ipswich

CONTENTS

PREFACE

Over the years that we have known each other and worked together, we have shared gardening experiences and gardening ideas. We have visited gardens and talked gardening up and down the land. We have exchanged plants and opinions and have been privileged, through 'Gardeners' Question Time', to share a great deal with you (although not, sadly, the plants!). We have been and continue to be extremely fortunate in enjoying each other's company and although we have each come into gardening from very different backgrounds, this has worked to our advantage. In facing audiences and questions week in and week out right across the phenomenally wide spectrum of gardening, we feel we have learned to appreciate just what gardeners, both experienced and not so experienced, really need to know. Thus it was that we decided to share a little more and write this very personal guide to gardening not just as we preach it but as we practise it.

Of course, we each have our favourites among garden plants and our favourites among the many facets of gardening. Rather than try to concoct a pot-pourri therefore, Stefan wielded his authority as overworked and unpaid Editor and Compiler, and decided to carve up the subject and apportion the various chapters, as far as possible, to those whose experience and tastes best fitted them. It has meant give and take; Geoffrey was saddled with modern roses because Stefan clung so tenaciously to old ones. Clay was planted firmly in his vegetable plot so that Geoffrey could roam through his alpines. Unfortunately, Geoffrey's alpines also swallowed his garden pool and Stefan was left, quite literally, to carry the can. But as compensation for being locked out of his greenhouse by Clay, he was given the entire fruit garden and lawn to indulge himself. Because it is a personal book and because no garden (or even three gardens combined) can ever be comprehensive, you may find a particular plant missing from our pages. This may be because we don't like it or because experience has pointed us to a better alternative. But you may be quite sure of one thing; every plant, tool, technique and tip in this book is there because we have used them and tried them. And we don't know of many other modern gardening books quite as personal as that.

I

SOILS & FERTILISERS

Stefan Buczacki

I have never known which old gardener first propounded the notion that 'the answer lies in the soil' (it certainly wasn't Clay or Geoffrey, old as they are), but with regard to a great deal of gardening's problems he was probably right. The world of the soil is a wonderful world and men could and, indeed, have, spent a lifetime trying to unravel its mysteries. I would not willingly condemn *you* to a life with your head in the soil, but nor should you bury it in the sand, turn a blind eye or adopt any other appropriate metaphor of ignorance. A modest understanding of what happens beneath your feet will add greatly to the efficiency and interest of your gardening.

You don't garden for long before you realise that soils are very variable in many respects but the most important features of which you should be aware are the advantages and disadvantages of acid and alkaline soil, of heavy and light soil and, implicit in the latter, of sand, loam and clay. First, therefore, the difference between an acid and an alkaline soil.

Acidity and alkalinity are measured on a scale called pH. It ranges from 1 (very acidic) to 14 (very alkaline), the mid-point of 7 being called neutral, but your garden soil is almost certain to lie somewhere between 4 and 8.5. Generally, the pH of a soil is dictated by the type of rock or other local materials from which it is derived; the soil of pH 4 will comprise moss peat and little else whereas that of pH 8.5 is very probably a thin soil overlying chalk rock. Different plants prefer soils of different pH and the vegetation growing naturally or in other gardens in your area may give a good indication of the local conditions. Rhododendrons and azaleas, heather, bracken and oak and birch woods suggest an acid soil while old man's beard (clematis), the polypody fern and ash woods are good indicators of alkalinity. You can also gain an indication of soil pH quite simply by using one of the test kits available from garden centres; but do take a good range of samples and don't expect the results to be very accurate. Having discovered the pH of your soil, what action should you take? If the soil is highly acid and you plan to grow acid-loving plants, clearly the answer is nothing, but most vegetables, fruit and flowers grow best in a soil just on the acid side of neutral, about pH 6.5. This provides conditions in which the majority of plants take up nutrients most efficiently. None the less, whilst it is possible to raise the pH of an acid soil by adding appropriate amounts of lime (see the graph on p.12), it is well nigh impossible to lower the pH of a highly alkaline soil. Adding large quantities of peat will help, but ultimately you should follow the old advice and 'go with your soil'; choose plants tolerant of high pH and make use of the chemical sequestrene at the start of each season. This contains the element iron in a form that plants can absorb in alkaline conditions – one of the major problems of chalky soils is that plants cannot take up iron naturally and hence are unable to manufacture the green colouring material chlorophyll. They grow inefficiently and turn yellowish as a result.

Heaviness and lightness of soil are expressions of its texture – the relative

proportions that it contains of sand, silt and clay. Pick up a few crumbs of soil and moisten them between your finger and thumb (what I really mean is spit on them). A soil with a large proportion of sand will feel gritty while one with a large proportion of clay will be greasy. A soil with a high proportion of clay (called, not surprisingly, a clayey soil) is likely to be heavy and laborious to dig, sticky when wet, liable to waterlogging in winter yet prone to set into brick-like clods when dry. None the less, because clay particles attract and hold nutrients, releasing them slowly for plants to use, such a soil is potentially fertile. To render it easier to work (in other words, to improve, not its texture, but its structure), no one, to my mind, has yet produced a better answer than organic matter and more organic matter, dug in thoroughly. It is hard, back-breaking work but it will, ultimately, pay you wonderful dividends. In individual cases, I am prepared to believe that adding sand, gypsum or even lime will have some benefit but in general it must be muck.

A sandy soil, by contrast, is light and easy to dig, free-draining but relatively deficient in nutrients, a situation compounded because any fertilisers added are rapidly washed or leached away by rain. But by one of those ironies of which a gardener's life is so full, a sandy soil, like a clayey soil, is also improved with

Acid soils, like these New Forest heaths (above) *provide ideal conditions for rhododendrons and others of the most choice garden shrubs* (below)

Limestone soils support a wonderful array of wild flowers (above) *just as a chalky garden soil can be turned to splendid advantage* (below)

organic matter, in this instance because the sand particles are bound together to help form soil crumbs by the natural glues present in the organic material which also adds its sponge-like properties to the enhancement of water retention.

I have referred to organic matter (and we shall all, time and again throughout the book, refer to it again), but organic matter comes in many different forms – garden compost, farmyard and stable manures, pulverised or shredded bark, seaweed, mushroom compost, shoddy, hop waste and, of course, peat. What, you will wonder, are their relative merits? As additions to soil for the reasons I have outlined above, they are all essentially similar, although I would add the proviso that any organic matter that is largely undecomposed (strawy manure or fresh seaweed, for instance), should be composted before digging in or, at least, only dug into the soil in the autumn. The reason I advise this is because the material will begin to decompose *in situ* and inevitably deplete the nitrogen of the surrounding region as it does so. It is much better, therefore, if the nitrogen is that supplied in an accelerator to a compost heap, rather than being taken from the valuable nutrients in your garden soil. There is, however, another side to organic manures and composts, besides their simple, physical bulk.

11

Most bulky manures, composts and similar organic materials, with the major exceptions of bark and peat, contain at least some plant nutrients; some, but not a very great deal and almost invariably less than 1 per cent of the major nutrients that all plants require. These major nutrients are nitrogen (N), phosphate (P) and potash (K), of the greatest importance respectively for leafy growth, for flower and fruit development and for root formation. Remember that the typical, balanced, general purpose fertiliser called Growmore contains 7 per cent of each, and more specialised fertilisers even more. Organic materials also contain greater or lesser amounts of minor or trace elements (seaweed is especially high in them), but I believe that the significance of these is often overstated, for most soils already contain ample reserves. Thus, whilst manure or composts will supply some nutrients to your plants, you will be a rare and very lucky gardener indeed if you can manage with them alone.

We now come to the subject of specific fertilisers; a topic with more than its fair share of contentious argument between gardeners, even (or do I mean especially?) between these three! There are several ways of considering fertiliser types and you will see them described as organic or inorganic, slow-release or quick-acting, solid or liquid and see them used as root or foliar feeds. How do you find your way through this maze of nomenclature and decide which to choose? An organic fertiliser is one derived from some once-living organism; their names, like hoof and horn, bone-meal and dried blood, betray this. An inorganic fertiliser is derived from somewhere else, which may be a chemical factory but might equally be a hole in the ground. Organic fertilisers frequently contain minor or trace elements which some gardeners believe to confer additional merit. Inorganic fertilisers are sometimes said to be washed from the soil more readily, to contaminate rivers and other watercourses and to cause despoiling of the environment in their manufacture or extraction. These are sweeping generalisations but contain some valid arguments. Ultimately, it is for each individual gardener to decide, for moral, economic or other reasons, which he chooses to buy and use but I do feel strongly that there is no intrinsic value in trying to argue that either organic or inorganic fertilisers give better results simply because they *are* organic or inorganic— each category contains too wide a range of substances, manufactured or prepared in too wide a range of ways for this to be valid.

And so to the other categories of fertiliser which cut across the organic/inorganic division. A slow-release fertiliser breaks down slowly in the soil to liberate nutrients over a long period of time. It is useful at planting time or early in the season therefore. A quick-acting fertiliser gives very rapid response when it is needed at the height of the growing season; while applying such a fertiliser as a liquid, and especially as a foliar feed, gives the fastest response of all.

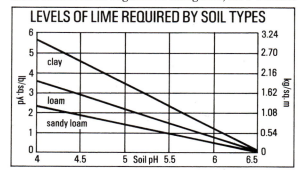

LEVELS OF LIME REQUIRED BY SOIL TYPES

By adding different amounts of lime to different types of acid soil, the pH can be raised to 6.5, the most suitable value for most garden plants

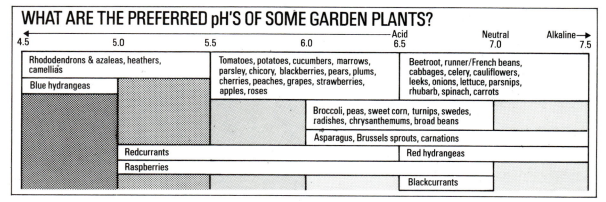

WHAT ARE THE PREFERRED pH'S OF SOME GARDEN PLANTS?

4.5	5.0	5.5	6.0	Acid 6.5	Neutral 7.0	Alkaline → 7.5
Rhododendrons & azaleas, heathers, camellias			Tomatoes, potatoes, cucumbers, marrows, parsley, chicory, blackberries, pears, plums, cherries, peaches, grapes, strawberries, apples, roses		Beetroot, runner/French beans, cabbages, celery, cauliflowers, leeks, onions, lettuce, parsnips, rhubarb, spinach, carrots	
Blue hydrangeas						
			Broccoli, peas, sweet corn, turnips, swedes, radishes, chrysanthemums, broad beans			
			Asparagus, Brussels sprouts, carnations			
	Redcurrants			Red hydrangeas		
	Raspberries					
			Blackcurrants			

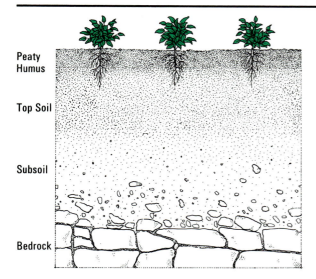

Peaty
Humus

Top Soil

Subsoil

Bedrock

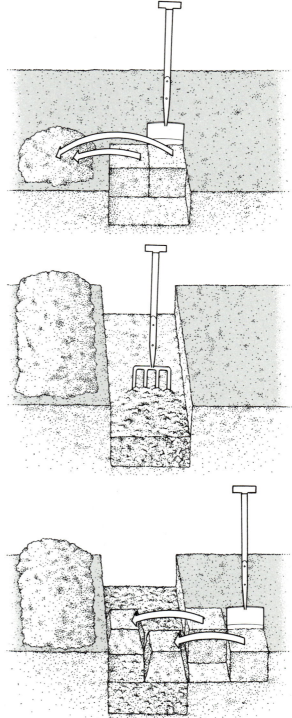

above, *A profile shows the layers of your soil*

right, *Double digging entails cultivating the soil to two spades' depth but ensures that each layer is returned to its original position*

I often draw the analogy between fertilisers and headache cures; the soluble aspirin gives the fastest results because it is much more rapidly taken into the body's tissues. Out of the innumerable fertilisers available however, and bearing in mind the considerations I have outlined, which do I use? I have the following short list of basics that I find satisfies 90 per cent of my fertiliser requirements and which I commend strongly:

A solid formulation of a balanced or other general purpose feed such as Growmore or Fish, Blood and Bone (the latter being Clay's staple diet!).

A balanced liquid fertiliser for general feeding during the growing season. One of the most popular contains N, P and K in the ratio 10:10:27, with additional trace elements.

A liquid tomato fertiliser containing a high proportion of potash for swift results on rapidly growing, flowering and fruiting plants.

A lawn fertiliser for spring use that contains a high proportion of nitrogen.

Sterilised bone-meal as a slow-release source of phosphate to aid root development; this is especially valuable when planting out perennials, but do note

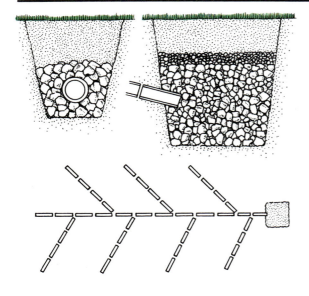

above, *Lay drainage pipes on beds of small stones in a herringbone pattern of trenches dug 60 cm deep and sloping gently to a 1 metre deep soakaway*

that steamed bone-flour is not the same substance. It is quicker acting and, unlike bone-meal, contains no nitrogen.

Finally, however, before we actually begin some gardening, I must add a word about what in polite circles is called soil management. Essentially, this means keeping your soil in good heart and health. The additions of organic matter to which I have referred are not once and for all exercises for they need repeating annually. The additions of fertiliser should be maintained as a routine; nitrogen in particular disappears from the soil with alarming rapidity through the action of rain alone, quite apart from the demands that plants place upon it. But it is in the vegetable plot that the soil really has to work for its living. Not only do nutrients disappear very rapidly as fast-growing vegetables use them, but such intensive cropping can provide ideal conditions for pests and diseases to build up in the soil. Hence the reasoning behind crop rotation – changing regularly the position in which particular types of crop are grown. Clay describes a suitable rotation system for the vegetable plot in Chapter 4.

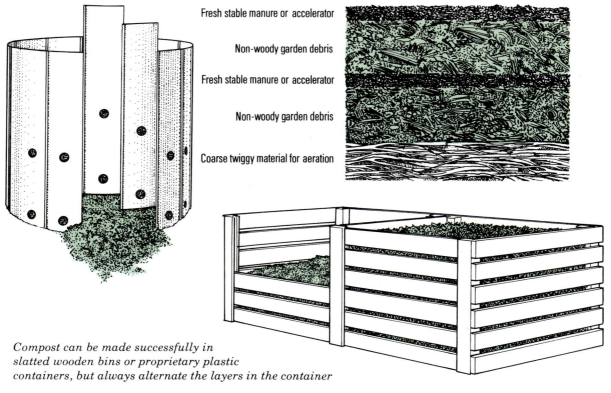

Fresh stable manure or accelerator

Non-woody garden debris

Fresh stable manure or accelerator

Non-woody garden debris

Coarse twiggy material for aeration

Compost can be made successfully in slatted wooden bins or proprietary plastic containers, but always alternate the layers in the container

2

TOOLS FOR THE TASK

Stefan Buczacki

No one can garden without a certain number of tools and appliances but, surprisingly, many gardeners manage with a very small range; the ability to improvise is a great virtue. As with almost any other hobby, it is possible to go to the opposite extreme and collect tools and gadgets as the fisherman collects floats; with no real likelihood that they will actually ever perform any useful function. In selecting the equipment to describe here, therefore, I have ignored the many strange and sometimes ingenious contrivances that have come my way over the years. I have, instead, prepared an inventory of the present contents of my garden, garden shed and greenhouse; an inventory of equipment that I find essential, and I shall base my recommendations on these, elaborating where necessary to include equally good alternatives and those items that I don't use simply because they are inappropriate for my own garden.

Tillage Tools

Tillage tools are those used to handle soil. They all have a business end and a shaft which ends in a handle, the former made from iron, carbon steel or stainless steel and the shaft from some type of metal, plastic or wood. I used to be somewhat critical of stainless steel tools, on the grounds mainly of cost, until I began using them regularly. For ease of maintenance, minimal soil adhesion and that indefinably welcome feel, I now greatly prefer stainless steel spades, forks and trowels, although I still don't minimise the cost. It is much more of a luxury for other tillage tools, however, where carbon steel, at about one-third of the price, is generally adequate. Perhaps it is merely that I have never given them a very thorough trial, or perhaps it is my unfortunate culinary experiences with 'non-stick' frying pans that turn me against tools with a black, plastic coating to the blade. Metal shafts also cause tools to be very heavy, whereas plastic shafts are often too light, too weak and have an unsatisfactory feel. There really is nothing better than ash, either treated for weather protection or sheathed in plastic. Ensure that the socket of forks and spades is forged as one with the blade, not merely riveted, but that the shaft is steel riveted into the socket. Although many older, not to say ancient, gardeners like Geoffrey prefer 'T'-shaped handles, these have largely been superseded with 'D' shapes and I generally find them much more comfortable. The basis of the handle is usually polypropylene, although some still have an ash cross-piece which can loosen, turn annoyingly and trap your fingers.

You will need full-sized tools if you have a large area to dig and especially if you plan to grow vegetables. Otherwise, the smaller and lighter border fork and spade will be adequate and some gardeners manage with these for all tasks.

A shovel is an important member of my gardening inventory but if you can find a large version that is tolerably lightweight you will be lucky. They are available in a range of sizes, so do try several first in order to select one that you can actually lift!

Even if you can't afford the luxury of stainless steel for the larger tools, do try to

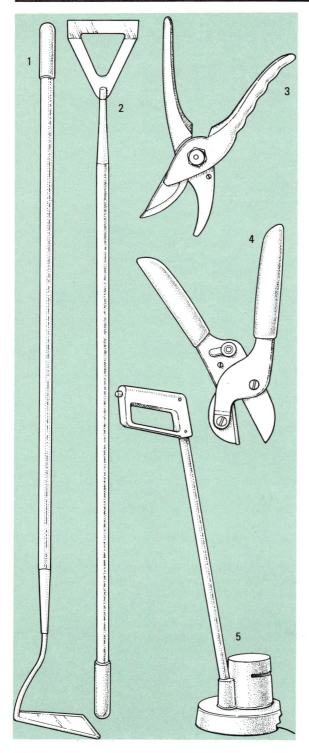

A selection of useful tools for the garden: 1 Swoe; 2 Dutch hoe; 3 Scissor-type secateurs; 4 Anvil-type secateurs; 5 Grass trimmer

treat yourself to a stainless steel, wooden-handled trowel and hand (or weeding) fork. They will 'come to the hand' like no other and, well cared for, will last for a lifetime.

Given a modicum of dry weather, a Dutch hoe is an essential weeding appliance. There are modern variants on the traditional pattern but the only one that impresses me is the swoe, a version shaped rather like a golfer's putter, which enables you to reach around the back of growing plants. A draw hoe will be needed for the vegetable garden but can be dispensed with elsewhere. A metal rake is a valuable tool and should have about twelve teeth, each presenting a slightly flattened face for efficiency of drawing action. The most recent introduction to the range of cultivating tools is the long-handled weeding fork; not essential by any means, but very useful for working the soil among herbaceous borders rather than actually digging up anything.

Two essential appliances for the lawn are a spring-tined lawn rake (the masochist's tool) and a half-moon lawn edger. I find a surprising number of other uses around the garden for the latter; it is also one of those exceptions where I find the 'T'-shaped handle is easiest to use. Finally, useful, but again not essential, is a bulb planter that enables a plug of soil or turf to be removed to a depth of about 15 cm (6 inches)*.

Cutting Tools

Whilst every garden has soil and needs some tillage tools, the range of cutting appliances necessary depends very much on the types of plant that you grow. Almost everyone will need secateurs but the choice is very large; one alone of the leading manufacturers offers at least ten different patterns. Always buy the best that you can afford and check the thickness of stem it is designed to cut; nothing so swiftly damages secateurs as trying to cut through wood too thick and twisting them in consequence. My own preference is for a scissor rather than an anvil action, for this is much less likely to bruise soft tissues; but a cheap pair of scissor-type secateurs is next to useless and you must be prepared to pay accordingly. For larger stems on larger shrubs and trees,

*We have given both metric and imperial measurements throughout the book. The conversions are for guidance and are therefore approximate rather than exact.

1 D-shaped handle; 2 T-shaped handle; 3 Curved pruning saw; 4 L-tines for a cultivator; 5 Slasher tines for a cultivator

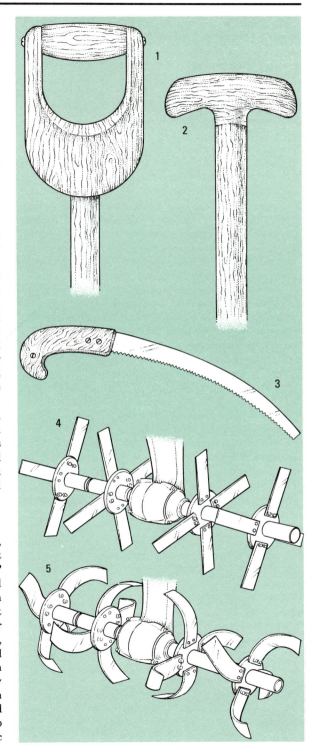

you will need loppers; again, I prefer a scissor action, and also the versions with extra-long handles for additional leverage. Regular pruning tasks in the garden will demand a pruning saw also; the curved forms are extremely useful but seem to be less readily available now, other than with the infamous black coating. A bow saw is always handy but you will need a large and continuing involvement with trees to need long-arm pruners, rope saws or chain saws.

Hedges, like lawns, positively demand attention, but shears, like secateurs, come in bewildering variety. The very best have blades about 20 cm (8 inches) long, cushioned hand grips and stops, adjustment for shearing force and a notched blade to cope with thicker shoots. My distaste for black plastic coatings which wear away in time, prompts me to choose chromed steel. Long-handled lawn shears are certainly a boon in saving your back but economy in buying them is false economy for the handles flex annoyingly on cheaper versions. If you can't afford the best, use normal hand shears and exercise your spine. Lawn edging shears, with the blades turned vertically through 90 degrees, are essential to give your lawn a completed look after mowing.

Most other cutting tools like scythes, slashers, sickles and billhooks will only interest you if you garden on a rural estate but a good pocket knife is invaluable; never mind the optional corkscrews and assorted contrivances for removing boy scouts from horses' hooves – put your money into a good steel blade.

Powered and Wheeled Tools

Anything for an easy life, if not exactly a quiet one, must be most gardeners' approach to power tools. But do they, in practice, make things so much easier? Powered lawn mowers most assuredly do and I shall refer to them and to other specialised lawn appliances in more detail in Chapter 12. But what about the others? I resisted buying a hedge trimmer for a long time but I now have so much hedge, and, more to the point, some of it once old, farm, field hedge and scarcely the most beautiful boundary in the world, that I found the need irresistible. My trimmer is a mains electric model, although I remain uneasy about long lengths of electric cable draped across the garden; even allowing for fail-safe trip switches and similar devices. Rechargeable electric trimmers are available but annoyingly only offer you about forty-five minutes' worth of cutting per charge. To my mind, if your hedge can be cut within forty-five minutes then you scarcely need a trimmer. I would prefer a petrol driven model were it not for the weight that also seems designed to restrict my arms to about forty-five minutes' worth at a time. But, for my yew hedges and certainly for the box topiary it is shears every time.

I also have an electric grass trimmer; a flail-like cutting tool at the end of a long handle for dealing with rough grass and similar areas. Mine is a modest model with a whirling nylon cord that gradually wears away and requires replacing from time to time (it is possible to rewind these yourself and I conjure up a vision of the modern rustic couple by the winter fireside; she with her knitting, he rethreading his trimmer). It is a valuable tool for anyone with rough grass (orchard grass, for instance) and more robust, petrol driven models are available with interchangeable heads that range in cutting power up to a wicked-looking contraption that is, in effect, a circular saw on a stick for even coarser, scrub-like vegetation. These larger models have a sling to spare your arms the weight.

Finally, among the powered category, to a contentious subject, electric or petrol engined rotary cultivators. I don't have one and even if I grew more vegetables than I do now, I wouldn't have one. None the less, I have had occasion to use them extensively and remain in two minds about their value. They perform a coarse cultivation that just about equates with very rough winter digging. They also perform splendidly the role of shredding and dispersing perennial weeds such as couch and, on a clayey soil, they can smear and cause a pan to form below the surface – although this can be circumvented to some degree by using straight 'slasher' rather than 'L'-shaped tines. Yet, given limited time for your gardening and a large vegetable plot or allotment that is basically free from perennial weeds, a rotary cultivator of some sort is probably essential. As with any power tool, do ensure that its engine is powerful enough for the job you have, check the range of optional attachments available and do ask for an opportunity to try one first. A surprising number of people, for lack of strength, dexterity, balance or other reason, never really learn to master a cultivator and I have seen many a gardener veering crazily across his allotment as he wrestled with a wayward machine.

Hardly powered, but at least wheeled, is a wheel-

barrow. Plastic models are available but my general and personal aversion to plastic prompts me to choose metal. The fairly recent introduction of roller-style wheels has proved useful on soft or wet ground and a traditional pneumatic tyre is an improvement over solid rubber. If you have a greenhouse, large shed, gate or archway to negotiate, do take a tape measure with you when you buy your barrow to check its width! You will find little use for a garden roller although a leaf sweeper is a boon if you have a large lawn in a wooded neighbourhood. Electric leaf blowers are now readily available too and the commonly-held belief that they disperse the leaves over the whole garden is far from true as they are surprisingly easy and accurate to direct.

Cloches are among the most underused of garden appliances but are invaluable for pre-warming the soil before sowing and for extending the growing season of many different types of vegetables. The modern version of the barn cloche (above) *is robust and gives good ground coverage although they are fairly expensive. The various types of plastic tunnel cloche* (left and far left) *represent excellent value although the so-called umbrella cloche* (above left)*, a modern equivalent of the old bell cloche, can be inconvenient to use.*

Propagating Equipment

The choice between clay pots and plastic pots has been largely resolved by the immeasurably lower cost of plastic. It does, however, have disadvantages; it is virtually non-porous and can give rise to problems of root asphyxiation if watering isn't carefully regulated. Although much lighter than clay pots, plastic is less robust when full and, picked up by one edge, will annoyingly part company with it, like a lizard with its tail. None the less, they are generally more durable (you only drop a clay pot once), and easier to clean thoroughly. Plastic now reigns supreme among seed trays too; wooden bloater boxes, regrettably like the bloaters they contained, are

largely things of the past and, for ease of washing and disinfecting, plastic has no rival.

At its simplest, a propagator need be no more than a seed tray covered with a plastic bag to retain moisture but one with a rigid, clear plastic cover is much more convenient. Always choose a version with small ventilators that permit you to regulate the moisture content of the atmosphere inside. Larger propagators comprise a covered container in which several seed boxes can be placed but seeds and cuttings need warmth as well as moisture so the ability to provide some additional heat is an enormous advantage. The most basic heating aids are flat pads containing heating elements, which are either placed inside the seed

19

A cold frame, with a top formed from an old greenhouse window frame is readily home-made

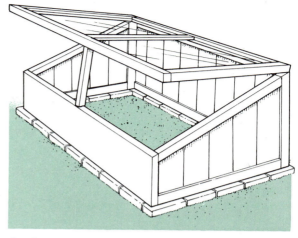

tray (and are, therefore, inefficient in that they cannot be reused until the tray is finished with), or are placed beneath several separate seed trays. The better types have thermostatic control and I have been especially impressed with the system I use now, which comprises low-voltage heating pads that operate through a mains transformer. This method is very much more versatile than the more complex propagators which have heating elements in the base and individual thermostats.

Cloches are perhaps the most underused of gardening aids. They are, in effect, miniature greenhouses and, although most frequently employed for extending the vegetable cropping season, they are invaluable for warming the soil before planting or sowing many outdoor plants. For cloches to use over individual plants, my preference lies with glass barn cloches, supported by a metal frame, but I accept that this may be because I am a traditionalist and that mine were given to me (although excellent, they are very expensive and can be fiddly to erect). Cheaper glass cloches can be made by buying separately sets of metal clips and sheets of glass (remember to ask for horticultural glass), but perhaps the best answer for individual cloches at a relatively low price is to use the various types composed of semi-rigid clear plastic sheets, supported in different ways with wire hoops. Plastic sheeting, supported by hoops (in effect, small tunnels), certainly represents the cheapest form of cloche for long runs such as you might use for vegetables, and it may just be that I am unusual in finding them fiddly too.

The cold frame is an essential adjunct to the greenhouse for hardening off plants before they are subjected to the rigours of the great outdoors, but it also has a valuable role to play in its own right for extending the cropping season of lettuce, for example, or for raising cucumbers, melons and other slightly tender crops. Many, perhaps most, cold frames, including mine, are home-made with glazed wooden window lights supported on a simple wooden frame. Wooden and aluminium cold frames can be bought but, large enough to be practical, these are fairly expensive and the construction of a basic cold frame should be within the scope of any handyman. Ensure, with bought or home-made models, that the lid can be raised, propped open to varying degrees, or removed entirely. A size of $1\frac{3}{4}$ m × $1\frac{1}{4}$ m (about 5 by 4 feet) should suffice for most gardens, but don't skimp on depth – 45 cm (18 inches) at the back is not too much.

Watering Systems

Not so long ago, a gardening watering system meant little more than a disgusting, black, rubber hose-pipe that left you with filthy hands. Now a clean, green, plastic hose is merely the core of a system that can include sprinklers, variable nozzles, trickle irrigation systems for the greenhouse, and even a microprocessor-controlled computer that can switch the water supply on and off for predetermined lengths of time at preprogrammed intervals; connected to a soil moisture sensor, it can even make up its own mind whether or not water is needed. I am still experimenting with such a computer and, combined with the trickle lines, it looks very promising for my holiday prospects; I may be able to leave the greenhouse in safe hands at last. I must advise you to decide early in your gardening life which of the leading brands of watering system you wish to buy because fittings for one can, very irritatingly, not work on another.

With any other than a very modest length of hose, I would most strongly commend a 'through-feed' reel that obviates the need to unwind the whole for each use. They are considerably more expensive than simple reels but, once used, they will count among the garden indispensables.

Sprinklers for lawns and other garden watering tasks are available in three main forms; the simple nozzle-constriction, fountain style with a soil spear for anchorage, the rotating arm pattern (sometimes working on a pulse principle) and the oscillating device. The given order of the three represents increasing cost and increasing coverage. Before you buy a sprinkler, therefore, pace out the size of your lawn or other area to be watered and check the coverage offered (which should be quoted on all good brands). Check with your water authority too; you may be in an area of low water pressure, which will restrict your choice of equipment and you may require a permit before using a sprinkler of any sort.

Even if you subscribe to the no-chemical school of gardening, you will need some form of sprayer; if only to direct soapy water at your greenflies. As with hose systems, there has been a minor revolution in the spraying business. They are not easy things to try out in a shop, for obvious reasons, although a garden centre might be more obliging. This is unfortunate, for even some quite costly sprayers have annoying dry areas in the middle of the pattern of coverage. For a really large garden, you may need to consider a knapsack style of sprayer but, whatever type you use, always wash it very thoroughly after use and, if you apply weedkillers in this way, always keep one specially for the purpose. The need for keeping weedkilling equipment separate also applies, of course, to watering cans. And do be sure that you can easily carry a two-gallon can before you buy it; many people find them too heavy and should buy a smaller one.

Sundries

To complete your basic gardening equipment, you will need a great many odds and several ends. First, plant supports of various kinds. Bamboo canes are invaluable but it is not often appreciated that they are sold in varying thicknesses as well as lengths, usually expressed as weight in lbs per 100 canes. Green-dyed, split canes, usually called flower sticks, are excellent in giving almost invisible support to weak stems and in marking unobtrusively the whereabouts of dormant bulbs. Various proprietary

devices are also sold for supporting herbaceous perennials but I haven't yet found one that didn't have its drawbacks. Hardwood dahlia stakes find all manner of uses apart from supporting dahlias (for which they are really too massive), and a stock of a few, stout, tree stakes is always valuable in a large garden; choose those that have been pressure-treated with preservative. For tying fairly robust plants such as climbing roses to supports, I have a stock of plastic-coated tying wire, but this must not be used where it will be left in place for more than one season. Then, plastic, belt-style shrub and tree ties are needed that can keep pace with the stem's expansion. For more lightweight tying, I must use miles of jute fillis, raffia and lightweight natural fibre twine. This twine virtually rots away after one season and is ideal for herbaceous perennials. Do join me in resisting like the plague the intrusion into gardens of luminous green polypropylene twine which calls out to you from afar and never rots away, but surfaces, year after year, as you dig out the compost. It is the bad penny of twentieth-century gardening. If you have climbing plants on walls, keep a box of lead-headed nails and vine eyes (metal pegs with a hole at one end) for driving into masonry to support wires.

Lightweight, plastic, fruit-cage netting is always useful to provide temporary bird protection over seed beds or newly-sown lawns, while a good garden line on a spool will be indispensable in the vegetable plot and elsewhere. For your greenhouse, cold frame, fruit store or almost anywhere else you care to place it, a maximum and minimum thermometer is invaluable in telling you exactly how high and how low the

The area of sprinkler coverage is about 50 square metres for oscillating types and a circle of about 120 square metres diameter for the rotating pattern and 60 square metres for the static spray

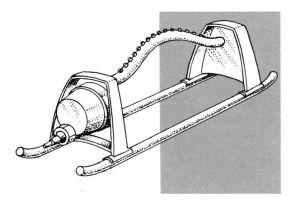

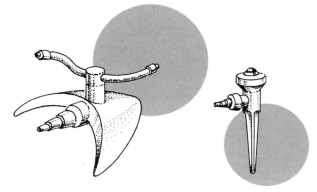

The watering computer brings microchip technology into the garden and enables the water to be turned on and off at predetermined intervals and for measured periods of time

temperature falls and will confirm if any particular spot really is frost free.

Gardeners fall into the labelling and the no-labelling categories; the former generally have poor memories whereas the latter seem to know off by heart the names of every plant in their gardens, know but don't mind if they forget, or never knew and don't care. I confess to being a labeller and I confess to using plastic labels because there really is no durable and inexpensive alternative. But I do have a stock of fairly dark green labels on which I write with a waterproof marker.

And, last of all, a hand lens; one item of equipment that accompanies me everywhere (I was once asked if I took it to bed with me and am still uncertain of the implication behind the question). A lens magnifying ten times is ideal for revealing features of your garden and plants that you didn't even realise existed, but gardeners never seem to know where to buy one. Some large garden centres certainly stock them, and I have seen them in some opticians too but if you cannot find one from either source, ask the science teacher at your local secondary school for the address of a scientific equipment company.

Lest you feel I have bankrupted you with my list, it is important to assess priorities and consider your real essentials first. And take very good care of any tools that you do buy. An annual servicing (or as frequently as the manufacturers recommend) is essential for the long life and safety of powered tools, a regular sharpening, properly done, is vital for all cutting equipment, while an oilcan and a cloth can help to add years to the life of almost all. Nor should you forget you can now hire almost any item of gardening equipment at fairly modest cost.

3

GO FORTH & MULTIPLY

Geoffrey Smith

Just as I find some plants more interesting and rewarding to grow than others, so there are some gardening practices which offer more enjoyment. I infinitely prefer construction to routine maintenance of a garden, and taking cuttings to weeding onions. Of all the varied aspects of gardening the propagation of plants, whether by seed or cuttings, offers at first a challenge, perennial interest, and as a successful conclusion, real satisfaction. No sooner is a plant to hand than I am searching for a method of turning one into several. Add to the sense of adventure the saving in money, and the argument in favour of propagating plants to stock the garden is irrefutable. I also need spares of choice plants to ensure that Clay and Stefan have well-stocked gardens!

Plants may be propagated by seeds, which are dormant young plants complete in embryo form, or by means of cuttings, budding, grafting, layering or division. Seed is the sexual method of reproduction by which the majority of plants ensure survival of a given species. Unfortunately, only true species can be relied on to reproduce seedlings identical to the parent. A seed sown from hips collected from a rose bush growing wild in the hedgerow for example will, as a rule, produce offspring identical to the parent plant. But collect a ripe seed-pod from a garden hybrid rose for sowing and every one of the resulting offspring would be different from the original. Nevertheless, seed is the cheapest and often the only way of raising large numbers of certain types of plants. The majority of vegetables and annuals are raised from seed with predictable results concerning the quality of the end-product.

The terms annual, biennial and perennial are gardeners' shorthand used to describe certain types of plants. An annual starts and completes the cycle of life, from germination through growth and flowering to seed ripening, in one year. This is in contrast to a perennial which lives for several years, completing a number of cycles of flowering and seed ripening. A biennial usually takes two years over the business of procreation – the first year being devoted to growing, the second to flowering and seed setting. Annuals are subdivided into hardy – those which can be safely sown outdoors without protection – and half-hardy which are started into growth under glass and are then moved outdoors when all fear of frost has gone.

Though it is possible to sow seed and root cuttings outdoors without any protection at all, the range of plants which can be grown is somewhat limited. A greenhouse and frame are such essential aids to my enjoyment and successful maintenance of the garden, I just could not manage to work without them. That they have repaid their initial cost several times over is a minor consideration though, nevertheless, true. The value of a greenhouse to be used for propagation will be increased immeasurably if some form of artificial heat is added. Here I must not trespass further except to refer you to Chapter 6 for Clay's piece on greenhouses.

Before getting down to the practicalities of seed sowing, I must add just a word or two on the harvesting and storing of the seeds which plants growing in the garden

Spacing large seeds evenly over the compost means each seedling gets its light, air and nutriment

offer in such abundance. Remember that although seed may appear to be totally devoid of life it is very far from dead, and unless harvested and stored correctly germination will be poor. Take seed only from clean, healthy stock plants. Choose a dry, sunny day and harvest the crop just as the capsules begin to open and disperse their contents – a sure sign of ripeness. To make sure the drying and ripening are complete, spread out the pods and capsules on sheets of paper in a dry, airy shed. Pods which on maturation explode to shoot seeds far and wide should be enclosed in a paper bag. Once the seeds are dry they can be cleaned free from dust and other fragments by first sifting through a sieve, then gently blowing across them. After the seeds are cleaned they may be stored in paper bags or envelopes clearly labelled with their name and date of harvesting.

Seeds bought from a reputable merchant will have been harvested in peak condition, cleaned, dried and stored correctly until despatched to the customer.If seed from a reputable source fails to grow, the fault lies in most cases with the purchaser not the vendor.

Open a packet of begonia seeds and compare it with, for example, sweet peas and the difference is obvious. Fine, very small seeds such as begonia should be sown soon after they ripen or they lose their viability and die. They must not be sown too deeply or the tiny seedlings may not have sufficient food reserves to push shoots into the light. Oily seeds of the magnolia type also lose viability quickly if stored too long so, irrespective of season, I sow them on receipt. Hard-coated seeds such as sweet peas, camellias and paeonies need help in germination: rubbing (carding) them with a wire brush, or chipping them with a nail-file to weaken the covering will suffice.

There are some seeds which need to absorb more than average quantities of water before shoot and root start to grow. Garden peas, beans, cucumbers and marrows tend to germinate more quickly if given a good soak in water for twenty-four hours before sowing.

Seeds of roses, hawthorns, apricots, peaches and holly need several months of a process known as stratification before they are capable of germination. Simply place the berries or stones in trays or boxes between layers of sand, and leave them in a shady corner covered in ashes or gritty sand for twelve months. The following April they can be sown, sand and all, in shallow drills on a sheltered border out-

doors. Raising plants from seed requires no special skill or knowledge except the understanding of the best conditions required for germination to take place.

All seeds need moisture to soften the seed coat and begin the chemical processes prior to germination. Warmth is another essential factor. How high the temperature must be depends on the type of seed. Meconopsis, Primula and a number of alpines have an inhibitor which is a built-in safety device to prevent germination until weather conditions are favourable for uninterrupted growth. Exposing such seeds to a spell of cold weather by sowing them early and leaving the pots outdoors to be frosted and snowed on is enough to break the dormancy and they will then germinate normally. At the other extreme, seeds of some tropical plants will only commence growth in very high temperatures. Fortunately, most seeds will grow in temperatures between 12 and 23°C (55–75°F).

Because a seed is a living organism, air is absolutely essential for germination and healthy growth. Once the shoots push up through the compost to unfold their first leaves, they need light to start producing food.

After years of mixing all my composts for seed sowing as and when necessary, I now prefer to buy both seed and potting compost ready-mixed, owing to the ever-increasing difficulty of obtaining the basic ingredients, particularly good-quality loam. There are several combinations to choose from:

Seed sowing is an expression of the gardener's confidence that spring will triumph over winter

general-purpose mixtures contain lime.

One thing I have noticed is that loam-based composts in plastic pots need careful watering or they become too wet. In contrast, peat composts in clay pots dry out quickly. So I use peat compost in combination with plastic pots, and loam compost with clay containers. I do not economise on either compost or containers. Pots and boxes designed for the raising of plants will have provision for drainage. Composts are specially formulated to provide the right conditions and food supply for healthy balanced growth. Yoghurt pots, margarine cartons, indeed anything capable of holding moist composts without disintegrating, will suffice as containers providing they are, like the pots or trays, thoroughly clean and provided with drainage holes.

Seed packets, pots, seed-trays, compost and potting bench are the paraphernalia which signal the start of another gardening year. Quite often the garden is covered in snow as I begin seed sowing, insulated from the chill outdoors in the greenhouse. Opening the first packet of antirrhinum seed becomes almost a ritualistic gesture of defiance. Seed sowing should be a leisurely operation. Fill the pot or seed-box with compost, lightly firming with the fingers particularly at the corners. A final levelling with a milk bottle bottom or smooth piece of wood should leave the compost surface about 1 cm (½ inch) below the container's rim. A smooth, flat seed-bed is important when sowing very tiny seeds: any unevenness could result in seeds being buried too deeply for germination to take

some with soil as the main ingredient based on a formula devised by the John Innes Horticultural Institute; the others with peat as the principal component. There are also specialised mixtures with a preponderance of bark in the formulation, designed for orchids and other such plants for those who dabble in exotics. The multi-purpose composts, whether loam- or peat-based, are suitable for the cultivation of the general run of plants likely to be grown in gardens. For rhododendrons, heathers, camellias, and other selectively fastidious plants, the specially formulated ericaceous composts will suit very well, being acid in reaction, whereas the

TWELVE INTERESTING PLANTS WHICH CAN BE GROWN AS AN INTRODUCTION TO SEED SOWING

1	Aubrieta	Sow in April–May in cold frame.
2	Campanula	Sow in spring–early summer in standard compost.
3	Dianthus	Sow in January–April under glass in standard compost.
4	Gentiana	Sow when ripe in lime-free compost. Exposure to frost improves germination.
5	Geranium	Sow in March–April in standard compost in a cold frame.
6	Lilium	Sow in spring–early summer in standard compost in a cold frame.
7	Paeonia	Sow seeds when ripe in standard compost in a cold frame.
8	Primula (hardy)	Sow when ripe using a peat-based compost in a cold frame.
9	Rosa	Sow seed after stratifying into standard compost or nursery bed outdoors.
10	Saxifraga	Sow in March in loam-based compost in a cold frame.
11	Rhododendron	Sow in March on to the surface of lime-free compost in a cold frame.
12	Viola	Sow in February–March in standard compost under glass.

place. I err on the side of caution with fine seeds by lightly dusting the compost surface with sand to leave a smooth bed. Then, instead of covering, just compress the seed gently into the sand using the milk bottle or wooden press. Mixing small seeds with fine sand or brick dust is another way of making sure they are spread evenly and buried to a suitable depth. All seeds whether large or small need to be sown thinly to avoid overcrowding at a later stage of growth. Large seed such as marigold or Capsicum can be picked up individually and spaced out at equal distance. In gardening terms, this is called space sowing and eliminates the need for later pricking out the seedlings into a larger container – a job I do not relish. Label all seed-pans with the name of the seed and date of sowing. Water them and cover them with first a sheet of newspaper, then a sheet of glass – a contrivance which really quickens germination. The coverings must be removed as the first shoots show above the compost.

There are propagators of various types which are useful both for seed raising and rooting cuttings – Stefan has described a range of them in Chapter 2.

Being of an economy-conscious persuasion, I use the house windowsills as seed nurseries.

The time seed takes to germinate depends both on its type and whether it has been freshly harvested and stored correctly. I have had Lavatera germinate within eight days of being sown, while delphiniums and other perennials usually take four to six weeks and shrubs, the really determinedly slothful, twelve to eighteen months. Do not be impatient and empty the compost – I once had Cyclamen coum seed germinate two years after sowing.

Once the seedlings are large enough, they must be pricked off (transplanted) into seed-trays where they will have space to grow, free from competition, and with an adequate food supply. Seedlings grown in the loamy John Innes seed compost can be transferred to John Innes No. 1 potting mixture. Usually the peat-based composts are of general purpose, suitable for seed sowing and pricking out with the qualification that after six weeks, and from then on at fortnightly intervals, they will require a liquid feed.

To prick out, fill a seed-tray to overflowing, then wipe off the surplus with a flat piece of wood to leave

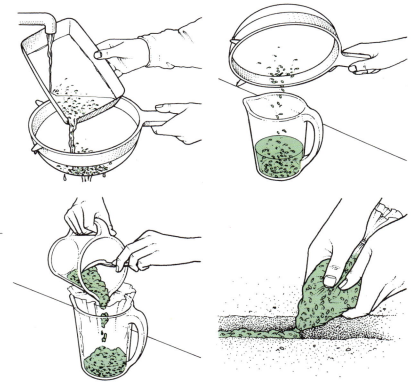

Fluid sowing is a cultivation technique which I use to persuade seed like those of the parsnip, which are often difficult or slow to start into growth, to germinate quickly. There is no need to spend money on special equipment, apart from the wallpaper paste – the other tools can be borrowed from the kitchen. In the interest of domestic harmony all the equipment should be returned after use clean and undamaged.

Pricking out needs to be done before the seedlings become drawn or disease ridden through overcrowding. It is one of the few gardening jobs which can be done sitting down with the potting shed bench comfortably adjusted at a convenient working height. The work is conducive to a reflective sense of well-being on the part of the gardener.

the surface loose and level. A dinner fork makes an ideal tool with which to lever out young seedlings. Insert the fork prongs right down well below the roots, then lever gently so the root system is lifted intact with the compost still adhering to it. With the handle of the fork make a hole large enough to accommodate comfortably the root in the fresh compost, then gently firm the compost around them. *Always* handle seedlings by a leaf tip, never by the stem or they may be seriously damaged. After all are pricked off, water them in, keep them shaded from direct sun for a few days, and have a well-earned cup of tea!

Sowing outdoors is common practice when growing hardy annuals, biennials such as wallflowers, hardy perennials, trees or shrubs. There is less control over temperature and moisture content of the soil than is possible in a frame or greenhouse. Nevertheless, I directly sow into open ground every year wallflowers, pansies and some score or more varieties of hardy annuals. Soil preparation includes digging in organic matter in the autumn. Then when raking down in the spring I work in a quantity of sharp sand, plus 50 g per square metre ($1\frac{1}{2}$ oz per square yard) of superphosphate. The soil is then left in a fine, friable condition to receive the seed which I sow into shallow drills. The depth of sowing varies according to the type of seed. I then shuffle the soil back over the seed using my feet, and rake down, not across, the rows to leave everything neat. April to late June is the time when soil and season are most suitable for open ground sowing; although the period can be further extended by using cloches or polythene tunnels to protect the seedlings.

Fluid sowing is a cultivation technique used to encourage quick germination and not, as Clay insists, ensuring the gardener is kept from dehydration by regular supplies of liquid refreshment. Seeds are chitted (sprouted) on moist tissue paper in a warm place indoors, using a plastic box with a close-fitting lid. Once sprouted, the seeds are carefully washed out into a flour sieve. They are now ready for sowing, and to do this mix them very carefully into one of the cellulose pastes used for hanging wallpaper, but make sure it is one without added fungicide. Tip the mixture into a plastic freezer-bag, cut off one corner, and gently squeeze the contents into well-prepared soil along a shallow drill. Then cover with soil.

Cuttings is yet another word from the gardener's dictionary of useful terms. This word is used to describe any part of a plant from root tip to the topmost leaf bud which, after being separated from the parent, can by the exercise of care and patience be persuaded to grow into a new plant capable of an independent existence. Usually a plant grown from a cutting is identical in every respect to the parent.

Before describing the different kinds of cuttings, I must say just a few words on the basic equipment and materials I use. In my own greenhouse there is an unheated frame measuring 2 metres ($6\frac{1}{2}$ feet) long by 1 metre (3 feet) wide, and two large seed-trays 61 by 33 cm (24 by 13 inches) complete with plastic domes. One of the trays is fitted with an electrically heated base which I use for cuttings which are not easy to coax into striking roots. Success can cost more than it is worth, so I forgo installing expensive mist units and soil warmed benches. In the majority of cases I want only enough plants for my own use, so why should I complicate my gardening life more than necessary? Simplicity after all is nature's first step, and the last of art, so why not combine the two and become an artistic simpleton?

Essential materials for taking cuttings are: first and most important a supply of clean, lime-free sharp sand which is a first-rate material for the task. Never

be tempted to use builder's sand which is soft, often contains lime, and is liable to cake into a hard, airless crust under the frequent waterings required to prevent cuttings drying out. A quantity of medium-grade, horticultural peat will also be needed to mix with the sand. The all-purpose cutting compost I use is two parts of sand to one part peat – measured by bulk not weight.

Pure sand on its own is the best rooting medium for silver-foliaged plants, Dianthus and houseplants. I keep one tray made up with three parts of sharp sand, two parts of sieved peat, and one part of sterilised loam for shrub cuttings, and roses in particular. Secateurs, a sharp knife or razor blades, and a dibber complete the list. Dibber, another of the words peculiar to gardening, refers to pegs, home-made in my case, of yew or hawthorn, of varying thicknesses, which are used to make the holes into which the

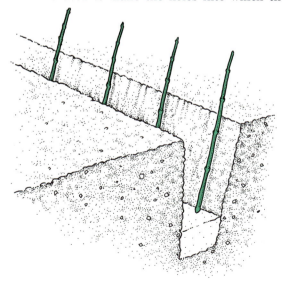

cuttings are inserted and for firming the compost around them afterwards.

There are several types of cuttings but, fortunately, the name used to describe each is usually self-explanatory. Stem or top cuttings are made from any non-flowering shoot. Those taken early in the plant's growing season are described as softwood cuttings. Similar cuttings, allowed to grow on the parent plant until the base of the shoot is mature while the top remains soft are classified as semi-hardwood. Delay removing the shoot until it is fully ripe and the wood hard throughout its full length, and it is then a hardwood cutting.

Softwood cuttings, because they are young and full of sap, will soon dry out, so they need to be off the plant and into the compost quickly. But I must add a cautionary word regarding all cuttings – never propagate from a diseased plant, use only material from healthy stock which is true to name. I find a razor blade in a holder the only instrument sharp enough for preparing softwood cuttings without bruising them and I make a clean cut just below a leaf joint (node in gardening language). This is a fairly general rule for most cuttings, although there are exceptions – Fuchsia, Clematis and Hydrangea are three.

The length of a cutting depends on the length of its parent shoot: a heather may offer only a niggardly 1¼ cm (½ inch), whereas a Delphinium generously contributes shoots for cuttings of 10 to 15 cm (4 or even 6 inches) in length. After removing all the leaves from

The juxtaposition of extremes: left, hardwood cuttings are rooted unprotected in a sheltered corner outdoors, with little more effort than the preparation of the soil and making of the cuttings; right, A specially designed propagator, even if it is no more than a seed tray with a plastic cover, is an invaluable aid

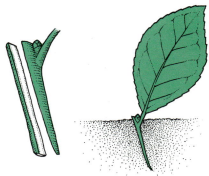

Sooner or later, preferably sooner in the interests of economy, the gardener will discover the need to take cuttings. This may be just as an insurance against the loss of some treasured favourite plant, or a means of stocking a garden. Softwood (left) or leaf bud cuttings (right) are just two of the possible methods.

the lower third of the stem and dipping the cut end in rooting powder, the cutting can be dibbled into the rooting compost and gently firmed in. Keep cuttings shaded and spray them with tepid water, although even then they may droop a little. Once the shoot tip straightens (becomes turgid) it will almost certainly root. Continue the spraying, shade from very hot sun, and in a month the cutting will be ready for potting off into a peat or soil compost.

Semi-hardwood cuttings are treated in the same way. A point worth noting is that cuttings from some shrubs will often root better if the shoot is gently pulled off with a heel (a piece of the old stem) attached, which is then trimmed wafer thin and dipped in rooting powder before being inserted in the compost.

Hardwood cuttings are available at the end of a plant's growing season, and are prepared from shoots

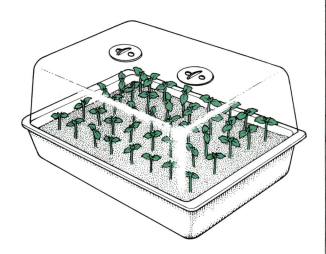

SIX SOFTWOOD CUTTINGS

1	Dahlia	Take in February–April.
2	Delphinium	Take in February–March.
3	Dianthus	Non-flowering shoots, take in summer.
4	Fuchsia	Non-flowering shoots, take in June.
5	Hydrangea	Take in May–June.
6	Penstemon	Take in summer.

SIX SEMI-HARDWOOD CUTTINGS

1	Camellia	Take in June–July.
2	Ceanothus	Take in July–August.
3	Cytisus	Take in July–August.
4	Potentilla	Take in June–July.
5	Rhododendron	Take in July.
6	Rosmarinus	Take in June–July.

SIX HARDWOOD CUTTINGS

1	Buddleia	Take in October–November.
2	Cornus	Take in October–November.
3	Deutzia	Take in October–November in cold frame.
4	Ilex	Take in September–October in cold frame.
5	Rosa	Take in October–November.
6	Weigela	Take in October.

SIX LEAF CUTTINGS

1	Begonia rex	Take in summer.
2	Camellia	Take in June–February, as a leaf or bud.
3	Ramonda	Take in June–July.
4	Saintpaulia	Take in spring–summer.
5	Sansevieria	Take in May–August.
6	Sinningia (gloxinia)	Take in April–May.

29

which are fully ripe during the period between October and December. Because the cuttings are prepared from mature wood, there is no danger of them wilting, so close, humid conditions are not just unnecessary but positively harmful. I root hardwood cuttings in a frame or on a sheltered border outdoors. Take out a shallow trench approximately half the cutting's total length. Hardwood cuttings can be anything in length from 10 cm (4 inches) upwards. A layer of coarse sand in the trench bottom will assist rooting and ensure that the drainage is good. Dip the cut end in rooting powder, push it into the sand, then replace the soil and firm it well down with your feet. In twelve months most hardwood cuttings will be sufficiently well-rooted for lifting and transplanting.

'Failures for gardeners are merely stepping stones to success', is a text which should be written in large letters over the potting shed door. If one part of a plant will not root, then keep trying until you discover a piece which will. Some plants, Begonia rex is a well-known example, will produce living young plantlets from healthy leaves, given the right conditions. 'Mother-in-law's tongue' (Sansevieria) is another and, the most popular of all, African violet (Saintpaulia) is a third. Just take a Begonia rex leaf from a healthy plant, turn it upside down on a sheet of glass then, using a razor blade or sharp knife, make cuts where secondary and main veins join. If the leaf

is pegged the right way up on top of a sandy compost, and kept in warm, humid conditions, it will sprout a plantlet at every cut. I am never in a hurry to pot these off until the old leaf has almost disintegrated. 'Mother-in-law's tongue' cut into 6-cm (2-inch) sections, then pushed into the peat/sand mixture will root well. However, this mass propagation only produces plants with mottled green leaves – the gold stripe is lost. African violet leaves will even grow when stood in a glass of rainwater, though I find the leaves transplant better when rooted in peat/sand compost. African violet leaves for propagation are pulled from the parent plant with a piece of stalk and are pushed into the compost so that the base of the leaf blade is just clear of the rooting medium.

Leaf bud cuttings are taken from ripe shoots which are cut into sections, each with a leaf and bud attached. Split the stem in half longitudinally, dust the wound with rooting powder and then bury the cutting in compost, leaving just the leaf exposed. Sometimes one branch of Camellia, Ficus or Vitis will provide a dozen leaf buds for rooting.

There are many plants, and I am adding to my list every year, that will grow from pieces of root when given the opportunity and encouragement to do so. Small plants to be used for propagation can be dug up to make selection of the most suitable, fleshiest roots easier. Larger plants are better left undisturbed. For

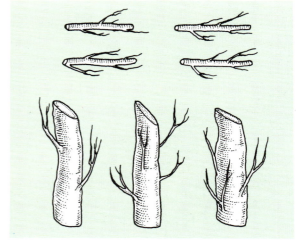

The gardener utilises every part of the plant in an effort to turn one into many. Some plants (left) *will produce a whole plant from one leaf.*
Others (above) *can be persuaded to grow from chopped-up pieces of root.*

these, I just scrape the soil away from the outer roots, choose the best of them as cuttings, and replace the soil. The cuttings should be prepared from the thickest roots – pencil-thickness for larger plants, but somewhat less in diameter for the fibrous-rooted Phlox, for example. Cut the roots into sections 4–8 cm (1½–3 inches) long – straight across at the top and slanting at the bottom. Varying the cutting angle is my way of making certain I can tell one end from the other! John Innes seed compost, or the all-purpose peat-based mixtures are quite suitable for root cuttings. The thicker root sections will, I have found, grow best when dibbled upright into 13-cm (5-inch) pots and spaced 6 cm (2 inches) apart. For the finer-rooted herbaceous plants, I just fill a seed-tray with compost, lay the cuttings on top, then cover them with more compost to the depth of 1½ cm (½ inch).

Layering, whereby a branch is persuaded to grow roots *before* it is detached from the parent bush, is a foolproof method of turning one plant into several. Early spring is my choice of season, though any time when opportunity offers will do as second best. Select a young stem, preferably non-flowering, which is supple enough to be bent to the ground. Prepare the soil below it by working in a generous supply of sand and moist peat. On the underside of the stem where it meets the soil make an incision 6–10 cm (2–4 inches) long and place a spent matchstick in the wound to

There are methods of rooting shrubs which reduce the risk of failure almost to zero. Ground layering (above) *and air layering* (right) *are two techniques which persuade a stem to root while still safely attached to the parent.*

top, *Making a cut in the selected shoot*
middle, *The wound is enclosed in polythene tubing which has been packed with moisture-retentive sphagnum moss*
bottom, *The sealed, airtight tube*

SIX ROOT CUTTINGS	
1 Anchusa	Take in February–March.
2 Anemone (japonica)	Take in November.
3 Eryngium (sea holly)	Take in November–March.
4 Phlox	Take in November–March.
5 Primula	Take in February–March.
6 Romneya (Californian tree poppy)	Take in March–May.

hold it open. Dust the cut surfaces with rooting powder then bury the stem in the ready-prepared soil. I put a heavy stone on top to hold the branch firm, although a wooden or wire peg would also work.

For air layering, the method used is similar to the technique employed in ground layering. Make a 6-cm (2-inch) cut in a pencil-thick shoot, treat it with rooting powder as described above, then enclose the wound in polythene tubing packed with moist sphagnum moss. Seal the tube with tape to prevent moisture loss. May or June is the best time to attempt air layering, when growth is active enough to promote quick root formation.

Plants which form several crowns or tufts of leaves, and are easily broken up into separate units are simple enough to multiply. Indeed, unlike mathematicians, gardeners can, in truth, multiply plants by simple division. Many herbaceous plants, bulbs and some shrubs lend themselves to this mode of propagation. Autumn or spring are the best times to lift and split up the crowns. In cold areas I would favour spring, just as growth begins, except when dealing with Primula, snowdrops and Pyrethrum which will re-establish more quickly if divided as the flowers fade. Stubborn crowns can be divided by means of two garden forks pushed through the root ball back to back then levered apart. As this is a process carried out for rejuvenation, take only the youngest outer growths and discard the rest.

The bearded or rhizomatous Iris must be divided every four or five years. In July, lift the mass of root-like stems (rhizomes) and cut off the youngest, outer rhizomes each with a fan of leaves attached and replant in well-drained, lime-rich soil, reducing the fans by half to prevent wind rock.

Lily bulbs tend to be expensive so I buy only a few of each variety, then increase my stock by means of scales

There are bulbs and corms such as Gladiolus, bulbous Iris and tulips which produce a mass of tiny potential adults, some of which are no longer than a rice grain. These can be separated then grown on in a nursery bed. They reach flowering size in three to five years.

Lilies are capable of being propagated from the fleshy, overlapping leaves which make up the bulb. When the bulbs are dormant in late autumn or winter, gently break off two or three of the overlapping scales. I am careful not to remove so many that the bulb is weakened, while choosing only those which are plump and disease-free. I then put the selected scales into a polythene bag (freezer-bags are ideal) along with some moist peat, shake them up to mix them well together, seal the bag and then hang it with its contents in the airing cupboard. After six weeks each scale should have grown roots and formed a tiny bulb, and can be potted off into a general-purpose compost. Some lilies form tiny bulbs (called bulbils) amongst the ripening seed-heads. I remove these just as they loosen to be shed naturally, and root them in pots with their tops only just covered in soil.

Budding and grafting are terms which send a shiver of apprehension through the tiro yet, given a little practice, they really are no more difficult than taking cuttings except in needing some advance preparation. Suitable rootstocks with which, in due course, the bud or graft will be joined, must be planted during the previous autumn and a suitable source of supply of bud wood or scion material will

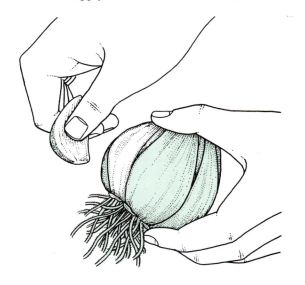

*Grafting is one of those invaluable gardening skills
that is well worth a modest amount of effort to acquire.
A 'Whip and Tongue' graft as illustrated is the one I
find the easiest to begin with.*

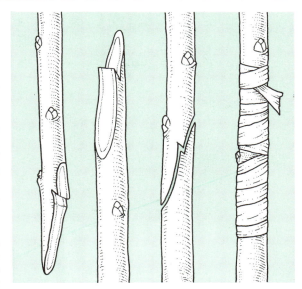

have to be located. 'Bud' and 'scion' are two more
words from the gardener's dictionary. A bud is just
what the name implies, and is usually taken with a
sliver of bark from the parent stem attached. A scion
is a young shoot of the previous year's growth which
is capable, when joined with a compatible root, of
growing into an exact replica of the tree or shrub from
whence it was taken. Compatible is the operative
word – bud or scion must be capable of union with the
stock, so rose with rose, apple with apple; like must be
placed with like always or it is so much wasted effort.

Roses are usually propagated by budding selected
varieties on to stocks of wild briar which can be
grown from seed. Should there be a commercial rose
nursery nearby then I would recommend buying
stocks. When planting the stock in the autumn prior
to working, do not bury the junction between root and
shoots as that is where the bud will be placed. The
budding operation is performed between mid-June
and August, for the work can only be properly con-
cluded when the rind or bark lifts easily from the
wood. Dry weather, by reducing the sap flow, tightens
the bark on to the wood, so when this happens delay
budding until after a good rain shower, or water the
stocks the day before work is to begin. The best buds
are usually found on a shoot which has carried a
flower – they should be plump and well-filled. The
thorns on a ripe shoot will break easily and cleanly

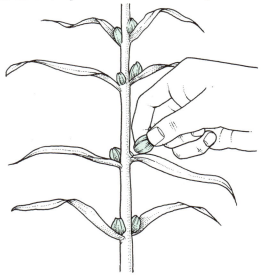

from the stem when they are pressed firmly sideways.

Grafting is spring-time work, done as the sap rises
during March and April. For a successful graft, the
scion (a one-year-old shoot, usually three to five buds
long) must be completely dormant, while the root
stock must be in growth. I gather scion wood from
healthy stock plants in January and keep it temporarily heeled in on the north side of the house.
Stocks to be grafted are lined out twelve months prior
to being worked. Ideally, the scion and stock should
be equal in size so that the two cut surfaces can make
maximum contact. Prepare the stock by making a
6-cm (2-inch) slanting cut upwards some 8–16 cm
(3–6 inches) above soil level, then cut a small nick
downwards in order to form a tongue on the cut surface. The scion is prepared by making a similar cut of
the same shape and length near a bud. Then, make a
nick to form a tongue on the cut surface the opposite
way to that of the stock so that they fit and are held
firmly together. Bind the joint with tape or moistened
raffia and carefully seal the tie with grafting wax to
render it waterproof. Many ornamental trees can
only be propagated by budding or grafting, so these
are skills worth the effort of learning.

Tissue culture was originally a technique
developed by botanists to study plant nutrient
requirements and absorption. Small pieces of plant
stem, leaf or root, placed on agar jelly enriched with a
nutrient solution, can be kept alive indefinitely. It

*Some lilies form embryo bulbs on the flower stems.
These can be grown on to flowering size in two years.*

Plant division requires ingenuity not brute force

was eventually realised that by introducing hormones into the culture medium the plant tissue could be stimulated into growth and multiplication and, in due course, into forming roots to become new plants capable of an independent existence. These were then potted off after a period of weaning, and grown in the normal way. At present, micro-propagation is beyond the scope and pocket of most amateurs, although in practical terms the techniques of micro-propagation and the allied embryo culture in commerce are exerting an increasingly powerful influence on our gardens.

Plants which in the past have proved very difficult and extremely slow to increase by vegetative means can now be propagated on a production-line scale. Nowhere are the results more apparent than in the price of some orchids. Varieties which only a few years ago cost anything from £50 to £500 for a very young plantlet, can now be bought in bloom for as little as £10.

Micro-propagation enables a new hybrid plant to be multiplied by the thousand in a matter of months.

I am thinking here in particular of Narcissus seedlings which first had to be grown on to flowering then, if judged worthwhile commercially, took up to twenty years before they could be made available in marketable quantities. Now, once the bulb is found to be commercially viable, enough stock for marketing can be made ready by means of micro-propagation in two to three years.

Even more important, virus-infected stocks of strawberry, apple and a wide range of valuable food crops can be cleaned up, for virus is not carried in the extreme growing tip of the shoot, and tissue taken from these points and grown under the micro-propagation technique will be disease-free.

The tissue used for propagation is taken from areas in active growth: buds in leaf axils, shoot tips and similar sources. This primary growth is then dissected under the microscope, sterilised and placed on the nutrient-enriched jelly. Then the hormone which stimulates root and stem formation is added, resulting in the production of a new plant.

Shoot tip culture is a form of micro-propagation and is, as the name implies, the selection of a growing point complete with leaves. This is really a mini-softwood cutting, although the material used may be only a centimetre long and only one new plant results from each.

Micro-propagation techniques are still in their infancy. They offer such a potentially profitable field of investigation that I am certain that as the process becomes better understood, and gardeners achieve a practical, working knowledge of the subject, this method of increasing plants will have a major influence on horticulture, both in the private and commercial fields.

Rose budding, left to right, *Use a sharp knife to remove a plump, well-ripened bud with a piece of bark attached; make a T-shaped cut in the bark of the stock at the junction between root and stem after first cleaning the area free of soil; insert the bud and trim bark to fit; secure with raffia or a purpose-made tie*

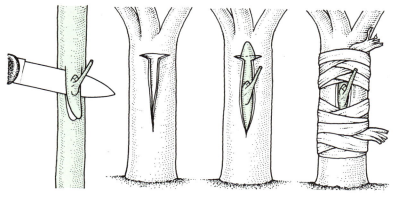

4

GROW YOUR OWN

Clay Jones

Sadly, vegetable growing is in decline and has been for over a decade. I suspect the reason lies in the ready availability of the so-called 'convenience foods' in the form of frozen, canned, dried or otherwise mutilated products. Read the labels on them and you will find that the vast majority contain preservatives and other additives. What, for instance, are monosodium glutamate, the stabilisers E450c and E339, and the colours E102, E160a and E127? I have no idea and as I have no wish to eat my food by numbers I thankfully grow my own.

From my modest plot my family enjoys a supply of fresh vegetables all the year round, produced at a fraction of their cost in the shops. Being fresh they retain their full, wholesome flavour, untainted by mysterious additives. Growing my own also affords the opportunity of choosing the varieties that are the best for taste, although they may not necessarily be the heaviest croppers. In addition I can practise pest control without resorting to the use of pesticides that I consider suspect. Finally there is the sheer pleasure of growing and reaping the results of one's own loving labours. I enjoy it all – the digging, sowing, feeding, hoeing and harvesting – all done as a means of mental and physical recreation in the open air.

My fellow gardeners, Geoffrey and Stefan, have covered elsewhere in this book the subjects of soil fertility, seed sowing and pest control in some detail.

On soil fertility I just want to stress that the soil in the vegetable plot needs to be the richest in the whole garden to yield its full potential. My soil feeding programme consists of digging in heavy dressings of manure and compost in the autumn and winter when the soil is frost-free, followed by a top dressing of Fish, Blood and Bone fertiliser raked into the surface, two to three weeks before sowing and planting. Anything that seems to be a bit slow on the uptake receives a feed or two of liquid fertiliser to start it moving. I begin sowing outdoors when Nature tells me that the soil is warm enough. I wait until the weed seeds begin to germinate, a sure sign that Nature has pressed the starter button and growth is under way. I have also learnt from experience that it is better to sow a little late rather than too early. The best plants and crops are those grown without any checks caused by adverse conditions, of which one is intense cold.

For the keen vegetable grower the plot is always too small and to use it to its full potential entails careful planning. So arrange your cropping system in such a way that you grow more of the vegetables you and your family like best and set out to provide them with a fresh vegetable from the ground every week of the year, even in midwinter. In other words, make the best possible use of the limited space at your disposal.

I shall first define and explain a few of the terms in common use in vegetable gardening and then proceed to outline my ways with individual crops.

Successional Sowing

The term 'successional sowing' has two meanings. First, it means sowing a vegetable variety at regular intervals to ensure a constant crop over a long period whilst avoiding a glut that is wasteful. Lettuce is a prime example. Unless you have habits like rabbits, a 4-metre (13-feet) row of lettuce all ready at once can be an embarrassment. It is better to sow a third of the row, wait until the seedlings have grown four leaves and then sow another third of the row and so on. Successional sowing may also refer to the sowing of different varieties of the same vegetable in order to achieve varying maturity times. For example, by selecting the right varieties and sowing them at the appropriate times it is possible to cut cabbages at all seasons.

Catch Cropping

Catch cropping involves growing a quick or early maturing crop, such as radish, harvesting it and then growing a second crop that year on the same piece of ground. For example, a row of early peas could be followed by a row of winter cabbages. Growing two or more crops in the same soil in one season exerts a heavy toll on plant foods so it is essential to apply a general fertiliser before the catch crop goes in.

Intercropping

Intercropping means growing an early maturing vegetable between rows of other vegetables that take longer to reach harvest time. The early cropper is ready and out of the ground before its growth can be adversely affected by the later crop. For example, a row of early sown lettuce may be grown in the runner bean row or Brussels sprouts may be planted between rows of lettuce, spinach or spring onions.

Crop Rotation

There are two reasons, one nutritional and one pathological, why every gardener should try to operate a simple three-year crop rotation, as Stefan explains in Chapters 1 and 15.

The following table illustrates a basic, three-year crop rotation that may be practised in quite small plots. To achieve good yields all the plots should be manured and fertilised as already advised. The only exceptions are the areas where root crops, that is, carrots, beetroot and parsnips, are being grown. These are not manured as the roots tend to fork and become misshapen in freshly manured ground. In addition, the brassica plots should be top dressed with garden lime every year, about two months after manuring. Liming 'sweetens' the soil, reduces the incidence and potency of club root disease and all the cabbage family like lime in their diet.

An A–Z of the Most Popular Vegetables

Bean, Broad (legume group)

Broad beans are delicious either cooked whole in the pod, or shelled. To enjoy them unshelled, pick the pods when they are no more than 10 cm (4 inches) long, boil them briefly, smear them with butter and revel in their incomparable flavour. Normal varieties grow to about 1–1½ metres (4–5 feet) tall and need supporting with strands of string on bamboo canes, running down each side of the row. For small and windswept gardens the dwarf varieties are ideal, growing to only 40 cm (about 15 inches) in height. There are also one or two varieties that may be sown in the autumn to crop in early summer, before spring-sown crops are ready. In cold districts and in severe winter weather, provide cloche protection.

Spring sowing can start under cloches in February and may continue at intervals until the end of April. Sow the seeds about 2½ cm (1 inch) deep and 20 cm (8 inches) apart, in alternate rows, in a spade-wide shallow trench some 2½ cm (1 inch) deep. Allow a good 60 cm (2 feet) between rows. In my experience, the dwarf varieties seem to escape the ravages of blackfly. I don't know why; perhaps the flies are short-sighted and fail to see the low-growing plants!

Varieties I grow: 'Aquadulce' for autumn sowing; 'Hylon', 'Jubilee Hysor', 'Rentpayer' and 'The Sutton' (dwarf).

Bean, Dwarf French (legume group)

I confess that dwarf French beans are not in the same

A THREE-YEAR CROP ROTATION

	Plot area A	Plot area B	Plot area C
1st year	peas and beans (legumes)	brassicas, swedes and turnips (cabbage family)	root crops, salads and others
2nd year	brassicas, swedes and turnips (cabbage family)	root crops, salads and others	peas and beans (legumes)
3rd year	root crops, salads and others	pears and beans (legumes)	brassicas, swedes, turnips (cabbage family)

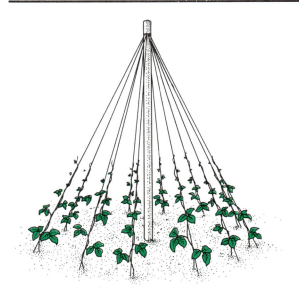

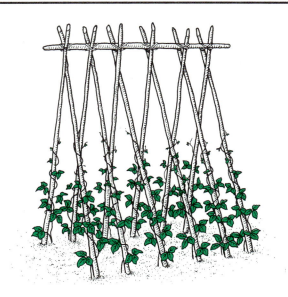

league as runner beans for flavour but I grow a row because they are ready for the pot when the 'runners' are only half-way up their sticks.

Seeds may be sown under cloches in early April or in the open ground from the end of that month until June. Sow them in a 2½-cm (1-inch) deep, 30-cm (1-foot) wide trench, spacing the seeds 10–15 cm (4–6 inches) apart. Although the plants grow to no more than 60 cm (2 feet) in height, a heavy crop may topple them. Support them either with short bushy twigs or by lengths of twine attached to short lengths of bamboo cane. To savour the earliest crops, sow the seeds in trays in the greenhouse in early March and plant out under cloches when four leaves are showing, or sow four seeds in a 25-cm (10-inch) pot of good soil. After germination, give liquid feeds weekly and keep them in the greenhouse until cropping is over.

Varieties I grow: 'Tendergreen'; 'Pros'.

Bean, Runner (legume group)

I can eat runner beans until my tummy touches the table! My enthusiasm for them is such that I have studied their habits and have reached a point when I can guarantee a good crop every year whatever the weather. The vital clue lies in their origins. Runner beans are subtropical plants and, at home, are accustomed to warmth and high humidity. We can do nothing to keep them warm but we can and should provide them with humidity.

This is what you do. In winter dig a trench 60 cm (2 feet) deep and 45 cm (1½ feet) wide. Into the bottom

left, Runner beans on the 'wigwam' support system

right, The traditional crossed canes support system

put a 10-cm (4-inch) layer of water-soaked old newspapers and on top a 30-cm (1-foot) layer of rich manure or compost, dusted over generously with bonemeal. Replace enough soil to level off but leave it unfirmed. By April the soil in the trench will have sunk quite a bit. Add more soil to bring the level up to within about 2½ cm (1 inch) of the surrounding soil, leaving a permanent shallow trough. Then insert the supporting sticks or canes 30 cm (1 foot) apart and cross them at the top to form a 'V'. Place horizontal canes along the 'V's and tie them in to the uprights. Finally, dust the row with Fish, Blood and Bone fertiliser at around 55 g per metre (2 oz per yard) run and hoe it into the surface.

For early crops sow seeds in mid-April in the greenhouse, one seed to each 8-cm (3-inch) peat fibre pot of peat-based compost and plant out in late May to early June when no more frost is likely. Outdoor sowings can be made in the period from the end of April to mid-May, sowing one seed 2½ cm (1 inch) deep at the foot of each cane and half a dozen extra at the end of the row to replace any failures.

From then on the plants need lashings of water at the roots. The abundance of organic matter in the trench will retain moisture but in dry weather extra and copious watering is a must. Put the end of the hosepipe at one end of the trough, turn the tap on and

37

Sow the seeds in a seed-bed in April and plant out in June and July, in rows 60 cm (2 feet) apart, and the same distance between individual plants.

Varieties I grow: 'Dwarf Green Curled'; 'Frosty'.

Broccoli (brassica group)

There are two kinds of broccoli. The first, and most familiar, is the sprouting variety that yields tender, tasty 'spears' in the early spring 'hungry-gap' when the winter greens have all been eaten and the spring cabbages are not ready. Sow the seeds in a seed-bed in April and plant out 60 cm (2 feet) apart all round (as for borecole) in June to July. Six plants or so are enough for the average family; any more and you'll be literally fed up with them. They are fairly tough plants but severe frost and high winds can play havoc with them. I protect mine by throwing a fine-mesh nylon net over the top.

The second broccoli type is a summer/autumn cropper called calabrese, and if you haven't slurped a forkful you haven't lived! It looks like a cross between a cauliflower and a sprouting broccoli, producing first a loose, green or greenish-purple 'curd', followed by a good supply of tender, short spears from the axils of the leaves. Sow the seeds in a seed-bed in April and plant out in June to enjoy superb meals from September well into October.

Varieties I grow: 'Early Purple Sprouting'; 'Mercedes' and 'Corvet' (all calabrese types); 'Romanesco'.

Brussels Sprouts (brassica group)

Brussels sprouts come in many varieties, some maturing earlier than others, to provide a continuous picking of tight, tasty buttons from September to March. I used to grow three varieties to ensure a long cropping period, until I realised that one was enough. In my garden, the variety 'Peer Gynt' will stand in tip-top condition until well into the New Year and I can pick as many as I like whenever I want them.

Sow the seeds in a seed-bed in April and plant out 60 cm (2 feet) apart all round in June to July. Do a war dance on the bed before planting out to ensure that the soil is really firm, otherwise the buttons tend to be loose and open. Stake each plant to prevent wind damage. Harvest the sprouts from the bottom of the stalk upwards. Remove yellow, dead leaves to prevent rotting and be patient – the sprouts always taste sweeter after a frost or two. When all the sprouts have been picked, don't throw the plants away before eating the top leaves – they're delicious.

Varieties I grow: 'Peer Gynt' (F_1); and sometimes the late variety 'Rampart' (F_1).

Cabbage (brassica group)

I seldom eat cabbage away from home. All too often it has been cooked for too long in too much water and sloshes on to the plate like a revulsion of seaweed. But when steamed gently for a few minutes in a little water cabbage retains its colour, texture and excellent flavour. By growing the right varieties it is possible to cut a fresh cabbage from the garden every week of the year. They need copious watering in dry weather and are better for earthing up as they grow. Earthing up helps to secure the plants, which also send feeding roots to the soil from the stems. After you've cut the cabbage, leave the stem in the ground and cut a 2½-cm (1-inch) incision in the shape of a cross into the cut end. In a few weeks, four mini-cabbages will grow from the cut surfaces and are as toothsome as their big brother.

Summer cabbage seeds are sown in a seed-bed from March to June and are planted out when about 10–15 cm (4–6 inches) tall. My favourite variety at present is the ballhead, 'Minicole'. It is just big enough for a family of four, is as tight as a drum and will stand in fine fettle without bolting for at least ten weeks, even in a hot summer.

Winter cabbage seeds are sown in a seed-bed from April to early June and are a valuable follow-on crop. I usually plant out in June and early July in ground left vacant after harvesting earlier crops such as broad beans or early potatoes.

Spring cabbage seeds are sown in a seed-bed in late July in the north and early August in the south, and the plants are then planted out in September or early October in reasonably good ground. They have to be tough to come through the winter so don't give them any fertiliser until March when a smattering of sulphate of ammonia will spur them into growth. In truth, I sometimes wonder whether it is worth growing spring cabbage at all. In some winters the weather reduces them to pathetic, naked stalks, or rabbits and pigeons have a go at them and even if they survive, against all the odds, they are loth to heart up before I need the space for something else. Instead, I sow summer cabbage in soil blocks in the greenhouse in January, grow them on in the cold frame, plant them out and cut good firm cabbages in twelve weeks or so from sowing.

Before closing the book on cabbages I must mention and commend a new variety that hearts up in the autumn. It goes by the name of 'Hawke'. It is shaped like a rugby ball and comes to cutting in the period between the summer and winter varieties. At home, I cut the first 'Hawke' in September and the last, which was still in prime condition, in late November.

Varieties I grow: Summer cabbage – 'Minicole' (F₁); 'Hispi' (F₁); Golden Acre'.
Autumn cabbage – 'Hawke' (F₁).
Winter cabbage – 'Celtic' (F₁); 'January King'.
Spring cabbage – 'Pixie'; 'Spring Hero' (F₁).

Carrot (root crop group)

Carrot varieties differ in the length and shape of their edible roots. The long, tapering varieties can attain a length of 90 cm (3 feet) and more, in the care of the keen exhibitor. Most of us are content just to grow good crops and in the average soil type the shorter, stump-rooted and cylindrical varieties are the better choice. For those of you gardening on shallow, stony or heavy clay soils there are globe-rooted varieties that don't need depth to yield a worthwhile crop, but they do need earthing up to prevent greening at the shoulders.

Sow the seeds successively from March to July. I sow thinly and leave the seedlings unthinned in order not to invite the ravages of the carrot fly. In areas where carrot fly is a real pest, and that means most of Britain, late June sowings will escape attention, as the fly has finished laying its first batch of eggs by then. It lays a second batch in August by

Plan for a productive back garden with a large vegetable plot

which time the carrots are big enough to cope. Earthing up also helps to keep the fly at bay. Lift the roots in November and store them in layers, in boxes of sand or peat. With the exception of the coldest areas and in very wet soils, carrots may be kept in the ground over winter, although there is a risk that slugs may eat some of them before you do.

Varieties I grow: 'St Valery' (long); 'Nantes Tip-Top' (cylindrical); 'Parmex' (globe) and 'Camus' (F₁) (stump-rooted).

Cauliflower (brassica group)

Cauliflowers are both popular and problematic. Time and again gardeners who grow them end up with curds no bigger than buttonholes. The reason is simply that cauliflowers are demanding plants. They must have a fertile, humus-rich soil, and gallons of water in dry spells. Following ten rainless days in summer a row of 'caulies' will need about three to four gallons of water per square metre (or square yard). It is a waste of time giving them just a splash from a watering can; they need a sprinkler left on for fifteen to twenty minutes to do the job properly. There is also an old gardeners' trick which not many people know of that is worth passing on. Just as the curd begins to form, cut a 2½-cm (1-inch) vertical slit right through the stem and half-way down it and insert a matchstick to keep the slit open. For some reason the curd

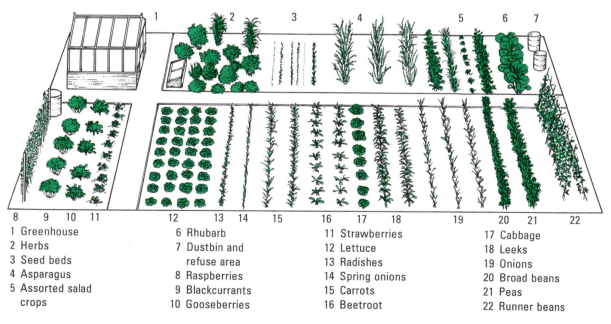

1 Greenhouse	6 Rhubarb	11 Strawberries
2 Herbs	7 Dustbin and	12 Lettuce
3 Seed beds	refuse area	13 Radishes
4 Asparagus	8 Raspberries	14 Spring onions
5 Assorted salad	9 Blackcurrants	15 Carrots
crops	10 Gooseberries	16 Beetroot

17 Cabbage	
18 Leeks	
19 Onions	
20 Broad beans	
21 Peas	
22 Runner beans	

41

Nowadays most of us grow our onions from sets. These are tiny bulbs in an arrested stage of growth. They are stored over winter under strictly controlled conditions and are planted in spring to begin regrowth. Good-quality sets from a reputable supplier are guaranteed to yield a good crop of onions that are less likely to run to seed than those grown from seeds, but handle them with care. Here are a few tips to ensure success: first, don't plant them too early. They will not be killed by frost but very severe weather may check them and cause them to run to seed. Wait until late March or early April before putting them in.

Second, don't push them into the soil. Take out a shallow drill, place the sets in it and firm them in by drawing soil around them with your fingers.

Third, before planting cut off the 'tails', the remains of the old leaves at the tips of the bulbs. If you leave them on they get wet, flop over and earthworms foolishly try to drag them below ground to line their nests, pulling the sets out of the soil in the process. Birds have also been known to yank them out by their 'tails'.

Fourth, always hand-weed onions in growth. Many of their roots are near the surface and will be cut and mutilated by hoeing.

Fifth, to assist ripening and to enhance their keeping potential give the onion-bed a light dusting of sulphate of potash in late June and water it in.

Finally, don't bend the necks over to hasten ripen-

above, Round- and long-rooted radishes add piquancy and colour to summer salads

right, Tomatoes and marigolds make a cheerful and colourful display in this greenhouse

ing. This damages the lower leaf tissue and may well lead to fungus diseases entering at the wound. Instead, place a fork under them when the leaves start flopping and ease the bulbs up a few inches, then leave them until the leaves keel over of their own accord. Lift them, dry them and store them in a cool and dry place. I used to spend hours stringing the bulbs à la Breton onionseller until I found that they kept just as well by cutting the shrivelled leaves off two or three centimetres (about an inch) above the bulb and storing them, bottoms upwards, in boxes kept in a cool, dry, frost-proof shed.

To grow onions from seed sow them either under glass in January and February or in open drills in March. Under glass, the seedlings emerge looking like small green hairpins and they are ready for pricking out when the hairpins begin to straighten out. At this stage transplant them to 8-cm (3-inch) pots, feed and then plant out in mid-April.

Varieties I grow: from sets – 'Sturon'; 'Giant Fen Globe'.
From seeds – 'Rijnsburger-Balstora'; 'Lancastrian'; 'Hyduro' (F_1); 'Robinson's Mammoth'.

All the above onion varieties are ones that are

spring sown or planted and will keep in good condition at least until April of the following year.

Japanese onions are entirely different. Their seeds are sown in August to give small, sturdy plants that overwinter to yield a crop of tear-jerking onions from the end of May onwards. They will not keep in store, but I value them highly as they provide a supply of home-grown bulbs when imported onions in the shops are expensive. Japanese onion sets are also available.

Varieties I grow: 'Express Yellow O-X' (F1); 'Extra Early Kaizuka'.

Spring onions are much in demand for salads and sandwiches. Sow the seeds in succession from March to August and leave the plants unthinned to be pulled and used as required. Seeds of the winter-hardy variety are sown in September to provide plants for early spring salads.

Varieties I grow: 'White Lisbon'; 'White Lisbon – Winter Hardy'.

Parsley

There is more superstition attached to parsley than there is to walking under ladders. I even know a lady who tells me she sows it at midnight at the full moon and to perform the ritual she strips to the buff. Unfortunately, I cannot vouch for the veracity of her claim! Me, I sow parsley, fully dressed, from March onwards and it comes up with no bother. Although I don't do it myself it is claimed that pouring a kettle of boiling water over the seeds after sowing assists and accelerates germination. We use a great deal of parsley and to get a supply all the year round I also sow seed in the greenhouse in February and plant out in March under cloches. Last sowings are made in August and these too are cloched in October to provide winter snippets. If the leaves of your parsley turn yellow or red the roots are probably being got at by the carrot fly so take the necessary precautions.

Varieties I grow: 'Bravour'; 'Moss Curled'.

Parsnip (root crop group)

Parsnips are precious. In winter the ground can freeze solid, yet the roots emerge unscathed. In fact, they are all the sweeter for a good touch of frost.

There is just one snag. Parsnip seeds are inherently poor germinators, no matter how carefully they have been harvested and stored. Therefore it is advisable to practise the station method of sowing. Take out shallow drills 25 cm (10 inches) apart and sow three seeds at each station spaced 15–20 cm (6 to 8 inches) apart. If more than one seed germinates, thin to the strongest. Parsnips are also prone to a condition called canker that usually appears as a rusty-brown discolouration of the root beginning at the shoulders. Late sowings at the end of April often seem to escape attack and a couple of varieties show a good degree of canker resistance.

Varieties I grow: resistant to canker – 'Avonresister'; 'White Gem'.
Non-resistant to canker – 'Tender and True'; 'Improved Hollow Crown'.

Pea (legume group)

Once, and without thinking, on a 'Gardeners' World' programme I solemnly averred that 'I like to have a good pea in the garden'. I've never lived it down but you know what I meant. Peas, dried, tinned or frozen, cannot compare with the taste of a plateful of freshly picked ones. By successionally sowing suitable varieties it is possible to spread cropping over several weeks from spring to late summer. For the first sow-ing choose an early variety, remembering that the term 'early' means that the variety comes into crop in a shorter time than second-earlies and main crops. For this reason, an 'early' is also the one to sow late – in July – so that it has a chance to reach maturity before shorter days and chilly nights affect its productivity. In fact, modern early varieties are so good and so prolific that I grow the same one throughout the season with one exception. I use 'Kelvedon Wonder' for my July sowing because it is a good pea and because it resists the mildew that is a hazard with the advent of autumn. There are also some varieties that may be autumn sown in November and overwintered under cloches to produce the very earliest pickings.

Like everything else, peas have undergone change of late. Mangetout or sugar peas are flat-podded, contain very small seeds and are topped and tailed, cooked and eaten whole. Now the plant breeders have developed a mangetout with a full-sized pod within which are fully grown peas encased in a sweet 'flesh'. They've called them 'snap' peas and they are absolutely delicious, eaten raw or cooked. The latest development is a pea that is virtually leafless, bred to make harvesting easier for commercial growers who supply the canning industry. The variety 'Poppet' needs hardly any support. The plants intertwine their abundant tendrils to such an extent that 60 cm (2 feet) wide rows are more or less self-supporting. It is a prolific maincrop variety with a fine flavour.

Varieties I grow: 'Hurst Green Shaft' (early); 'Kelvedon Wonder' (early); 'Sugar Rae' (snap pea); 'Poppet' (semi-leafless).

Potato

In the average garden, maincrop potatoes are hardly worth the space they occupy. It is more economical to devote the room to other vegetables that are expensive to buy in the shops and better eaten fresh from the soil but early potatoes should be in every garden bigger than a window box. One of the greatest pleasures in life is the incomparable taste of the first 'lift' in June. The tender, parchment-skinned tubers don't have to be eaten, just put them in your mouth, close your eyes and drool as the tender flesh dissolves in a mush of sheer ecstasy.

Coming down to earth, literally and metaphorically, potatoes in good, fertile soil give a high return for little outlay. Buy the early seed potatoes as soon as you can, in January if possible, and 'chit' them by putting them 'eyes' end upwards in a shallow tray in a light, warm room to start the tubers into growth.

Seed potatoes that have been chitted come into crop a week or two earlier than those that haven't. Plant them from mid-March to mid-April and be prepared to protect the leaves from frost, either by earthing up, or by throwing sheets of newspaper over them. Should you be taken unawares and the leaves do get frosted all is not lost, provided you can leave your bed before morning sun strikes the leaves and hose the frost off with cold water. Earthing up is vital. It helps to support the plants and it prevents the tubers turning green and it is worth bearing in mind that green potatoes eaten in any quantity are poisonous and have been known to kill.

Inexperienced gardeners are sometimes puzzled by the small, green, tomato-like fruits that some potato varieties produce after flowering. Potatoes are closely akin to tomatoes and the green 'marbles' are fruits and contain true potato seeds. They, too, are poisonous. The seeds are not worth sowing for two reasons: first, they will not come true to variety; and second, it will be two or three years before they will yield a worthwhile crop. As a rough guide early potatoes are ready in twelve weeks from planting and maincrops are ready for lifting and storing when their haulms have died down completely. Store potatoes either in sacks or brown paper bags to exclude light and prevent greening; never in plastic bags where they will sweat themselves to rot.

Varieties I grow: 'Maris Bard' (early); 'Pentland Squire' (maincrop); 'King Edward' (maincrop).

Pumpkin (cucumber family)

I once grew a pumpkin that weighed in at 55 kg (121 lb). I asked my wife what I should do with it. She told me, but I didn't and it eventually ended up in pieces on the compost heap. Therefore I shall not dwell on pumpkins except to say that they are grown in much the same way as marrows and the more they are fed, the bigger they get.

Varieties I don't grow: 'Hundredweight'; 'Mammoth'.

Radish (root crop group)

Whether you wish to grow long- or round-rooted radish give them the best patch of soil in the vegetable garden. The secret of growing crisp, crunchy roots lies in humus-rich soil that is never dry, so that they grow quickly without check. As the seeds are fairly large, I take the trouble to sow them individually 8 cm (3 inches) apart to save thinning. First sowings are made under cloches in early March and then at two- to three-week intervals until the end of June.

After June the seeds will germinate readily enough but the plants hardly ever yield a crop of edible roots.

Varieties I grow: 'Cherry Belle' (round); 'French Breakfast' (long).

Rhubarb

Rhubarb may be grown either from seed or from one-year-old plants bought from a shop or garden centre. From seed it takes two years before the plants are well enough established for cutting to begin. If roots are planted they should be left untouched for one whole season and only moderately cropped in the second. Once established, rhubarb may be forced to provide very early pullings. One way is to cover a clump with a thick dollop of manure or compost and then place over it an upturned bucket with a hole in the bottom, or use a cloche. Another way is to lift a clump in December, put it into a deep box of soil and leave it under the staging in the greenhouse. After indoor forcing the clump is of no further use.

Clumps of rhubarb last a lifetime so give them a good start when planting. Dig in plenty of manure and plant in well drained but moist soil. Top dress every spring with lashings of manure or compost. Pull the sticks when they are young and juicy but leave a few to feed the plants. Stop pulling in June and give a liquid feed or two. A smaller, second crop comes ready in August.

Varieties I grow: 'Champagne'; 'Timperley Early'; 'Cawood Delight'.

Shallots (onion group)

Ploughmen knew a thing or two. For them a pint of ale, a hunk of cheese and a pickled onion was a feast, the pickled onion being a shallot preserved in vinegar.

Plant the bulbs at any time from the end of February, spacing them 20 cm (8 inches) apart all round. Remember to plant enough to allow for some to be pulled before they start bulbing, to use chopped up in salads and sandwiches. The mature bulbs are ready for harvesting when the leaves have dried and died back, when they should be lifted and dried off in the same way as onions. For a very early crop of 'scallions' or 'jibbons' plant a few bulbs in January, in compost in seed-trays, in the greenhouse.

Varieties I grow: 'Longkeeping Yellow'; 'Hative de Niort' (red-skinned).

Spinach

Spinach worked wonders for Popeye. Its strong

flavour is not to everyone's taste but there are few more health-giving vegetables and by careful planning a fresh cut of spinach can be an all-year-round event.

Seeds of summer spinach are sown from March to June in a soil that is rich in humus and never dry. Like lettuce, spinach must never go thirsty and needs a lot of water in dry weather. In thin, dry soils it runs to seed before it is ready for cutting. Like beetroot, the seeds are in clusters so sow them 15 cm (6 inches) apart and then thin to one seedling. When cropping fully grown plants, cut two or three leaves only and wait until more leaves grow before cutting again. Each plant will provide a cut-and-come-again supply of leaves for a period of three to four weeks from the first to last cuts.

Varieties I grow: 'Norvak'; 'Sigmaleaf'.

Winter spinach is very similar to the summer variety except that it is hardier and its season of use extends from November to April. Sow the seeds from July to September. When cutting take no more than two leaves from each plant and in severe weather cover the plants with cloches to keep them clean and usable.

Variety I grow: 'Broad-leaved Prickly'.

New Zealand spinach will put up with hot, dry summers and is less likely to run to seed than the ordinary summer spinach. It is therefore the better choice for light soils that drain quickly. The plants have a low-growing, spreading habit and need a lot of room, an all-round spacing of 90 cm (3 feet) between plants is about right. There is only one variety and that is just called 'New Zealand'.

Swede (brassica group)

Although swedes bear little resemblance to cabbages they are nevertheless of the same family and therefore they are prone to the same pests and diseases. They are also something of a mystery. I have never understood why the farmers all around me grow swedes 'as big as your 'ead' with no difficulty, whilst mine are all shapes and sizes, ranging from footballs to tennis balls. It is so frustrating I have totally retired from swede production and I buy what I need from the farmer down the lane.

Another consideration weighing heavily against serious swede growing is the space they occupy. They need 60 cm (2 feet) spacing all round which makes them hardly worth growing in small gardens when they are so inexpensive in the shops. If you do grow them sow the seeds in March and April and lift the roots in late August or early September before frost or mildew get at them.

Varieties I have grown: 'Acme'; 'Marian' (resistant to club root and mildew).

Sweet Corn

Sweet corn has been adapted to suit our uncertain summers and modern varieties are reliable croppers providing they are treated properly. The first essential is to avoid any kind of root disturbance and this means sowing the seeds in such a way that the seedlings need not be individually transplanted. The best way is to sow them singly in 8-cm (3-inch) peat-fibre pots in early April in warmth, standing the pots on a base of moist peat or perlite. The primary root is quite thick and grows quickly until it penetrates the bottom of the pot and meanders its way into the base material which should be kept moist to prevent the root drying out. The plants are ready for planting out in their pots in pre-warmed soil under cloches in mid-May. Another method is to sow the seeds outdoors in May, spacing them 45 cm ($1\frac{1}{2}$ feet) apart and placing an inverted jam-jar over each. Either way, the plants never suffer root disturbance.

To ensure a successful crop of full, fat cobs it is essential to sow, or plant, sweet corn in blocks, never as a single straight row. This is because each plant carries both male and female flowers, the males at the very top and the females lower down as long, silky hairs sprouting from the tips of oval, pointed sheaths. The pollen is as light as gossamer and in a single row of plants it can be carried away from the expectant female flowers by the merest breeze. In a block formation the chances of cross-pollination are greatly enhanced.

The cobs are ready for gathering when the colour of the silky hairs or 'tassels' turns to dark brown, almost black. A further check for ripeness is to peel back the sheath and press your thumb into one of the golden yellow grains. If it oozes a milky liquid it is not quite ready, but if it has the consistency of clotted cream, cut the cob where it joins the stalk, peel it, boil it, butter and salt it and enjoy it.

Varieties I grow: 'Aztec' (F_1); 'Sundance' (F_1).

Tomato

I could write a whole book on my favourite fruit – the tomato. In fact I once did but I must here confine my enthusiasm to the salient pointers to success.

Growing under Glass

Tomatoes are prone to a number of soil-borne dis-eases. As a result, plants grown year after year in the same greenhouse soil-bed gradually deteriorate to the point where they show prolonged periods of wilt and yield very poor crops. There are ways of solving the problem. The soil can be steam or chemically sterilised, methods that are tedious and not really the answer for amateur gardeners. Or the soil can be changed, taking out the old and replacing it with new from the garden. This is no more than a temporary solution and is a tiresome, toilsome task that needs repeating every two years at least.

The answer therefore is to grow tomatoes in a soil-less and/or sterile medium where fungal root diseases cannot get a hold. One way is to use specially pre-pared growing bags filled with peat-based compost. They are first class with one proviso. They have no drainage holes and need to be watered with extreme care; too much will result in waterlogging and poor root development, while too little will result in inci-pient wilt and restricted growth. But once you get the hang of it you will grow good crops in growing bags. Another way is to remove the soil to a depth of 30 cm

right, *Home-grown, fresh and tasty*

below, *A well-set 'cob' of sweet corn just right for eating*

(12 inches), lining the resulting trench with polythene sheeting along the bottom and up the sides. Then fill the space with a fairly fine 5-mm ($\frac{1}{4}$-inch) down grit to form a sterile base. The tomatoes are grown in special bottomless rings filled with a good growing compost and watered and fed to a set plan. After planting, the tomato is watered-in but thenceforth it derives its water from the aggregate

right, *The pattern of winter removal of shoots on an established open-centred bush apple tree*

below, *The removal of dead and crossing branches on a neglected tree should be a gradual process*

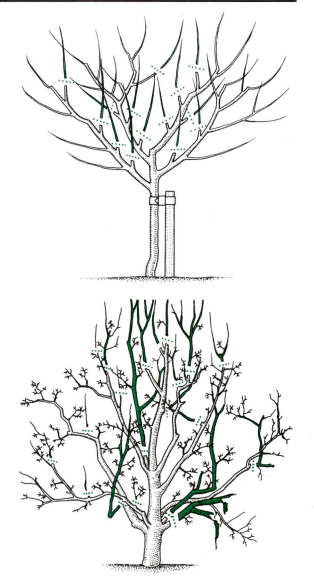

against a wall, fence or training wires. Apples, pears, plums and cherries respond well to both systems, damsons are best grown as free-standing trees whereas peaches are much better against a wall. A sunny position is important for both free-standing and wall-trained plants; in my experience peaches rarely succeed at all outdoors unless they are against a warm, south- or south-west-facing wall. As free-standing plants, pears require a warmer spot than apples for they come into blossom earlier and are more prone to spring frost damage. For this reason, they are less successful than apples in the north of Britain where the provision of wall protection will give very much better results. Quite honestly, in any cold area, wall protection and/or a choice of later flowering varieties of apples and plums makes sound sense.

In all instances, the same basic soil preparation may be used and I can do no better than recommend the advice that Geoffrey gives in Chapter 9. The spacing between the planting positions will vary with the rootstock and training system used but plants for wall training should be planted about 25 cm (10 inches) away from the wall. Although it is now possible to buy fruit trees in containers for planting all year round, they will generally establish better when planted in a dormant state at the traditional time; between November and March, provided the soil is not frozen.

Apart from the regular attention to pruning described below, it is a mistake to imagine that a fruit tree, especially a young fruit tree, will take care of itself. After planting, it is essential to keep the area around the base of the trunk free from weeds and, if the tree has been planted in a lawn, a circular area about 1 metre (1 yard) in diameter around the trunk should initially be kept free from grass too. This will facilitate the application of spring mulches, fertilisers and water. After about five years, however, I prefer to grass over this area, an operation that limits over-vigorous growth.

Although the fertiliser demands of all types of fruit tree and, indeed, of all varieties are not the same, I am well satisfied with the results from forking an annual fertiliser dressing into the soil surface around the young trees (or watering it into the turf with

those that have already been grassed down) in late February or March. I give each tree an application of a balanced general fertiliser such as Growmore or Fish, Blood and Bone at about 100 g per square metre (3 oz per square yard); my older trees in fertile soil are much better able to fend for themselves. With stone fruits, it will repay you to ensure that the soil does not become more acid than about pH 6.5.

Nor should watering be forgotten; the water loss through the leaves of a tree in midsummer can be prodigious and, especially until it has a well-

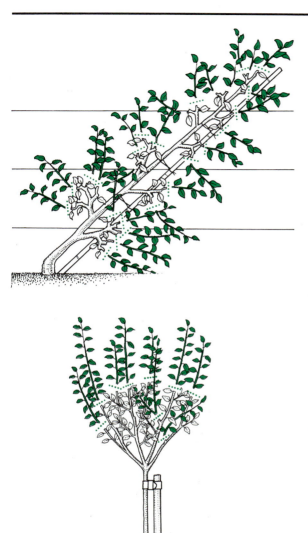

left, *Pruning on a cordon apple tree is a summer process; see text for details*

below, *Final stages of formative pruning on an open-centred half standard plum; see text for details*

written on the many methods available and I have neither space nor inclination to give chapter and verse on them all (indeed, I must confess that after years of trying I still find some of the more obscure and Gallic among them to be beyond comprehension). I have selected therefore those that I find most satisfactory for the needs of the average gardener.

Fruit tree pruning can be divided into two aspects; the formative pruning that shapes the plant in its early years and the maintenance pruning that keeps it in shape and maintains its cropping efficiency. I shall describe both from the standpoint of a gardener starting with new trees as this will be many people's introduction to pruning and is certainly the ideal way to ensure that your tree has the form most appropriate to your needs, that it gives the minimum of trouble throughout its life and, of course, that you learn most about the principles of pruning and how the plant reacts to it. I shall also add a few comments for those, like me, who have moved to a garden with existing and neglected trees.

Apples and Pears
The conventional way to grow apples and pears is free-standing in the open, with no support other than a stake and this is still the most widely used technique. I have long believed that the simplest and most convenient form into which to train such a tree for general garden purposes is the open-centred bush (or dwarf bush if a dwarfing rootstock is used). Although some summer pruning is sometimes advocated in addition to the regular winter treatment needed, I never summer prune my trees for this seems to add an unnecessary complication; most varieties, in most gardens, will crop perfectly well without it and there are so many other more gainful pursuits to occupy our short gardening summers.

The commonest, and probably the best way to start is with a 'virgin', 'unpolluted' or 'fresh' tree (all dictionary variants on 'maiden', which is the name generally applied to a one-year-old with a straight stem) planted in the autumn. In the first winter, cut or 'head-back' the single shoot to a strong bud at the height above ground required for the stem (normally, this will be between 60 and 90 cm (2 to 3 feet)).

By the second winter, several upright shoots will

established root system, you must make allowance for this. Small, garden trees will need watering throughout their lives during very dry periods to enable the fruit to swell and ripen satisfactorily; remember that the bulk of apple, pear or plum fruit is actually water, which must come from somewhere!

Pruning Top Fruit
Few subjects in gardening are endowed with more myth and mystery than the pruning of fruit trees. Entire books, both large and numerous, have been

have grown. The central one of these should be cut out completely in order to give the tree its open centre, and the strongest four well-placed shoots among those remaining should be cut back by about half (more if the tree is growing weakly, less if growing strongly), always cutting to an outward-facing bud. If choice is possible among several shoots, select those that leave the stem at an angle of about 45 degrees as they will be inherently stronger than those with upright growth and better able to support the crop as the tree matures. Remove completely any other long shoots and, at the same time, cut back laterals to about three buds. Some nurseries routinely sell so-called two-year, cut-back trees which will have had two years' growth after grafting and will already have had the leading shoot headed back. The pruning of these should be commenced at the second winter stage, just described.

In the third and subsequent winters, maintenance begins to take over from formative pruning and I am convinced that the most useful system of maintenance pruning for gardens is that known as established spur pruning. Cutting back of the leading shoots by a quarter to a third should be continued, but gradually lessened each year until the leaders are merely tipped back by a few centimetres, and some left altogether unpruned. The aim, with this leader shortening, is to strike a balance between stimulating too much leafy growth with hard pruning and causing bare lengths of shoot with dormant buds as a result of too little. The laterals should be cut back to about three buds and sub-laterals (shoots produced from the laterals pruned in the previous winter) cut back to one bud. This pruning of laterals stimulates the formation of fruit buds and spurs close to the base. If lateral pruning is neglected, the result will be the same as with unshortened leaders – the basal buds will remain dormant, those near the tip of the shoot will break and thus a long length of useless bare stem will result.

In due course you will need to remove any branches that cross or touch each other and you may also need to thin out the spurs to prevent overcrowding, too much blossom and fruit, and a reduction in quality. New laterals may arise after spur clusters are removed and these can be retrained to stimulate the production of new spurs by shortening in the usual way.

I must now qualify my advice, however, regarding some of the more important exceptions to these general guidelines. A few apple varieties ('Beauty of Bath', 'Lane's Prince Albert' and 'Blenheim Orange'

most notably), have a naturally spreading habit and can be damaged by the weight of fruit on the branches as they mature if this is not offset to some degree. To encourage a more upright growth, therefore, the leader shortening on these varieties should be to an inward-, not an outward-facing bud.

Time and again, we are faced with gardeners who have the problem of tip-bearing apples. These are varieties that bear the fruit at the tips of one-year-old shoots instead of on spurs at the base. 'Blenheim Orange', 'Bramley's Seedling' and 'Worcester Pearmain' are among the commonest of them. Clearly, my normal established spur pruning technique will remove most of the potential crop but, having anguished over the years about the best remedy, I am sure that the simplest solution is to restrict pruning to about half of the laterals each year.

When moving to a garden that already contains mature and well-cared-for trees, the established spur pruning method may be used, more or less regardless of the system used previously. If, as is often the case, however, the trees have been seriously neglected, a judgement must be made over the likelihood of ever inducing them to come back into full cropping. Provided the trees don't form an important feature of the garden structure, it is often better to cut your losses, cut down your trees and start afresh. Otherwise, a process should be begun of gradually cutting away dead, diseased or crossing over branches, as shown in the illustration on page 56. This is best spread over two or three winters to enable the tree to adjust to the new conditions.

The cordon is a form of fruit tree particularly suited to small gardens, to very windy sites, and to instances where several varieties are required in a restricted area. It is the simplest of the many methods used to train apples and pears against walls.

A strong framework of posts and wires will be needed against which the plants are placed. They may be grown vertically, but more usually, and more economically in terms of space, they are planted at an angle of 45 degrees. It is always easiest to start with a maiden plant and, for once, the best system of pruning is a summer system (and a French one to boot) known, after its inventor, as modified Lorette. (I have often thought that there must be a story to tell about the unquestionably tortured mind of Monsieur Modified-Lorette, but that is for another book.) Each summer, starting around mid-July, cut back all mature laterals arising directly from the main stem to three leaves (not counting the basal cluster). As you are wondering, quite reasonably, what consti-

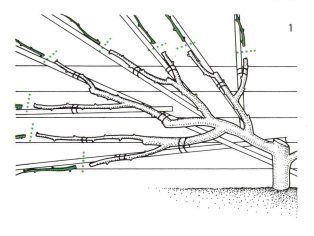

On a fan-trained Morello (1), winter prune leaders by half for three years, then (2) thin out new shoots in spring and (3) cut out fruited laterals in summer

tutes a mature lateral, it is one at least 20 cm (8 inches) long, bearing dark leaves and woody at the base. Any mature shoots arising from existing laterals or from spur clusters should be cut back to about 5 cm (2 inches) or one leaf beyond the basal cluster. Soft, immature laterals should be left until mid-September, when they should be treated in the same way. At this time, any new shoot growth on the July-pruned shoots should be cut back to one bud. The leader is not cut until the plant has filled its allotted space, when it should be cut back by the required amount in May. And you now know why I steer clear of most other French pruning systems!

Plums, Gages and Damsons
Although plums will need careful attention in the early, formative years, they are immeasurably easier than apples and pears thereafter. They differ also in that all pruning must be done in the spring or immediately after fruiting in the early autumn. If plums are pruned in late autumn or winter, they run a high risk of being infected by the fungus causing silver leaf disease. I prefer to see garden plums grown as open-centred half-standards for this is a form of growth particularly suitable for the most widely used varieties and for the popular rootstock, 'St Julien A', although bush trees may be grown successfully on the more dwarfing 'Pixie' rootstock.

A maiden tree, having one year's growth since grafting, should have its single shoot cut back to a good bud 25 cm (10 inches) above the height required for the stem; about 1½ m (5 feet) for a half-standard and about 1 m (3 feet) for a bush. This should be done just before growth starts in the first spring after planting. In the second spring, choose four of the strongest and most evenly placed of the new shoots that developed during the previous season and cut them back by between a third and a half, cutting each time to an outward-facing bud (except with 'Victoria' and those other varieties with a naturally spreading habit, when cutting to an inward-facing bud will help develop a more upright tree). Ideally, these shoots should arise from the stem at intervals of about 8 cm (3 inches) and, as with apples and pears, the best and strongest are those formed at an angle of about 45 degrees. If the tree has been bought as a two- or three-year-old, I suggest that you leave it unpruned for one year to help it establish.

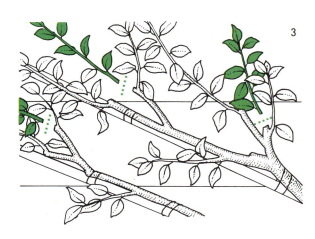

Continue the selection of well-placed shoots in the third spring after planting, shortening all branch leaders by between a third and a half. By this time, seven or eight main branches will have developed and the cutting back can thereafter be discontinued, unless, as with 'Victoria', it is still needed to shape the tree.

Once formed in this way, you should treat your plums to what is known in polite circles as regulated pruning or, translated into the language so beloved of one of my colleagues, do nowt.

Cherries

Although sweet and acid cherries can be grown as bush trees, I have always believed that the advantages of fan-training them against a wall are very much greater in respect of protection from the worst of the weather and the ease of netting against birds. Yet, when I said this to Clay, his response was that it might put people off growing cherries for ever and as he keeps his 'Stella' free-standing, poor girl, I shall modify my advice. I still think that wall-training is the best plan, but free-standing trees are possible if you have the cosseted climate of Chepstow!

Space and patience limitations preclude me from giving step-by-step advice for establishing the fan but the accompanying diagrams should make this clear. Always bear in mind that acid cherries fruit only on the previous year's wood and the pruning regime must be performed with this in mind. The fruiting habit of sweet cherries, however, is different from that of all other top fruit. They bear their fruit on spurs formed along the entire length of the two-year-old wood and although the basic formative pruning of the fan is the same as with acid cherries, the maintenance pruning is very different, therefore.

After the third year of plant establishment, the laterals should be shortened to about five leaves during July and then shortened again in September to four buds. At the same time, cut out any old wood that has already borne fruit. Although it will be necessary to rub out any buds facing the wall, there will generally be far fewer laterals than with other tree fruits. The major problem with sweet cherries, even on 'Colt' rootstock, is that they require a very tall wall because laterals are so few, leading shoots so vigorous and yet, as with climbing roses, cutting back the leader only compounds the problem, producing more and more upright growth. The only real way to overcome this is to bend the leader back on itself and tie it in so that new laterals will be produced. It can then be cut back to a weak lateral in the following year.

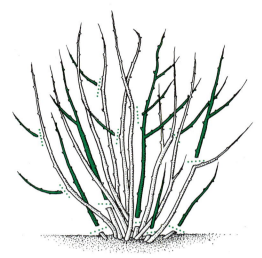

Peaches

I believe that growing peaches as free-standing trees is a waste of time in all except the extreme south of the country and they should be fan-trained and pruned in exactly the same way as acid cherries. You will find that some careful pulling and tying back of leaves to expose the fruit to the sun will aid the ripening process greatly.

Storing Top Fruit

Although plums, cherries and other top fruit can be frozen, bottled or otherwise preserved, fresh storage is limited to apples and pears. The main criterion is to select fruit that are as near blemish-free as possible. Always pick them very carefully by hand, therefore (certainly don't use windfalls), never pull out the stalk, and examine each very closely for evidence of bruising or pest and disease attack.

The fruit store can be a small shed, part of the garage set aside for the purpose, a spare bedroom or the loft. Mine is an old conversion of what our forebears called a garden closet. The term convenience food has taken on a new meaning in our family. As this building is some distance from the house, however, even I think twice about the desirability of satisfying my longing for a crunchy pippin on a late night in mid-February when the snow lies thick and the east wind howls. I have great sympathy for former owners of the house who may have had a more pressing need for the journey in such conditions.

The main criteria for a fruit store are that it can be kept at a uniform temperature as close as possible to about 5°C (40°F) and that it is free from contaminat-

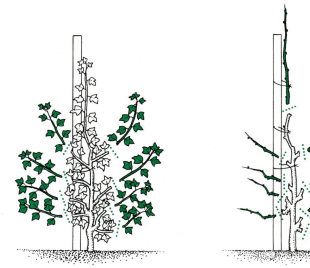

left, *Blackcurrants fruit mostly on the previous year's wood, so a proportion of this must be cut out each summer after fruiting*

right, *On redcurrants, shorten the laterals to five leaves in summer and then in winter, to basal buds. Cut back recent leader growth by half in winter.*

ing odours of paint or other chemicals. The latter may be difficult to ensure in a garage, and care should be taken in a shed to keep fruit away from garden pesticides. The fruit should be arranged on slatted shelves or in fairly open boxes with good air circulation. I store apples either unwrapped and singly on slatted shelves or as dozens in clean plastic bags either perforated or with the tops left partly open; I am unsure which is better. I have been disappointed with following the suggestion to wrap each fruit in newspaper because it seems to draw out the moisture. If possible, pears should be stored separately from apples; they will keep at lower temperatures but are best laid singly, unwrapped on shelves where they can be inspected regularly and used as they reach optimum ripeness. 'Conference' and 'Williams' store well but should be picked when still fairly hard.

Soft Fruit

If I had to forfeit any aspect of gardening, the soft fruit cage would be almost the last thing to go. It was certainly the first thing that I built in my present garden. Although soft fruit belong to two quite distinct families of plants (currants and gooseberries in one and the remainder in the other), a more natural division from the standpoint of cultivation and pruning is into the four groups of blackcurrants; redcurrants, whitecurrants and gooseberries; blackberries and their allies; and raspberries.

Although some gardeners still adhere dutifully to the range of soft fruit varieties that they or their fathers and grandfathers grew years ago, there is so much greater disparity between them and the more modern types than there is with top fruit that, almost without exception, I commend the modern varieties, bred largely in this country for our climatic conditions and to combat our pest and disease problems. As with top fruit, it is important to decide the period over which you wish the fruit to mature, but remember that as you are able to have many more bushes than trees, a much greater range may be chosen. Consider too whether you plan to freeze some of the crop, for varieties differ in their success when frozen. There are no complications to take into consideration with regard to pollination or rootstocks.

My recommended soft fruit varieties:
Blackcurrants: 'Ben More' (early–mid-season); 'Malling Jet' (late season).
Redcurrants: 'Stanza' – the one plant, even among soft fruit, that I would not be without (one day, if you take Clay or Geoffrey aside, they just might tell you something about my fondness for redcurrants that not many people know about!).
Whitecurrants: 'White Versailles'.
Gooseberries: 'Invicta' – best as a culinary variety and with the important advantage of resistance to gooseberry mildew; 'Jubilee' – primarily a culinary variety but sweet enough for dessert use if left to ripen. 'Leveller' is perhaps the best dessert variety but I hesitate to recommend it widely as it needs good conditions to give of its best.
Raspberries: 'Glen Clova' – a very widely grown, fairly early variety with the major merits of high yield and a long cropping season that starts early, but

Some recommended soft fruit varieties – strawberry 'Royal Sovereign' (above) and the much smaller fruited alpine, 'Delight' (left), the 'Medana' Tayberry (above right), and the raspberry 'Malling Joy' (right) with arching laterals

definitely not the best for flavour; 'Malling Joy' – my real discovery of recent years – high-yielding with the fruits produced on widely arching laterals and thus easy to pick, although requiring wider spacing between the rows. Very good for freezing and with good flavour. This is my choice if you wish to grow only one variety. 'Zeva' – probably the best overall autumn-fruiting variety and certainly the best for the north but nowhere should you expect anything approaching the yield of the summer-fruiting types. I no longer grow it and struggle with the yellow-fruited 'Fall Gold' which doesn't crop well but is fun. *Blackberries and Hybrid Berries*: Blackberry – 'Merton Thornless', one of the more compact varieties (many of the others will soon subjugate the entire fruit cage, and, indeed, 'Himalayan Giant', the rest of the garden too). As it is thornless, the fruit is easy to pick. Loganberry – 'LY 654' is completely thornless and easily the best loganberry for gardens. I can't understand why it has never been graced with a proper name. Tayberry – the 'Medana Tayberry' is easily the best of the modern raspberry/blackberry

hybrids with elongated, rich-purple fruits which may be eaten fresh or very successfully frozen.

There are two main siting considerations for soft fruit; the position must be sunny and it must (in most parts of the country) be such that the plants can be protected from birds, which will relish both buds and mature fruit. Although a netting fruit cage of the type illustrated is fairly expensive in capital outlay, it will more than repay you in the satisfaction of your actually being able to eat the fruits of your labours. The preparation of the soil is essentially as described for top fruit and the more thorough and well-planned this preparation, the more will the plants benefit. Again, as with top fruit, late autumn is the best planting time and this is when nurseries will be lifting plants for despatch. November is the ideal planting month but the operation may be continued until well into December, provided the ground is not frozen. A few additional points should be noted. Blackcurrants differ from all the other fruit in that the young bushes must be planted deeply; the bases of the young branches should just be covered with soil in

order to stimulate the production of new basal shoots. Raspberries are most easily planted into a narrow trench, placing each so that the upper roots are about 5 cm (2 inches) below soil level. Care should be taken, if possible, to align rows of raspberries north to south to obtain maximum sunlight. It may be convenient in some gardens to grow raspberries and other cane fruits along a fence, but it is important that they face predominantly south or south-west and that the training wires are attached to posts sited in front of the fence rather than on the fence itself.

Redcurrants, whitecurrants and gooseberries need no support if they are grown as bushes but as cordons they are most conveniently supported trained against a system of horizontal wires similar to that used for raspberries, with the addition of strong bamboo canes to aid the tying-in, especially when the plants are young. Loganberries, blackberries and their relatives all require strong supports and, again, the system suggested for raspberries will be suitable – I find they grow very well along the south-east-facing side of my fruit cage which happens to be the

garden fence. Blackcurrants require no staking or other support. In a very restricted area, I have grown perfectly good raspberries around a single, vertical post. I placed one plant on each side and trained a total of nine or ten canes.

Most soft fruits are predominantly surface rooting and are very prone to suffer checks to growth during dry weather therefore. This carries two messages; first, don't neglect the soft fruit garden when using the hosepipe in the summer and second, mulch the plants in early spring using well-rotted manure, compost, peat or bark. Blackcurrants, above all, benefit from this treatment. The main fertiliser requirement for established plants is potash but most gardeners, including me, find it simplest to apply a balanced fertiliser such as Growmore at the rate of about 50 g per square metre ($1\frac{1}{2}$ oz per square yard) in early March. Raspberries are especially prone to the leaf yellowing known as lime-induced chlorosis and routine application of sequestered iron is important early in the season.

Pruning Soft Fruit
There are only three basic pruning methods to remember for soft fruit and these depend principally on the age of the wood on which the fruit are borne.

Blackcurrants
Blackcurrants bear their flowers and fruit predominantly on wood produced last season. I still do all my pruning in winter and it really is very simple as blackcurrants can only be grown as bushes, their fruiting habit not being amenable to cordon training. On new bushes, cut down all shoots to within a couple of buds of ground level after planting in the autumn. After one year, cut out any weak shoots and also one of the new stronger shoots, with the objective of encouraging more young growth to form. Thereafter, each winter, cut out weak new shoots and, as the bush develops, cut back older shoots to a good low lateral shoot, or, if none is present, to ground level. In practice, with modern varieties you can adopt the Welsh autumn technique of pick and prune – Clay assures me that he has results just as good as mine simply by cutting out the old shoots as he completes the fruit picking.

Red and white currants, and gooseberries
Unlike blackcurrants, red and white currants and gooseberries fruit mainly on spurs produced on the older wood and also at the base of last year's shoots and there are both summer and winter pruning oper-

ations to consider. After planting, shorten all lateral shoots by about a half to an outward facing bud (the objective is to produce a vase-shaped bush). New leaders and laterals will then form; the latter should be shortened to five leaves during the summer when the fruit first begins to colour, but don't cut the leaders at this stage. The following winter, the leaders should be shortened by half (again cutting to an outward facing bud) and the laterals cut back close to the basal buds. These processes should be continued annually until the bush has reached its required height, when the leaders should be treated in the same way as laterals, shortening them to five leaves in the summer and to the basal buds in winter. I now grow all my red and white currants and gooseberries as cordons and essentially the same pruning method is followed except that only one, two or three leaders are trained vertically upwards. Laterals are shortened in summer and winter as I have described and the leaders are annually cut back by half in winter until they have reached their allotted height, when they are treated in the same way as laterals.

Raspberries

Summer-fruiting raspberries bear their flowers and fruit on the canes produced in the previous year. Immediately after planting, cut the canes back to about three buds above ground level. In the first year after planting, merely remove any weak canes, but thereafter, cut out completely all two-year-old canes immediately after they have fruited and thin the new canes to leave no more than eight per stool. It is most important to tie in new canes promptly to avoid wind damage; in years when I have neglected this, the drop in fruit production really has been very marked. Suckers will arise freely from established plants, often at some distance from the row. If they are really dense, you may need to take a spade to sever them but I manage by cutting them off just below ground level with an old pair of secateurs. And I mean an *old* pair of secateurs!

Autumn-fruiting raspberries produce a small amount (quite often, if I am honest, a pitiful amount) of fruit at the tips of the current year's canes and these should be pruned in late February by cutting all canes back to the base.

Blackberries, Loganberries and Hybrid Berries

Adopt the same general principles suggested for summer-fruiting raspberries; cut out all canes after they have fruited, but take care to leave young canes untouched. Tie in the young growth and gradually re-tie the canes outwards as they mature during the following season in order to keep the new non-fruiting wood in the centre.

Strawberries

I still have my doubts about strawberries as garden plants. A strawberry bed in a small garden takes up a fair proportion of valuable space if it is to supply more than a few token plants and most of us are now within reach of a good Pick Your Own fruit farm. Although various extraordinary contraptions rejoicing under the name strawberry tub have appeared in recent years, purporting to provide an answer to the problems of strawberries in small areas, I am convinced that they are far more trouble than they are worth.

However, if you have the space and you fancy a proper strawberry bed, read on. Although everyone classes them with soft fruit (they are, after all, both soft and fruit), strawberries are grown quite differently from all other soft fruits and I prefer to think of them as long-rotation vegetables.

Consider first the choice of plants. There are three main ways in which strawberry plants are sold. First, plants freshly dug from rooted runners in the open ground; these are usually available from October to April. Second, plants dug early in the spring from the open ground, kept in a cold store and sold during the summer, and, third, plants raised from runners rooted in small peat pots or more conventional plant pots and sold all year round. My preference has always been to establish a bed in late summer with plants raised in plant pots. These generally have a much more well-developed root system, will establish better and are easily worth the additional cost. Whichever type you choose, however, always obtain plants of defined quality raised by a reputable nursery from virus-free stock.

There are many varieties of strawberry and most, in my opinion, are little more than red pulp. The following, very short list comprises the few to which I would now give garden space: 'Cambridge Vigour' – best grown as an annual as it really yields well only for one season. 'Royal Sovereign' – a very modest yield and a very old variety, outcropped by most modern types and fairly disease-prone, but matchless for flavour. 'Aromel' – a 'perpetual' fruiting variety, best grown as an autumn-fruiting annual. Its yield is modest but the flavour good.

The cropping period of both earlier and later varieties can be extended by a few weeks with the aid of cloches but, in addition to the above, the so-called Alpine strawberries such as 'Baron Solemacher' produce a good and interesting crop of small fruit from early July until well into the autumn. I grow them very successfully at the front of a partially shaded herbaceous border and they seem to excite less attention from birds than do conventional large-fruited strawberries. Clay, as befits his seedy background, is an advocate of raising strawberries from seed and once, during the course of a programme recording, muttered 'Sweetheart' in my ear. I think (I hope) he was referring to a variety of that name which I tried a few years ago and which ultimately made excellent compost. He keeps promising me a sample of fruit but, like the word in my ear, I rather suspect that it amounts to sweet nothings.

Strawberries require sun and a well-drained site. A soil with tendencies to be heavy or waterlogged must be lightened with organic matter well in advance of planting, therefore. It is also most important to ensure that the bed is free from any perennial weeds. By planning at least a season in advance, it should be possible to clean even the most overgrown site with a combination of chemical weedkiller and cultivation. The planting bed should be prepared in exactly the same way as you would prepare a seed-bed but rake a 2:2:1 mixture of sulphate of potash, Growmore and superphosphate into the soil at the rate of 100 g per square metre (3 oz per square yard) shortly before planting. Once established, a bed of 'Royal Sovereign' should crop reliably for about three or possibly four years. Throughout its summer-fruiting period, any strawberry bed will need water and benefits from a straw mulch to help retain soil moisture and keep the fruit clear of the soil. Immediately after the fruit has been picked, work over the bed carefully and remove all old foliage by cutting just above the crowns with shears. This will expose the new growth to light and minimise the onset of disease problems. The only fertiliser necessary is a top dressing of about 50 g per square metre (1½ oz per square yard) of sulphate of potash in February.

Figs

Regularly staying in hotels with someone can teach you a great deal about human nature. You wouldn't think, would you, to look at Geoffrey, that here is a man who will do most things this side of the law to be served a dish of green figs for breakfast? Yet, poor fellow, his windy garden is no place for this windiest

A fruit cage of 3 by 3 metres can supply a family of four

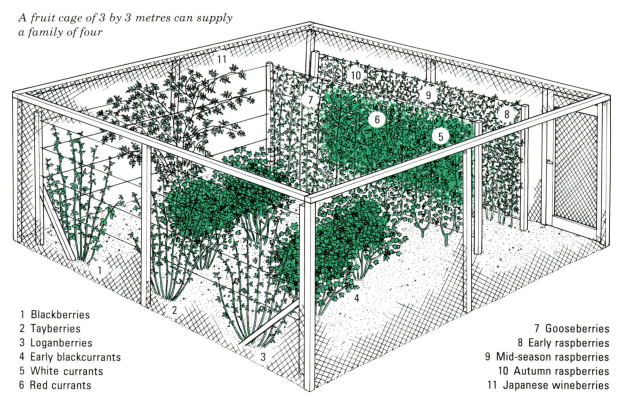

1 Blackberries
2 Tayberries
3 Loganberries
4 Early blackcurrants
5 White currants
6 Red currants

7 Gooseberries
8 Early raspberries
9 Mid-season raspberries
10 Autumn raspberries
11 Japanese wineberries

come to appreciate how much growth is put on by your plant each year and be able to judge how much cutting out and cutting back is needed in order to produce the correct balance of new and old wood.

Grapevines

The last grapevine that I had was in an old lean-to greenhouse. (I jest, for it had seen many and better days and strictly was a lean-from.) I never produced crops approaching Bacchanalian proportions but they are fun and I am currently musing over whether to plant one in my present greenhouse – as much as a living shade as a producer of fruit. Certainly it is possible to grow grapevines very successfully in this country, both in greenhouses and outdoors, as evidenced by the recent expansion of commercial British vineyards. However, they will not thrive in the north of the country or at a height over about 90 metres (300 feet) above sea-level and it would be misleading to suggest that, almost anywhere, you will obtain outdoor crops approaching the quality of the imported fruit to be seen on greengrocers' shelves. For greenhouse cultivation, 'Black Hamburgh' is far and away the most widely grown variety and generally the easiest too. For outdoor cultivation, choose 'Muller Thurgau', a very good white wine grape and one that can be eaten as a dessert also.

Outdoors in gardens, grapevines are best trained against a warm wall and even for greenhouse culture, a lean-to structure against a wall is the most straightforward system. I shall concentrate on these methods but my comments on training and pruning can be adapted to growing the plants outdoors against wires or in other types of greenhouse.

The major soil consideration is that it must be free-draining and at least 30 cm (1 foot) deep, for vines are deep rooting. A light dressing of well-rotted manure or compost should be incorporated but it is a mistake to make the soil too rich. (There are those, especially those from certain northerly regions, who advocate planting a grapevine over a dead sheep but these are not so easily acquired in civilised parts of the realm!)

For greenhouse cultivation, much the best plan is to cut a hole about 5 cm (2 inches) in diameter and at soil level through the wooden end wall of the greenhouse, plant the vine outside and train its leading shoot through to the inside.

As with figs, confining the roots will help restrict the plant's ambitions to produce masses of leafy growth and the best plan is to dig and line a hole as I have described. Fill this hole with a mixture of four parts of loam to one part of well-rotted manure and incorporate a generous dusting of bone-meal. Most gardeners will buy their young vines as container-raised plants but it is a mistake to plant them other than in the dormant season. Late autumn is the ideal time for planting.

Perhaps more than any other fruit, a greenhouse vine has a quite staggering demand for water and it is almost impossible to overwater one during the summer when the fruit is swelling. If local regulations permit, allow a hosepipe to trickle on to the soil at the base of the plant for at least one day a week.

Fertiliser requirements of vines are best summed up as little nitrogen but considerable potash. This is ideally provided by hoof and horn at the rate of 70 g per square metre (2 oz per square yard) early in the spring.

Pruning Grapevines

The easiest technique to adopt for a greenhouse vine is that known as the rod and spur system. After planting, carefully pass the main stem through the hole in the side of the greenhouse. In the first year of growth, train the leader within the greenhouse as shown on page 67, stopping it when it shows signs of becoming thin and straggly. This leader, known as a rod, will produce laterals along its length and these should be thinned to leave one every 45 cm (18 inches) or so and carefully tied-in as shown. Sub-laterals growing from these should be pinched out at one leaf. In December, when the plant is fully dormant, cut back all laterals to two buds from the base and shorten the leader by a half. This cutting back of laterals should be continued annually and, each December, the previous year's extension growth on the rod (not the entire shoot!) should be cut back by half until it has reached its allotted limit. Thereafter, it should be treated as a lateral.

Each spring, two new laterals will arise from the buds at the bases of each old shoot but only the strongest should be allowed to elongate, the other being pinched out. Continue to stop the sub-laterals at one leaf. It is also very important to thin the fruit trusses in order to obtain a few good, rather than many pitiful bunches. After fruit set (and I always shake the rods gently when the flowers are open to aid pollination), remove some of the young trusses to leave one for about every 30 cm (1 foot) of rod length. Thereafter, thin the individual bunches by removing up to half of the immature fruits. Use a blunt-ended pair of scissors and do not touch the grapes with your fingers as this will damage their protective bloom.

6

THE SMALL GREENHOUSE

Clay Jones

Having decided on the chapter heading I am now confronted with its definition. How small is small? The dimensions of the greenhouse may be determined by the total area of the garden or it may be as big, or as small as its price. One thing is certain. It is too small if it cannot house all the plants you wish to grow. So before buying and investing in a structure that is more or less permanent, pause with pencil and paper and give thought to your requirements.

My own greenhouse is a 5½ by 3 metres (18 by 10 feet) affair with a soil bed down one side and staging across the gable end and all the way down the other side. In its warmth I aim to grow a variety of vegetables, an all-the-year-round supply of pot plants for the house and it also serves as a propagating unit for seeds and cuttings. These are the bare essentials. It is adequate for my needs but there is hardly ever an inch of room to spare.

It is well-known that a greenhouse measuring 2½ by 2 metres (8 by 6 feet) is Britain's best seller. Its popularity is partly due to its economical price and also partly because it fits snugly into the average suburban garden. Furthermore, by careful planning and good management it should produce sufficient material to satisfy the garden and its occupants, the traditional family of four. It should and it will, unless the gardener gets bitten by the greenhouse bug, an incurable condition that only progressively larger greenhouses will ever ameliorate! I know from experience and observation that the casual greenhouse gardener can become converted to a dedicated enthusiast by the first ripe tomato, so be warned. If you are considering getting a 2½ by 2 metres (8 by 6 feet) structure, buy a 3 by 2½ metres (10 by 8 feet), you will be surprised how little more it will cost.

Having decided finally on dimensions you now have a choice of construction materials. The frame of modern greenhouses is either aluminium or cedarwood treated with a preservative as protection against the elements. Aluminium is, of course, the more durable of the two as it does not rust and needs the minimum of maintenance. Cedarwood greenhouses need looking after. They should be painted with a proprietary wood preservative every other year, quite a pleasant job on a warm summer's day. The preservative that should never, ever be used is creosote. Its fumes are fatal to plants growing anywhere near the treated area. The least expensive greenhouses are large tunnels covered with a 'skin' of heavy-gauge polythene supported on a framework of tubular aluminium. I look upon them as overgrown cloches but they are certainly better than nothing. Their major draw-backs are their vulnerability to wind damage and the necessity to renew the polythene skin at least once every three years. In addition, polythene does not retain heat as well as glass, and condensation can be a very real problem. Glass is definitely better and here again there is a choice to make between glass-to-ground structures and those that have walls, or part-walls of brick, wood or concrete sections. Quite frankly, I am not sure which is best and that is why my greenhouse has glass-to-ground on the soil bed side and concrete half-walls on the other sides.

The bed needs maximum light especially when plants are young and low on the ground, whereas the spaces under the staging are used mainly for storage and overwintering plants such as fuchsias, geraniums and dahlias.

Greenhouses come in two basic shapes – ones that mimic houses, with a ridged roof, four sides and a front door; and ones that are circular. The choice is yours and must depend on personal taste. Both types admit good light and are equally efficient at their allotted task of growing strong, top-quality plants. Lean-to houses cost less for the simple reason that they have two ends and only one side, the house wall acting as the fourth dimension. They are also cheaper to heat because the house retains warmth. It is possible to connect a lean-to greenhouse to the dwelling

above, *Lean-to greenhouses can be built into odd corners*

right, *Beat the clock with early strawberries under glass*

far right, *Tiered shelving adds more space and interest in greenhouses and conservatories*

house heating system, the only snag being that the house heating is usually non-operational at night, so some supplementary source of heat becomes necessary.

Siting the greenhouse correctly is vital, whichever type it is. A lean-to on a north-facing wall will lack adequate sunlight, whereas on a south-facing wall it will be bathed in sunlight all day. On east-facing walls plants can enjoy the morning sun and be in the shade from midday onwards and on the west side they will sunbathe in the afternoons only. The south wall is obviously the best, with east walls second best because plants seem to be more active before lunch than after, a trait I have noticed in some people I know! So pick the sunniest spot in the garden for the greenhouse and if it is the traditional ridge type, try to site it so that the ridge runs north to south. The sun beating its path across the sky from east to west will then smile equally on both sides.

Whatever you do don't put the greenhouse anywhere near trees. When in full foliage they can cast deep shade and they also have a nasty habit of dropping branches and other bits big enough to break the strongest horticultural glass. There's another thing: if a pane breaks, replace it with horticultural glass which is thicker and stronger than the normal household grade.

Do you suffer from wind, or rather, is your garden short of shelter? If it is, try to site the greenhouse well away from the brunt of north and east winds. The cold air they carry will not only force its way into the greenhouse, it will also suck warm air out as the gusts sweep past. In other words, the exposed greenhouse will prove far more costly to heat than ones that are sheltered in a warm corner of the garden.

Having bought and erected your greenhouse, there are a few extras needed; the accessories that make greenhouse management easy and efficient. All plants need water and ideally the water should be at greenhouse temperature to avoid checking growth. The very best arrangement for a small greenhouse is a 90-litre (20-gallon) galvanised tank, or a plastic water-butt positioned adjacent to and inside the door. In this position it can be conveniently refilled every morning, after watering, from a hosepipe attached to the nearest water point which could well be at the kitchen sink. If, for some reason, you reject the idea of having a water reservoir in the greenhouse, you will need at least two watering cans. The exotic plants in the greenhouse are not accustomed to having their

roots doused with cold water and react unfavourably to such harsh treatment. So the watering cans will have to be refilled and left to stand in the greenhouse for a few hours to acclimatise their contents to the ambient temperature before giving the plants a further drink. All things considered, a stand-pipe positioned just outside the greenhouse is a wise investment. It makes can and tank filling quick and easy and in addition the tap can be used to supply water to the whole garden during long spells of dry weather. A stand-pipe is also an aid to marital harmony! Before I had one installed I used to attach the hose to the kitchen tap which, frankly, was not a good idea. Once, I turned the tap on and by the time I had reached the greenhouse the din coming from the kitchen made a present-day disco sound like a chapel of rest. The hosepipe, of course, had sprung several leaks at the tap connector, spraying my wife, the cats and also the lunch with cold water. It was a time to retreat into the garden shed and when the dust had settled to promise to install a stand-pipe.

The next accessory for your greenhouse is electricity. Do you need it if, for example, you propose to provide heat by some other means or not at all? In my own greenhouse, an electrical supply is a must for

left, Automatic ventilators ensure fresh air

below, One of the many types of greenhouse heater

three reasons. First, I am often away during the day and on my return I like to nip up to the greenhouse to have a chat with my family of plants and to do those things that should not be left undone and I need electricity to lighten the darkness. Second, there are two electrically-powered propagators on the staging which I use for seed germination and for rooting cuttings. Third, the greenhouse is never empty in winter. It is a storehouse for frost-tender, overwintering plants, the bed is full of winter lettuce and on the staging are a number of pot plants coming on and scheduled for the house when they come into flower. To achieve all this, frost must be kept at bay and to prevent its ingress I use a fan heater, but more about heating later. I will tackle any job in the house and garden except one – I will not tamper with electricity. It is a job for a trained expert and although it will cost money, better a poorer gardener than a dead one.

Adequate ventilation is another necessity. First-time greenhouse gardeners often labour under the impression that the higher the temperature the better the plants like it. They keep the door and vents closed, so inside the conditions on summer days are comparable to a steamy Burmese jungle at the height of the monsoon. The net result is over-lush growth which is susceptible to infection by the first fungus spore that comes along. Every greenhouse must have at least one, preferably two, roof vents and ideally one or two side louvres as well to ensure free circulation of air and a healthy, buoyant atmosphere. These are the conditions enjoyed by the vast majority of the plants we grow in our greenhouses, with the exception of those such as some orchids, epiphytes and others whose origins lie in the humid, steamy forests of our globe.

Nowadays ventilation control presents no problems. For a few pounds you can buy automatic vent openers. They are fitted in minutes to either wood or aluminium frames and they cost nothing to run. They depend for their operation on the simple principle that some substances expand rapidly as the temperature rises and contract just as rapidly as it falls. In short, the only source of operative power they need is the sun. Automatic ventilators are a boon to gardeners who spend all day away from home, when the weather can change from cold and overcast to near equatorial in a matter of minutes. On the very hottest days, I leave the door wide open as well to avoid excessive temperatures and to ensure maximum aeration. If you think I'm exaggerating consider this, under excessively high temperatures the ripening of tomatoes is inhibited and the associated high trans-

danger of drying out and shrivelling. I use perlite because I find it lightweight, clean and highly absorbent. At the end of the season, I clean out the old perlite and spread it on the vegetable garden as a soil conditioner and replace it with fresh perlite to maintain hygienic growing conditions.

Under the heading of greenhouse equipment I include shading. At the height of a summer's day, temperatures under glass can soar to well over 38°C (100°F) and this, coupled with the very high light intensity, is not conducive to optimum growth. In unshaded greenhouses in summer you may have noticed the edges of tomato leaves curling inwards, an indication that the plants are trying to protect their leaf surfaces from over-exposure. For shading, use either a weak suspension of lime in water or one of the proprietary shading substances diluted as required. They will remain on the glass throughout all weathers and are easily wiped off with a dry cloth towards the end of August or early September as the sun dims its power. The very best shading is provided by green blinds that may be rolled up or down at the pull of a cord and at the whim of the weather.

Finally, I come to the question of heating and the cost involved which can be prohibitive. My advice to the gardener with a small greenhouse is this – in the dank depths of winter provide enough heat to ward off frost and to enable you to store tender subjects safely. From mid-March onwards, aim to maintain a minimum night temperature of 7°C (45°F) which will be high enough to sustain good growth of half-hardy annuals, tomatoes, peppers, cucumbers and all but the more exotic pot plants. For the small greenhouse there are two main heat sources – paraffin and electricity – and of the two paraffin is, or can be, marginally the cheaper but it has its drawbacks. It is messy, the reservoir has to be filled at regular intervals and its heat emission is constant, irrespective of external temperatures. A paraffin heater also increases condensation levels that can in combination with bright sunlight result in leaf scorch. For these reasons, I opt for electricity as my source of greenhouse heating. It is clean and by installing thermostatic control the appliances are operational only when the temperature falls below the thermostat setting.

Greenhouse electrical heating appliances are of two main types, namely tubular heaters and forced draught, fan heaters and there is much to be said for both. Tubular heaters are either free-standing or fitted to the walls a few centimetres above ground level. They are available in varying lengths and when present in sufficient numbers and strategically sited will provide an even distribution of heat. Fan heaters blow hot air and to achieve maximum efficiency they need to be positioned in the centre of the greenhouse, at ground level just inside the door. Their one advantage over tubular heaters is the buoyancy they create: even when the heating element is switched off by the thermostat the fan will continue to circulate air, keeping the atmosphere fresh and preventing the formation of moulds and mildews. My greenhouse and I live by the banks of the Severn estuary in an area of high humidity. Before I resorted to a fan heater, my overwintering pelargoniums, begonia tubers and such like became covered in mould despite dusting with fungicide. Since its introduction they have remained fungus-free. Having extolled the virtues of electricity, I must condemn its infidelity. It has a habit of going absent when it is most needed. Power cuts tend to occur in cold weather which is why I have kept the old paraffin heater as a standby for use when electricity lets me down.

Anything that can be done to reduce heating costs is a bonus and lining the greenhouse with polythene sheets is definitely a cost saver but it has its hazards. First, it increases condensation to dangerously high levels in areas where humidity is already high. Second, it is a two-person job. When I tried to line my greenhouse singlehanded I finished up in a cocoon of polythene and a filthy temper. Third, ordinary polythene is not good enough. You need the special lining grade that is air-permeable. In gardening terms it 'breathes', and prevents excessive condensation by being porous. The lining material should be put in place in October as temperatures drop and removed in March as they rise.

I also commend to you a heating system I saw recently in a DIY gardener's greenhouse. He had converted the entire staging area into one large propagator. He began by inverting all the aluminium trays so that he had a flat, even surface which he covered with lengths of capillary matting. He then constructed a wooden frame some 15 cm (6 inches) high around the whole thing and into one end he fitted a thermostat. To this, he connected a soil-warming cable in parallel loops about 15 cm (6 inches) apart and covered this with 3½ cm (1 inch) of quite fine sand. The next step was to find a suitable shroud to cover the construction and for this he used quite a heavy-gauge polythene tacked on to the side of the wooden frame nearest the glass, leaving the end nearest the greenhouse path free and mobile. At

Start broad beans in peat pots under glass for earlier crops. From seed sowing to planting takes about four to six weeks.

the free end he doubled back about 5 cm (2 inches) of polythene and stapled it to form a hollow tube into which he inserted a length of fairly heavy bamboo cane. The weight of the cane kept the polythene sheet taut over the wooden frame and when he wanted to see how his seeds and plants were doing it was a simple matter to roll the polythene back using the bamboo cane as a guide rod.

His greenhouse was 6 metres (20 feet) long, so for convenience and versatility he had subdivided his home-made propagator into four 1½-metre (5-feet) sections, each of which was independently shrouded with polythene. He has a large garden so in spring all four covered compartments are full of seeds and bulbs, corms and tubers – all being nudged into growth at a minimum temperature of 18°C (65°F). After germination and when there is visible growth on his begonia and gloxinia tubers, for instance, they are moved into an open compartment where they still have the benefit of basal heating and they grow apace. It works so well that he germinates traditionally difficult begonia seeds with ease and every year raises between 8000 and 9000 top-quality bedding plants, not to mention pot plants and a few hundred vegetable plants. All this is achieved with no other form of heating and he told me that in a power cut the covered compartments retain enough warmth to

keep all the plants happy until power is restored. When I have the time, I must follow his example.

At this point I must assume that either you have a small greenhouse or, having read this far, you will dash out and buy one. Either way it is now necessary to obtain the maximum return from your investment and the greenhouse can and must pay for itself in no more than two or possibly three years. It must be made to work all the year round and it should never be idle and empty. My pet hate is the sight of a greenhouse in abandoned retirement, from October to March, with the wizened remains of tomato plants standing like sentinels of death in offensive isolation. What a criminal waste. The greenhouse year begins in December with a thorough clean-out. I remove the remaining pot plants and provide them with temporary accommodation in the frame. The only plants that can't be moved are the vine and the winter lettuce in the soil bed. I cover the latter with a sheet of polythene before washing down the complete structure, inside and out, with a solution of a proprietary garden disinfectant, and pressure-spraying the area under the staging with the disinfectant. Empty pots and seed-trays come next. They are also washed in disinfectant and left to drip dry before being stacked in the garden shed. When the job is done and the greenhouse has the sweet smell of sterility, I bring all

77

the plants back in and lift the polythene sheet off the lettuce. All is set for the great spring surge which begins gently in January with a sowing of onion seeds in one of the two propagators and the taking of cuttings of 'indoor' chrysanthemums, that is, the ones that are summered in the open and brought into the greenhouse in September for flowering.

February is not a hyperactive period in the cool greenhouse. I sow seeds of fibrous-rooted begonias and geraniums because they need an early start to bring them into flower by June, but there is no advantage to be gained from sowing the main batch of half-hardy annuals so early. I also sow a few seeds of summer cabbages, cauliflowers and lettuces in peat pots for planting out in the cold frame or under cloches later on. Broad bean seeds are sown 5 cm (2 inches) apart in seed-trays for planting out and early cropping. Finally, with a gastronomic delight in mind I plant two seed potatoes of an early variety in the soil bed by the door. They will obligingly yield a reasonable lift of hen's egg sized, supremely delicious tubers in May, at least two weeks before the outdoor ones are ready. That's about all I do in February except to keep an eye on the overwintering plants and take anything that's coming into flower into the

above, Schizanthus, the 'Poor Man's Orchid', fills its pot and is easily grown from seeds

opposite above, Cinerarias in flower in early spring from a July sowing

opposite below left, Coleus or 'Jacob's Coat' comes in many colours, with lovely serrated and wavy leaves

opposite below right, Exacum affine, the Persian violet, is pretty and perfumed and grows easily from seeds

house to bring cheer to the winter windowsills. The look of appreciation in my wife's eyes is reward enough for the months of care I have lavished on the hyacinths, irises, cyclamen, calceolarias and cinerarias. They come in handy as peace offerings too on occasion!

Things really start happening in March. I sow the main batch of half-hardy annual seeds in the third week, as well as tomatoes and peppers, together with seeds of several pot plants for summer colour. We all have our special favourites and one I will always grow is Coleus. The multi-coloured leaves make Joseph's coat look drab by comparison and some of the newer varieties such as 'Milky Way' are so bushy and compact that they are just the things for window boxes as well as pots. I also grow a few pots of the lovely Exacum affine, the 'Persian violet', for its delicately scented, lavender-blue flowers. Another regular is Thunbergia alata, 'black-eyed Susan'. It is a darling little climber needing a 13-cm (5-inch) pot and a small plastic trellis that you can buy from any garden centre or shop. The single flowers are deep orange with a prominent black eye in the centre. My other choices for summer flowering are Hypoestes sanguinolenta – the 'polka-dot plant'; ornamental peppers; Schizanthus – the 'poor man's orchid'; and Solanum capsicastrum – winter cherry, for its winter berries. All these are easily grown from seed at a fraction of the cost of buying houseplants. Early in the month, the new growth on overwintered pelargoniums and fuchsias is a source of endless cuttings that in due course will furnish patio containers and pots with a riot of colour. It is also time to box up dahlia tubers in peat or compost for a supply of cuttings as soon as they are big enough to handle. It is all go and exciting and I am sustained with regular cups of tea as time slips by unnoticed.

The cups of tea continue throughout April when I have been known to eat my lunch in the greenhouse in between sowing and urgent pricking out. The begonias and gloxinias are ready for potting-on and so are the dahlia, pelargonium, fuchsia and chrysanthemum cuttings. The tomatoes and peppers are just right for planting in 'rings' on the soil bed and as the sun soars higher and higher the watering can gets busier and busier. I paint the glass with 'shading' and leave my bed an hour earlier to commune with the pulsating plants and to damp down if it looks like being a hot, sunny day. A yell from the back door signals breakfast, then I go back to the greenhouse where I find one of the cats asleep on a box of seedlings. It takes off at the speed of light and I resolve to

put netting over the open door to exclude pussies yet admit air. I calm down, rescue the seedlings and sow runner beans, melons, ridge cucumbers, bush tomatoes and sweet corn in peat pots, and wonder where I'm going to put them. The greenhouse is chock-a-block, bulging at the seams with the staging full, the shelves sagging and seed-trays along one side of the path. Luckily, some of the half-hardy annuals are mature enough to be moved into the cold frame for hardening off so I make space for more trays and pots.

May is the month of the great exodus. Tray after tray of bedding plants are moved from the greenhouse to the cold frame, and the various vegetables are ready for planting out. The tomatoes are way up their canes and call for regular tying-in and sideshooting. I notice that the first flowers are open on the bottom trusses and give them the first of their weekly feeds. I also notice that the whitefly have turned up and wait until evening before giving them a rapid burst of insecticide.

Work in the greenhouse eases off in June. There is plenty of room to rearrange the pot plants and allow adequate space for development. I am glad I installed automatic vent openers as the temperatures hit the roof, despite the shading. I sow cinerarias and cal-

below, *The greenhouse in early March is crammed full with seed trays;* right, *Sweet, juicy melons in the cold frame in late August/early September*

ceolarias for winter flowering and put the trays down at ground level between the tomato plants. I take leaf cuttings of Begonia rex and saintpaulias and put these also in the shade of the tomato plants. Tomato feeding is now a twice-weekly event and side-shooting is a daily task. The second-generation whitefly have been joined by greenfly and I decide to smoke them out after the sun has set.

July is more or less a repetition of June with the addition that it is time to restart resting Cyclamen corms into growth. These days, the door is left wide open all day and an inch or two on balmy nights. Having beaten the aphids, I now find a colony of ants in business under the staging and I dust their runs and the top of the nest with Phoxim.

August arrives and I find that something is eating the cineraria seedlings. I search but can't find the culprit. I return at dead of night, switch on the light and discover a fat snail in full munch. I remove him and take him up the grass bank to cool off and change his diet. I disbud the chrysanthemums and plant a few Freesia corms in the soil bed for winter-scented flowering. I sow Cyclamen seeds, take pelargonium cuttings and sow seeds of the lettuce 'Kwiek' to raise plants to grow on in the bed for cutting between November and February.

Frosts are certain in September and it is time to house tender plants including Azalea indica and winter cherry, and to bring in pelargoniums, fuchsias and begonias from their patio containers. I pinch out the growing tips of the tomato plants, now up to eight or nine trusses, and start the drying of gloxinias and Achimenes. The 'Kwiek' lettuces are ready for planting in the soil bed and their space on the staging is taken over by Cyclamen, calceolarias and cinerarias brought in from the cold frame. At the end of the month it takes but a few minutes to wipe off the glass shading with a dry rag. I reduce the frequency and volume of watering and feed only winter-flowering plants, including late chrysanthemums which are now indoors and ready for disbudding. I search frantically for my bulb bowls and find them in the shed under a pile of sacking. I plant them with irises, narcissi, early tulips, hyacinths and crocus.

In November and December I keep an eye on things and tidy up generally. On sunny days you could well find me in the greenhouse puffing at my pipe, basking in the warmth and just meditating!

To close the chapter on the joys of greenhouse gardening I hesitate, but must, exhort you to buy a garden frame as a very necessary adjunct. It will serve to harden off greenhouse-grown plants before

simple matter to restore the balance by liquid feeding. Before sowing, rake the bed to remove stones and to reduce soil to a fine, even texture. Then turn the rake upside down and use the end of the handle to mark out the sowing sections and sow in evenly spaced drills. I prefer sowing in drills, rather than broadcast, because it makes thinning the seedlings easier and it is also easier to recognise them among the weed seedlings that inevitably appear. To save time, combine the job of hand-weeding with thinning out and don't waste the thinnings but use them to fill gaps. After thinning, the remaining seedlings miss the support of their departed neighbours and tend to flop over. To prevent this happening, push them upright, draw a little soil around them and water them in.

Hardy annuals sown in late March to early April will come into flower in June and most will continue to flower right through the summer with a little help.

They need deadheading at regular intervals. This involves nipping off the faded flowers before they set seeds, so that the plants continue to produce more, and still more, flowers in a valiant attempt to guarantee their survival. When the summer show is eventually over, pull the plants up and put them on the compost heap to rot down into food for next year's plants. A good gardener wastes nothing, not even a dead hardy annual.

Hardy Annuals of Particular Interest

Clary (Salvia horminum). A close relative of the red bedding salvia to which it bears little resemblance. It is a beautiful, elegant plant grown for its colourful leaves or bracts, that at first sight look just like flowers. The colours are blue, pink and white marked with pretty and intricate veining. Very popular and useful in flower arrangements, the bracts will retain

SOME HARDY ANNUALS

Botanical Name	Common Name	Colour	Height
Alyssum maritimum	Sweet Alyssum	White, pink and violet	8–15 cm (3–6 in)
Amaranthus caudatus	Love-lies-bleeding	Green or crimson	60 cm–1 m (2–3 ft)
Bartonia aurea	Blazing Star	Golden-yellow	60 cm (2 ft)
Calendula officinalis	Scotch Marigold	Yellow and orange	30–60 cm (1–2 ft)
Calliopsis drummondii	Gold Crown	Yellow with deep purple centre	45–60 cm (1½–2 ft)
Centaurea cyanus	Cornflower	Blue, red, pink and white	60–90 cm (2–3 ft)
Centaurea moschata	Sweet Sultan	Pink, lavender, purple, blue and white	45 cm (1½ ft)
Chrysanthemum tricolor	Annual Chrysanthemum	Yellow, red, orange and white in concentric bands	30 cm–1 m (1–3 ft)
Clarkia elegans	—	Shades of red, pink and purple	60 cm (2 ft)
Convolvulus minor	—	Blue and rose with yellow and white centres	30 cm–1 m (1–3 ft)
Dimorphotheca aurantiaca	Star of the Veldt	Yellow, orange and white	25–30 cm (9–12 in)
Echium plantagineum	Bugloss	Lavender, rose or white	30–45 cm (12–15 in)
Eschscholzia californica	Californian Poppy	Red, pink, orange, yellow and white	15–30 cm (6–12 in)
Gypsophila elegans	Fairy Flower	Pink or white	45 cm (1½ ft)

their colour for several months without fading.

Godetia (Godetia whitneyi). Bearing the apt and enchanting name 'farewell to spring', the godetia is among the most colourful of all hardy annuals. The plants are neat and bushy and in full flower resemble a mass of azaleas.

Larkspur (Delphinium consolida). This is the annual equivalent of the perennial delphinium. It grows in stately spikes to a height of 1¼ m (4 feet) and is ideal for the back of the border. It is claimed by some that the liquid distilled from the flowers improves vision, so larkspurs are a sight for sore eyes in more ways than one.

Mallow (Lavatera rosea). Did you know you can grow a 1 to 1¼ m (3 to 4 feet) summer hedge from seeds of a hardy annual? With Lavatera you can. It grows rapidly, forming tall plants with strong, woody stems. The large, apple-green leaves are a perfect foil for the open, trumpet-shaped flowers in shades of rose-pink with deeper-coloured veins radiating from the centre.

Scarlet Flax (Linum grandiflorum rubrum). I include Linum among my specials for its brilliant red colour, the petals overlaid with a sheen as though they were highly polished, a rare colour among hardy annuals.

Poached Eggs (Limnanthes douglasii). A low, spreading annual in the colours of poached eggs. The flowers are faintly scented and attract bees in large numbers. They seed themselves with gay abandon and come up year after year.

Nasturtium (Tropaeolum majus). Nowadays, nasturtiums are vastly improved. The older climbing and rambling varieties are still around and very useful they are for covering trellis-work and dry banks on poor soil. The more modern varieties such as 'Whirlybird' are nice, compact plants bearing their many-coloured flowers well above the foliage and are ideal for bedding. The leaves and seeds are good in

Botanical Name	Common Name	Colour	Height
Helianthus annuus	Sunflower	Yellow and bronze	60 cm–6 m (2–20 ft)
Iberis umbellata	Candytuft	Shades of blue, pink and white	25–40 cm (9–15 in)
Layia elegans	Tidy Tips	Yellow-tipped with white	30–40 cm (12–15 in)
Leptosiphon hybridus	Stardust	Red, pink, orange, yellow and mauve	25–30 cm (9–12 in)
Linaria maroccana	Toadflax	Blue, red and yellow	25–30 cm (9–12 in)
Nemophila menziesii	Californian Bluebell	Blue with white centres	15 cm (6 in)
Nicandra physalodes	Shoo-fly Plant	Lavender	60 cm–1 m (2–3 ft)
Nigella damascena	Love-in-a-mist	Blue, pink and white	30 cm (1 ft)
Papaver rhoeas	Shirley Poppy	Salmon, pink and white	60 cm–1 m (2–3 ft)
Phacelia campanularia	Heavenly Bells	Gentian blue	25–30 cm (9–12 in)
Reseda odorata	Mignonette	Insignificant, strongly-scented	30 cm (1 ft)
Saponaria vaccaria	Soapwort	Pink	60 cm (2 ft)
Tropaeolum peregrinum	Canary Creeper	Yellow	Climbing
Viscaria vulgaris	—	Blue, pink, red and white	30–40 cm (12–15 in)

right, *Grown closely together, delphiniums may not need staking except in windswept gardens*

far right, *Achillea 'Gold Plate' is a bright border flower and dries well for winter arrangements*

below, left to right, *The cool blue flowers of Campanula lactiflora look good in the summer border; Linum narbonense from southern Europe flowers right through from June to September; Rudbeckia 'Goldilocks'; Hemerocallis 'Burning Daylight'; Tagetes 'Starfire Mixed'*

salads, having a very slightly peppery flavour.

Night-scented Stock (Matthiola bicornis) and Virginian Stock (Malcomia maritima). I couple them together because that is how they should be sown – as a mixture. By day, Night-scented stock is a drab nonentity, but at dusk it is transformed into a sweet-scented beauty. The advantage of sowing the two stocks together is that the one provides colour by day and the other a perfumed garden by night.

Butterfly Flower (Schizanthus pinnatus). Sometimes called 'poor man's orchid', Schizanthus has been widely grown as a pot plant. The hardier mixtures are also superb in warm borders, exotically lovely in soft, pastel shades, the flowers attractively veined and spotted in the throat.

Sweet Pea (Lathyrus odoratus). The doyen of hardy annuals. It has everything, an incomparably lovely form, a gorgeous range of colours, a heady perfume and an amazing diversity. If you want tall plants to grow as a decorative hedge, or for cutting, choose the tendril-climbing Spencer hybrids. Lower down the scale are the shorter 'Jet Set' sorts, at 1 metre (3 feet) they are the best for forming flowering hedges. Virtually hugging the ground at a mere 15 to 30 cm (6 to 12 inches) are varieties such as 'Cupid' and 'Patio'. By choosing the right varieties you could clothe your walls, cover your fences and fill your borders and patio containers with sweet peas that will bloom all summer long.

The list of hardy annuals on pages 84–5 contains many little beauties that tend to be neglected. Try a few. Echium will bring bees and butterflies all a flutter, and the dainty Gypsophila is the perfect complement to a vase of sweet peas. Canary creeper is a really beautiful climber and a clump of mignonette here and there will scent the whole garden.

Half-hardy annuals differ from the hardy kinds in their places of origin. Their forebears were found in the tropics and subtropics and their seeds find our springtime soil temperatures too low for germination. To get them sprouting they need extra warmth which inevitably means extra cost but it need not be prohibitive. The easy way out is to nip along to a garden centre and buy boxes of them as 'bedding plants'. Then half-hardy annuals *are* expensive and, with respect, I cannot abide having someone else's plants in my borders. I prefer to grow my own.

To achieve good germination of half-hardy annual seeds a minimum temperature of 18° to 20°C (65°F plus) is essential. In fact some, such as Salvia and Begonia, will not break their dormancy under 21° to 24°C (70° to 75°F). Therefore, I suggest you invest in a thermostatically-controlled, electric propagator. It is, I admit, a fairly expensive item but, once bought, it should last for many years and its daily operating costs can be counted in just a few pence. Once the seeds have germinated, the seedlings will grow on quite happily at the much lower temperature of around 7° to 10°C (45 to 50°F). If your garden is small and you need only a few plants to fill it, use your airing cupboard as a propagator. To avoid soiling your 'smalls' sow the seeds in a half-sized seed-tray, water them, then put the tray in a polythene bag with the open end tucked tightly underneath. This also prevents loss of moisture. Don't forget about them. Examine them every day and the moment the seedlings start pushing through, take the tray out of the airing cupboard, discard the polythene bag, and put the seedlings by the sunniest window of the house.

The important question is, when is the best time to sow seeds of half-hardy annuals so that they will flower to their full potential all summer? Traditionally, they were sown in early February in what has proved to be the mistaken belief that the earlier they were sown, the earlier they would flower and the more flowers they would bear. Admittedly, a very few of our summer 'bedders' are slow beginners and do need an early start. This is true particularly of begonias and zonal pelargoniums, but most others will flower just as profusely and just as early when their seeds are sown at the end of March. Obviously, the later they are sown the less will be the heating cost involved in raising the seedlings to planting-out maturity.

Having raised the plants in warmth, continue to be kind to them. Don't take them straight out of the warm greenhouse, or from the sunny windowsill and stick them in the comparative chill of the outdoor soil. The shock would be great, so great that they might turn up their tips and die. At best their growth would be severely checked and their flowering seriously affected. Before planting, give them a hardening-off period of at least a week in the garden frame, leaving the top open during the day and closed at night. In the absence of a cold frame, harden them off under cloches but if you don't have cloches, take the trays outdoors every morning and bring them in again just before the sun dips over the horizon.

Further Pointers to Success

1 Sow thinly, cover the seeds lightly and evenly and don't overwater.

2 Use a fine-mist hand-sprayer for the first watering.

A coarse sprayer may wash the seeds into a heap in a corner of the tray.

3 Always use a good seed-compost.

4 Prick out the seedlings as soon as they are large enough to handle.

5 Treat them with loving care and talk to them. A journalist from *The Times* once came to interview me. Among other things, he wanted to know what I said to plants that were tardy and reluctant. My spontaneous reply was 'Grow, you buggers, grow' and these immortal words appeared as a bold headline to his article in that august newspaper.

Planting-out time varies from north to south depending on the weather. In the south the end of May or beginning of June is usually about right; it should be a week or more later in the north. There is always the risk of a late frost. I remember a year when I lost all my planting on a freak and frosty night on the 20th of June! Before planting, mark out the beds as I described for the hardy annuals and apply a dressing of general fertiliser forked in just below the surface. Having grown good plants, treat them with tenderness as you take them out of the trays. The best way to do this is to give the tray a sharp tap or two at one end which will loosen the plants so that you can remove them in a solid block. Then tease them apart with your fingers, keeping as much compost as possible around the roots. With a trowel make a hole big enough to take the roots, ease the plant in and firm it gently, ever so gently, with your fingertips. The very

SOME SUGGESTIONS FOR YOUR HALF-HARDY BORDERS

Name	Variety	Colour	Height
Ageratum	'Blue Mink'	Azure blue	25 cm (9 in)
Antirrhinum	'Floral Carpet'	Mixed	30 cm (12 in)
Antirrhinum	'Bright Butterflies'	Mixed	80 cm (2½ ft)
Aster	'Dwarf Bedding'	Mixed	15 cm (6 in)
Aster	'Princess'	Mixed	80 cm (2½ ft)
Cineraria maritima	'Dwarf Silver'	Silver-leaved foliage plant	30 cm (12 in)
Cleome (Spider Flower)	'Colour Fountain'	Shades of rose and purple	1 m (3 ft)
Helichrysum	'Bright Bikini'	Various – good for cutting and drying	35 cm (15 in)
Lobelia	'Cambridge Blue'	Azure blue	15 cm (6 in)
Lobelia	'Crystal Palace'	Deep blue	15 cm (6 in)
African Marigold	'Inca'	Gold, orange and yellow	30 cm (12 in)
African Marigold	'Climax'	Shades of yellow and orange	1 m (3 ft)
French Marigold	'Naughty Marietta'	Deep yellow with maroon blotch	15 cm (6 in)
Mesembryanthemum	'Livingstone Daisy'	Carmine, pink, salmon and orange	8 cm (3 in)
Nemesia	'Carnival'	Mixed	30 cm (12 in)
Zonal Pelargonium	'Sundance'	White and all shades of red and pink	30 cm (12 in)
Petunia	'Resisto'	Mixed – rain resistant	30 cm (12 in)
Petunia	'Picotee'	Mixed with white edges	35 cm (15 in)
Rudbeckia	'Goldilocks'	Gold with deep-brown centre	80 cm (2½ ft)
Salpiglossis	'Friendship'	Mixed, veined in black	60 cm (2 ft)
Salvia	'Blaze of Fire'	Scarlet	30 cm (12 in)
Statice	'Colour Blend'	Mixed, good for cutting and drying	50 cm (1½ ft)
Ten-week Stock	'Dwarf Mixed'	Mixed pastel shades	30 cm (12 in)
Tagetes	'Lemon Green'	Lemon-yellow	25 cm (9 in)
Verbena	'Showtime'	Mixed	30 cm (12 in)

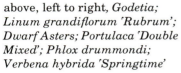

above, left to right, *Godetia; Linum grandiflorum 'Rubrum'; Dwarf Asters; Portulaca 'Double Mixed'; Phlox drummondi; Verbena hybrida 'Springtime'*

right, *Filipendula ulmaria 'Aurea' or 'Golden Meadowsweet' is aglow with colour all summer long*

far right, *Spencer hybrid sweet peas have no equal for perfume and the more you cut, the more they flower*

below, *Alchemilla mollis or 'Lady's Mantle' is a superb plant for sun or shade*

best time to plant is in the cool of the evening and then finish off the job with a thorough watering. After that it is a question of controlling the weeds, dead-heading and admiring the patchwork of colour that is your own creation.

Some Highly Commendable Half-hardy Annuals

The number of species and varieties available from shops, garden centres and seedsmen's catalogues is vast, yet so many gardeners seem loth to try new things. Look around suburban gardens and what do you see? Mile upon mile of neat rows of alyssum, Lobelia, Salvia, a few marigolds perhaps and little else. Pretty, but pretty boring too. Why not have a go at Nicotiana? The tobacco plant was once a tall plant which had a limited range of colours but the new F_1 hybrid 'Domino' varieties are neat and tidy, 30-cm (1-foot) beauties, and their colours encompass everything except blue. There is even a soft lime-green and they all have a superb scent.

Busy Lizzies too have changed out of all recognition. No longer are they the lanky occupants of cottage windows, fed with cold tea. Varieties such as 'Blitz' and the 'Elfin' strain are low and compact plants with large, brilliantly-coloured blooms, but the best for bedding is 'Accent'. It has a fantastic colour range and in my garden it will bloom come rain or shine, in sun or shade and it won't give in until hard hit by frost.

For carpet bedding, the Afro-French F_1 hybrid marigolds in orange, gold and lemon are warm and wonderful. The short-stemmed plants are a mere 30 cm (1 foot) tall and cover themselves with powderpuff blooms as much as 8 cm (3 inches) across. Being F_1 hybrids, the plants are of uniform height and habit, very desirable attributes in massed bedding.

Fibrous-rooted begonias are quite incredible. They will start flowering in June from February sowings and will be massed with blossom to summer's end. But they are not finished then. Lift a few plants before the first frost, pot them singly, cut them back by about half, keep them warm and they will burst into bloom again as winter houseplants. Who can ask for more? In addition, many varieties have glossy, bronze-coloured leaves to set off the reds, pinks and whites of the flowers.

Portulaca has never attained popularity yet it is a useful, ground-hugging plant with brilliant colours. It has succulent, tubular leaves and double flowers like lovely miniature roses. The variety 'Sunglo' is only 15 cm (6 inches) in height, but what it lacks in stature it makes up for in display. Portulaca revels in full sun and is ideal for those empty pockets in the rock garden, and on top of walls and dry banks.

If you listen to 'Gardeners' Question Time' you will know that I am a dazzled devotee of the annual phlox – Phlox drummondii. Every year I grow the 'Carnival' mixture and every year I am amazed that a single mixture of anything can come in so many colours – pink, salmon, red, white and blue, many of them with a darker, contrasting 'eye' colour. It will grow anywhere that gets a fair share of sunshine, its flowers gazing upwards to the heavens, even in the rain.

I find zinnias fascinating but frustrating. Started off in the greenhouse they are as temperamental as tennis stars (but a lot prettier). The trouble is they tend to develop blackleg, a fungus condition that blackens the seedling stems and kills them. I lost countless seedlings until, in desperation, I tried sowing direct outdoors in early May under small propagating cloches. They germinated like mustard and cress, grew at an astonishing speed and flowered profusely by early July. I have grown them this way for several years since and I never fail to get good plants and plenty of flowers to spare for cutting. There are many varieties ranging from the little 'Thumbelina' at 15 cm (6 inches) up to the tall 'Dahlia-flowered' and 'State Fair' at 80 cm (2½ feet), in every colour.

In this book there is room only for a brief reference to biennial and perennial flowers, though their value in our gardens is inestimable. A biennial is a plant whose seeds are sown in the early summer of one year to produce plants that will flower in the early summer of the following year. In a sense they are annuals that need an overwintering period. They are the ones that fill the colour gap between the great spring show of daffodils, narcissi, crocus and snowdrops and the even greater summer show of annuals and perennials. Heading the popularity list of biennials are wallflowers, filling our borders with colour and scent in May, closely followed by double daisies, Canterbury bells, Brompton stocks, forget-me-nots, Iceland poppies and sweet Williams. The trouble with biennials is that people forget to sow them; next year seems a long way off and it is hard to remember that biennials need about twelve months' growth to make good flowering plants. Sow the seeds thinly in rows, in May or June in a seed-bed and thin and transplant the seedlings to 15 cm (6 inches) apart when they are big enough. By late September or early October they are ready for their final move into beds recently vacated by summer bedding. Bearing in mind that these young plants have to survive the harshness of winter, the only fertiliser they need is a little something to encourage root growth, so dust the soil with bone-meal just before planting.

Perennials are our garden 'regulars'. They grow and flower every year, die back in winter to reappear the following spring from subterranean food stores, or from dormant rootstocks. They encompass the vast bulk of our permanent plants, ranging from the tiniest bulbs and alpines to the mightiest trees. In gardening terms, perennial is normally meant to refer to herbaceous plants that bring colour to our

borders season after season, year after year.

Unlike trees and shrubs that, once planted and established, are more or less self-sufficient, herbaceous perennials need a little more of our time. To begin with they respond to a rich, fertile soil, well-prepared before planting, bearing in mind that their tenancy is, in a sense, permanent. However, like most tenants their premises need a spring-clean from time to time. They are normally planted in their youth as youngsters with a few leaves and a primary root system. Over the years they form large and ever larger clumps, with new growth appearing annually from the periphery. The net result is a clump that is devoid

SOME LOVELY HERBACEOUS PERENNIALS IN FLOWER DURING THE PERIOD JUNE TO SEPTEMBER

Botanical Name	Common Name	Height	Description
Achillea filipendulina	Gold Plate	150 cm (5 ft)	Good for drying for winter arrangements
Alchemilla mollis	Lady's Mantle	45 cm (1½ ft)	A plant for all places, small pale-yellow flowers
Anemone hybrida	Windflower	60–80 cm (2–2½ ft)	White or pink flowers, good for cutting
Astilbe×arendsii	Goat's Beard	60–80 cm (2–2½ ft)	Likes moist soil and light shade, white, cream and pink flowers
Astrantia major	Masterwort	90 cm (3 ft)	Good for drying, attracts bees, pinkish-green flowers
Campanula lactiflora	Bell Flower	100 cm (3½ ft)	Lavender-blue bells
Coreopsis grandiflora	—	70 cm (28 in)	Golden-yellow
Delphinium hybrids	Belladonna	120–150 cm (4–5 ft)	Long spikes of white, pink and blue florets
Filipendula ulmaria 'Aurea'	Meadow Sweet	45 cm (1½ ft)	Grown for its lovely golden-yellow leaves
Gaillardia aristata	Blanket Flower	90 cm (3 ft)	Orange-yellow with darker centre
Geranium sanguineum	Crane's-bill	25 cm (10 in)	Magenta-purple flowers, excellent ground cover
Gypsophila paniculata	Baby's Breath	90 cm (3 ft)	A mist of white flowers, good for cutting
Hemerocallis hybrids	Day Lily	60–90 cm (2–3 ft)	Shades of yellow, orange, red and white
Linum narbonnense	Flax	45 cm (1½ ft)	Brilliant blue flowers
Lupin hybrids	Lupin	100 cm (3½ ft)	Almost every colour and bicolours
Nepeta mussinii	Catmint	30 cm (1 ft)	Grey leaves, pale-blue flowers
Ophiopogon planiscapus nigrescens	—	45 cm (1½ ft)	An unusual mass of spiky black leaves
Phlox paniculata	—	80–90 cm (2½–3 ft)	All the colours of the rainbow, good cut flower
Phormium tenax	New Zealand Flax	100 cm (3½ ft)	Imposing foliage plants, some with variegated leaves
Sedum spectabile	Ice Plant	35 cm (14 in)	Heads of light-pink flowers, attracts butterflies

of life in the older centre, and ringed on its circumference by new shoots that become progressively weaker as the soil and the clump become 'worked-out'. To restore a herbaceous border to its prime is a job that needs doing once every three to five years when it is apparent that the quality of growth and bloom is on the decline. The best time to tackle the task is during a mild period in March just before growth gets going in earnest. Start by lifting all the clumps and put them in groups with their labels somewhere out of the sun and safe from frost and drying winds. In the right place they will survive for days until the refurbished bed is ready for their return. I once had to regenerate a huge herbaceous border which, coupled with other day-to-day jobs, took two weeks to complete. During the entire period the lifted clumps were stored under the shade of a north-facing hedge with sacks thrown over the roots as protection and they didn't mind a bit. Once the border is clear of plants, dig it to a good spade's depth, at the same time putting in as much well-rotted compost or manure as you can possibly spare. After digging, leave it for a day or two, then tread it, rake it and, as a final touch, top dress with a general fertiliser. The one I use is Fish, Blood and Bone because, being organic, its action is gentle and it contains a goodly amount of the nitrogen the plants will need to make leaf growth and the phosphate required for rapid root development.

The border is now ready for rehabitation. From each old clump either chop off small, fist-sized pieces from the younger parts around the edges, a job I do with an old bread knife, or you can first break up each clump with two garden forks as Geoffrey has described in his chapter on propagation. Then plant them in groups of three to six in their allotted places according to your plan. At this stage some books advise inserting canes to support tall plants such as delphiniums later on. I don't, for the very good reason that a forest of bamboo canes sticking up out of bare ground offends my eye. I prefer to put the canes in when there is sufficient foliage to camouflage them.

For gardeners contemplating planting a perennial herbaceous border for the first time, I suggest you choose your plants on the three 'S's principle. The first 'S' stands for simplicity of design. A straightforward, rectangular bed is easier to mow around and maintain and after all it is the plants that provide the display, not the shape of the border. The second 'S' is for suitability. In a sunny border, plant sun-loving plants, and plant shade-tolerant ones where trees or walls and fences blot out the sun. Suitability, for me, also means planting wisely, siting tall subjects at the back of the border and short ones in front and also selecting perennials that all come into flower at the same time to give a great and glorious show at the height of summer. If you attempt to plant with spring, summer and autumn colour in mind the end-result is 'bitty' with large gaps of nothing all the year round. The third and final 'S' stands for sufficiency. If there is one thing I detest it is a border with a single Delphinium spike, or a solitary lupin groping for prominence among other lovely denizens of the herbaceous border.

I have used the herbaceous border to illustrate the needs and uses of perennial in the garden but I recognise that the trend nowadays is towards mixed borders. In these, a variety of perennials is planted and positioned to complement foliage and flowering shrubs and very nice they look. They are perhaps the answer to today's life-style where the garden often has to take second place to work or other leisure pursuits. Mixed borders mean less maintenance, an important consideration when equating time and space.

8

ROSES BY ANY OTHER NAMES
Introduction & Modern Roses

Geoffrey Smith

Forty years' experience of growing roses in gardens where the soil varied from blow-away sand to glacial clay has only served to demonstrate that they do function best on heavy land. Soil preparation, be it sand or clay, consists of forking organic matter into the top 45 cm (18 inches) of the area to be planted, as I describe in Chapter 9. Do this in the autumn, then in January perform a soil test to find out if the soil needs lime.

Some ten days before the actual planting takes place, a dressing of complete fertiliser worked into the soil surface with a fork makes certain there is a balanced food supply available for the roots. Roses are usually sent out from the nursery with top growth pruned fairly hard back, but if they are not, cut strong shoots back to three buds. Remove weak growth completely, and lightly trim the roots back by an inch or two. Root trimming encourages rapid growth of new fibrous rootlets, which ensures the bush quickly establishes itself in the new quarters. Planting distances must be adjusted according to the variety. A strong growing rose such as 'Southampton', or 'Robusta' will require 60 cm (24 inches) between individuals, at least, whereas a variety modest in stature and less vigorous in growth will need only 35 cm (14 inches). When judging distance remember that all the routine work of feeding, pruning, mulching and deadheading is much easier amongst bushes which are correctly spaced. Dig a hole large enough for the roots to be comfortably spread out and deep enough so the union between stems and root is buried 5 cm (2 inches) below the soil surface.

All roses need regular pruning, feeding and mulching to keep them in good health and flowering well. Gardeners argue interminably about how, when, and with what severity to prune. My advice is, decide which style of pruning suits your plants and is most convenient, and stay with it until proven wrong by subsequent events. As a general guide only, choose a warm day in March so the work can be done in comfort. Then with spring burgeoning all around, adjust the severity of the pruning according to the vigour of the variety undergoing surgery. First, remove all weak, dead or diseased wood completely to reveal the general framework of the branches which will carry the year's flowers. With hybrid tea roses, cut strong shoots back to seven buds and weaker growths to five.

Floribunda roses are pruned like hybrid teas in the first year. In the second year, cut back all shoots to approximately half their length. In the third year, cut approximately one-third of the shoots back to within four or five buds of the base; the rest should have the previous year's growth reduced by half. In the next year, cut more old wood hard back while only lightly pruning the young shoots. In this way floribunda roses are rejuvenated on a three-year cycle.

opposite, Queen Mary's rose garden in Regent's Park, London is a celebration of colour

'Albertine' (above left) is still one of the most popular scented climbing roses; 'Wendy Cussons' (top right) remains a prime favourite, with well shaped damask-scented blooms; 'Fantin Latour' (left) in shape, colour and delicate perfume is a most desirable shrub rose; 'Reine des Violettes' (above) is a fragrant hybrid perpetual

There is one form of pruning common to all roses – deadheading. Spent blooms should be deadheaded as the petals fade. Do this with a pair of secateurs or a sharp knife, cutting each stem back to a strong bud. Suckers, which are unwanted shoots produced from the rootstock, are not cut off; they should be pulled right away from the base.

Feeding established roses is essential to balance the removal of top growth in the annual pruning. In spring apply a balanced, special rose fertiliser immediately after pruning at a rate of 70 g per square metre (2 oz per square yard). If top growth is slow due to adverse weather I supplement this with a nitrogen foliar feed. Then in July as the first flowers are pruned off, another 70 g per square metre (2 oz per square yard) should see them through to autumn. Always adjust the feed to the state of growth and weather conditions.

Two weeks after the pruning and first application of fertiliser I put on a mulch of organic material. This keeps the soil in good structure and helps it to hold moisture against drying winds.

Many years ago I came to a decision regarding the most effective role the modern rose could successfully fill in the garden design. The majority of roses, out of flower, offer neither interesting shape nor attractive foliage; they are, in a word, nondescript. Why, then, emphasise this obvious deficiency, a total lack of quality other than loveliness of flower, by growing them segregated in beds divorced from other plants? Only in a large garden can a part be set aside specifically for the cultivation of roses, to be visited and enjoyed only when the plants are in bloom. Rosarians argue that grouping roses together makes pest and disease control easier and certainly this is true. Equally, 'togetherness' makes ideal conditions for both pests and diseases to proliferate, so that Stefan can potter happily for hours conversing with ladybirds and toadstools; (unless the subject for knife and fork dissection is a mushroom, Clay, like me, soon loses interest).

I was faced, then, with a problem: roses there must be, for no garden is complete without them. Yet to grow either hybrid tea or floribunda roses as a separate feature in the average-sized garden is unbecoming to the plants themselves, so why not treat them like any other shrub as part of the overall design? There is no need at this stage for the dedicated, embryo rosarian to scream heresy and throw this book away. Cultivation and after-care are the same for roses confined to beds or allowed their freedom in the garden.

But if roses are to be grown in beds, the layout and design of these is usually dictated by the overall size and structure of the garden, with just a leavening of personal preference. Regarding the planting plan, I would suggest keeping hybrid tea and floribunda roses in separate beds; they rarely complement one another. Also, I do not mix different colours because, as in a kaleidoscope, the end-result is a shapeless jumble.

Instead of growing roses apart from the rest of the garden, try planting groups of them in the mixed border where when in flower they can be appreciated, and when out of bloom remain unnoticed.

To avoid reproducing a catalogue of roses, let me offer my top six hybrid tea, floribunda and miniature varieties which, like all freely expressed preferences, are wide open to criticism.

Hybrid Tea Roses

'Peace' I always plant to grow as a lightly pruned shrub. Treated like this, flowering is almost continuous and although the individual blooms are smaller the yellow-edged, pink petals are deeper and more intensely coloured. I overlook the lack of scent on this occasion only.

'Red Devil' I have grown for twenty years; the well-shaped, fragrant blooms, light-red in colour, do not fade like some to a vinous purple.

'Wendy Cussons' replaced a very old variety called 'Hector Deane' in my affections. The flowers are deep-pink with a true damask scent and are less prone to attack from that scourge of roses – black spot.

'Admiral Rodney' planted alongside a glaucous-green-foliaged Hosta fortunei 'Robusta' is now an integral part of my summer scene. The light rose pink flowers are well-formed, and carry a pervasive fragrance.

'Double Delight' also exudes a subtle fragrance from flowers which are cream coloured, faintly flushed with pink and rimmed red. It needs a dark-foliaged evergreen to show off the colour to advantage, so I grow the low-growing Hebe buxifolia alongside.

'Grandpa Dickson' came to me on trial exactly twenty years ago. The lemon yellow flowers of the true high-budded shape look most attractive with red or copper foliage behind. I use a Prunus 'Crimson Dwarf' and keep it well-furnished with bright, young leaves by hard pruning.

So much then for the hybrid tea roses.

Floribunda Roses

Floribunda roses will continue to have a succession of flowers from June until the first frost, so they are good value no matter what size the garden. Here, then, is my selection of six.

'Anne Harkness' is fairly tall-growing with saffron-yellow flowers which I grow as a companion to Lilium regale.

'Anna Ford' is more compact; the deep-orange flowers share company with lavender, and gain from the association a more luminous quality.

'Southampton' with scented, apricot-shaded, orange flowers is a useful, not too tall-growing bedding variety convenient for edging a patio or terrace.

'Matanga' is the pick of what were once termed the hand-painted roses, and has petals which are a pleasing compilation of vermilion red and white.

'Iceberg' I remain convinced is a scented white rose, although no one agrees with me. It is lovely in the herbaceous border.

'Trumpeter' in orange-red took my eye in the trials eight years ago as a disease-resistant, free-flowering, bedding variety, and each year which passes only serves to cement this first opinion.

Miniature Roses

I grow the miniatures for a season as terrace decoration, then transfer them to the garden.

'Magic Carousel' is a two-tone, red/yellow reverse, and the only one with scent.

'Angela Rippon' is a tallish variety with salmon-pink flowers.

'Starina' is in miniature terms an old variety of over twenty years' service, and is still hard to beat for vermilion, scarlet blooms.

'Rise 'n' Shine' I think is the best yellow-flowered sort.

'Apricot Sunblaze' as the name implies is a pastel-shaded combination of colours, best grown in a corner shaded from the noon sun.

For those who, like me, need white in a garden to provide a foil and contrast to hotter colours, 'Pour Toi' serves very well.

Old Roses

Stefan Buczacki

It is often said that old men hanker for the things of their childhood, so why my colleagues extol the virtues of twentieth-century roses is something of a puzzle! I am on record as having said that rose breeding could have stopped around the year 1910 and that I would have been no less happy a man. Perhaps I was provoked into overstating my case by a bed of the stridently orange floribundas that besmirch so many of our urban parks. I used to mutter something about how the man who introduced that particular orange gene into rose cultivation had a great deal to answer for, but now that I know it was the finest of all rose breeders I hold my tongue and say that even the best of breeders can have their off-days! But I still don't have to like it.

I do, of course, accept that it is the twentieth century that has produced 'Peace' and, indeed, a handful of other virtuous varieties, a few of which I actually grow. But they are very different plants from those that make up the bulk of my collection. I have been delighted at the increasing availability, thanks to the devotion of some very talented and dedicated nurserymen, of some of the thousands of rose varieties that preceded the hybrid tea and the floribunda. Sometimes, these varieties are called 'old-fashioned' roses, an insult to as graceful a race of garden plants as you will find. Old, I will accept, although I approve most highly of the expression classic roses, for this does admit the few choice moderns too.

There is nothing mysterious or difficult about the culture of old roses; they require precisely the same site and soil conditions as Geoffrey has described, with the proviso that whilst some of them are as tough as nails, a few, like the tea roses, are a wee bit tender for very exposed gardens. In their pruning, they are simplicity and co-operation itself for, unlike the modern varieties which need an annual manicure to maintain them, all that is needed with the majority of old roses is an occasional removal of dead and worn-out wood. And what do they give you in return? They give you perfume beyond compare. They give you divine simplicity of bloom; the singles are the queen bees, chosen from the countless workers of the

above, 'Cupid' – large, single and flowering for a fairly short period, but a beautiful and vigorous climber for a large wall or a pergola; left, 'Iceberg' – arguably (powerfully arguably) the best white floribunda, although the strength of its fragrance is a matter for dispute; right, 'Zéphirine Drouhin' – well over one hundred years old but still a gem, free and repeat flowering and, most unusually among roses, thornless

hedgerow roses while the doubles have none of the sculptured perfection that so pleases the show-bench judge. They are large and loose, shaggy and carefree. They shake their heads and shed their petals with all the nonchalance you would expect of a flower that has seen more suns than you or I ever will. Many of them are fleeting but, to my mind, none the worse for that. How much more do I treasure a plant that displays its glory for a few wonderful weeks than one that continuously thrusts forth flush after flush of production-line perfection. But the old roses have one thing most of all that elevates them above the earthly world of my other garden flowers; they have history. To sit on a balmy summer's evening and drink in the beauty of a rose that the Elizabethans saw puts a little magic into my gardening.

But, back on terra firma, what of the drawbacks? That ephemeral existence over which I wax lyrical – surely a problem if you really do want colour right through the season? Not a bit of it; either choose a succession of varieties to give you continuity or select those that do, indeed, have repeat or recurrent flowering – my rose season begins with Rosa primula in May and ends with the China, 'Gruss an Teplitz', which peters out at the beginning of November; and there is never a day in between when one or more of my shrubs isn't in bloom. So, to progress to some varieties. Clay is helping himself to some classic climbers, so I will restrict myself to ten of the shrubs, the real heart of the very best that the wonderful genus Rosa can offer and with representatives of most of the main groupings. All are white, pink or a shade of red; this is partly personal preference and partly because these colours tend to be associated with the best roses. But seek out a catalogue and you will find some good yellows here and there.

My Chosen Ten

'Blanc Double de Coubert' – Rugosa, white, repeat-flowering.□'Reine des Violettes' – Hybrid Perpetual, violet, repeat-flowering.□'Great Maiden's Blush' – Alba, pink, summer-flowering.□'Roseraie de L'Haÿ' – Hybrid Rugosa, crimson-purple, repeat-flowering.□'Gruss an Teplitz' – China, crimson, recurrent-flowering.□'Fantin Latour' – Centifolia, pink, summer-flowering.□'Mme Isaac Pereire' – Bourbon, crimson-purple, repeat-flowering.□'Duchesse d'Angoulème' – Gallica, pink, recurrent-flowering.□'Alfred de Dalmas' – Moss, white/pink, recurrent-flowering.□'Frau Dagmar Hastrup' – Rugosa, pink, repeat-flowering.

Up the Wall
Clay Jones

The vast majority of Britain's people live in urban and suburban areas, confined on all sides by brick and mortar and more often than not the building materials have been assembled in identical fashion. Huge housing estates sprawl outwards from our towns and cities with a timeless monotony that profits no one except the builders. No. 1 Acacia Avenue is an exact replica of No. 2 and No. 3 and so on 'ad infinitum', except perhaps for the paintwork and curtains; yet it need not be so. Occasionally I come across a façade beautifully camouflaged behind a cloak of climbing roses and what a difference they make. As far as I am concerned, house walls perform three functions. They support the roof, they repel the elements and are just perfect for climbing plants, and what better to clothe them than the rose – the doyen of all climbers.

Geoffrey has already dwelt on the basics of planting and supporting. All I need add is that the support structure for climbing roses should be at least 15 cm (6 inches) clear of the walls, preferably more. The reason is that roses are prone to fungus diseases, notably black spot and mildew that are at their worst in the airless atmosphere close to walls. I have also found that roses and clematis have one thing in common; they both like a cool root run and my climbing roses have always done better with a few low-growing shrubs planted near their feet to provide shade.

Having prepared the site then comes the moment of decision, what is the best variety when there are so many to choose from? Let's begin by considering availability. Consult a catalogue or visit a garden centre and you will find many climbing roses labelled as 'continuous-flowering'. From this you may be forgiven for assuming that they will be in bloom from June to September without a break. This does not make sense. It will be obvious that no rose can bloom endlessly, it must have time to make new growth after flowering before giving a repeat performance. Truer descriptions are 'repeat-flowering' and 'recurrent-flowering'. In the former, the roses will bloom early during June, have a rest and then bloom again later in the season; in the latter, they will bloom intermittently during the summer giving a certain amount of colour for a great deal of the time. Most modern varieties are of the latter inclination, but neither new nor old varieties will give much of a show in the autumn if they have put their main effort into the June burst of bloom. Another truism is that those varieties that are rampant growers produce fewer blooms than the slow but steady growers.

I confess that choosing the right climbing rose is a difficult business although there are obvious pitfalls to avoid. If your house is built of red brick, a red rose would be lost against its background colour and similarly a white variety on a white-washed cottage would be equally unimpressive. It is also worth remembering that some of these gorgeous roses climb to a modest 3 metres (10 feet) or so, whilst at the other extreme a few will grope for the stars up to a height of 15 metres (50 feet) or more. Furthermore, we all have different ideas of beauty and at times I am prepared to plant an indifferent grower if it is blessed with an exquisitely shaped bloom, subtle colouring and an all-pervading perfume. The next consideration is whether to buy a rose listed as a climber or one which is a rambler. Ramblers in bloom are breathtaking, their foliage submerged under a mass of blossom, but

then – nothing. They give their all in one glorious show, but the period from overture to finale is all too short for my liking. I have a hazy recollection of the garden of my childhood and the two ramblers by the pigsty – 'Dorothy Perkins' and 'American Pillar'. Their glory was brief and poor Dorothy was a martyr to mildew, all of which explains why I went off ramblers at an early age. The pigs didn't think much of them either!

So my choice of climbers for walls falls on the varieties that are 'sports' of their bushy counterparts. A sport simply means that someone, somewhere, spotted a very strong-growing branch, or branches, on a bush rose, capitalised on its vigour and from it bred a climber. This is why you can buy the multi-coloured 'Masquerade' as a floribunda or as a climber and the same applies to the brilliantly-coloured 'Allgold'. Varieties that are superb and not too tall include 'Crimson Shower'; 'Cupid' – peachy pink; 'Handel' – creamy white, edged with pink; 'Maigold'; 'New Dawn' – silvery-pink; 'Zéphirine Drouhin' – carmine-pink, thornless; and 'Gloire de Dijon' – buff-yellow and fairly vigorous.

This leaves a number of varieties that are more vigorous and therefore more suitable for growing up

left, *The climber 'Paul's Scarlet'*

below, *The sweetly-scented 'New Dawn'*

105

and though treating the soil with special fertiliser restores them to good health it is only temporary and the medication has to be repeated at regular intervals. So my advice would be to find out what suits your soil, climate, situation and depth of pocket and let these plants form the framework of the garden, then introduce less easy plants as a challenge to your increasing skill.

Your list needs to contain a careful blend of deciduous and evergreen plants, with just a sufficient leavening of coloured foliage: purples, yellow or variegated to add piquancy without reducing the garden to an irritating patchwork of a Joseph's coat. Neither should it contain flowers alone; berrying shrubs extend the interest, while the shades of leaf and stem colour, though less assertive, light up the border in season or out.

Few of us are lucky enough to find that the soil in our garden is of such quality as to be incapable of further improvement. Equally, there is no soil in my experience so poor that it cannot be improved considerably by the expenditure of effort and the application of manure. The word manure when used in the context of soil preparation can mean any organic matter which will break down fairly quickly into humus which is that black, crumbling, peat-like material that makes even the most recalcitrant clay workable, and the most porous of sand moisture-retentive. Farm manure, compost, peat, pulverised bark and spent hops are all potential humus-forming soil improvers and should be worked in during the pre-planting operations. There is no better way of ensuring that a soil will be in first-class condition than can be achieved by working it to a depth of 40 to 50 cm (15 to 20 inches), mixing in whatever organic matter is available at the same time. Turning tons of soil with a spade is hard labour, yet I take consolation from the knowledge that work done thoroughly at this stage will show benefits in the years to come. Soil which is rough dug in the autumn and then left for the winter frosts to work on should be in suitable condition for planting into when spring comes.

Planting is one of the most satisfying gardening jobs, so in order to extract the maximum pleasure from laying down what is after all going to be the permanent framework of the design, I choose a warm, calm day for setting out. Shrubs despatched, if other than container-grown, may have suffered damage

Basic rules of tree planting: make sure the hole is large enough, deep enough and the stake accurately positioned.

either in lifting or in transit. All damaged roots are best trimmed back to sound tissue. Indeed with some shrubs, roses in particular, I tip prune all the roots as this makes them produce masses of fine, feeding rootlets which quickly establish into the fresh soil. Container-grown shrubs should be well-watered to make absolutely certain the root ball is thoroughly wet before planting. Never leave shrubs with roots exposed to drying winds prior to being planted – always keep them covered with soil or wet sacking. Five minutes' exposure to the drying wind will reduce appreciably a shrub's chances of survival. In a well-prepared soil, digging is easy, but there is a temptation when breaking up unprepared soil to keyhole a plant, that is to make the hole just large enough to fit the root. In each case make the hole sufficiently large to accommodate the roots completely when they are spread out.

Depth of planting depends very much on the character of the shrub or tree. In general, the soil is back-filled up to the mark on the stem which indicates the original planting depth in the nursery. The exceptions are rhododendrons, where the mark can be left a little above soil level and the plant then given a thick mulch of peat or leaf soil; and heathers

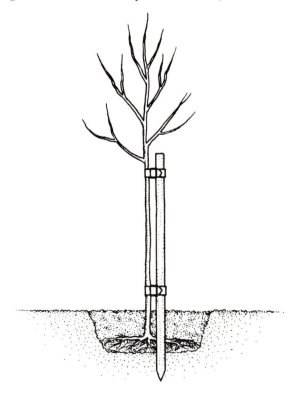

which, on the other hand, should be inserted deep enough so the base of the stems are covered – these will then produce roots which result in greatly increased growth. When back-filling the hole, firm the soil enough so it is in close contact with the roots leaving no air pockets, but leave the top layer loose so that rain can penetrate easily. Finish the operation with a moisture-conserving mulch. In poor soils, use one of the specially-formulated planting mixtures.

Trees are planted in the same way except that when required a supporting stake is driven into the bottom of the hole before covering the roots. Stake and tree are then linked firmly together, using a purpose-made fastener rather than string. Cut off the top of the stake 15 cm (6 inches) below branch level (the tree head) to prevent damage to the tree from rubbing against the stake.

There are some golden rules: keep newly-planted stock well-watered; protect evergreens from drying winds; do not let grass or weeds grow closer than 60 cm (24 inches) to the stem for the first three years. A layer of compost, well-rotted manure or similar moisture-holding material spread over the soil surface above the roots as a mulch each year provides very effective protection against water loss.

Pruning at this stage needs to be confined to establishing a framework of branches which will preserve the characteristic outline of the tree or shrub. When in doubt about what to prune, *don't*. Always remove obviously dead, diseased or damaged wood, and branches which cross over, are crowded or weak.

One other important point is concerned more with moving shrubs or trees already growing in the garden. If possible, dig a trench around the specimen to be moved twelve months before lifting, some 45 cm (18 inches) from the stem, cutting all the roots at that point. Fill the trench with moist peat and keep it well-watered. Before lifting the specimen a year later, prepare the hole ready to receive the root ball in advance, making it at least 30 cm (12 inches) larger all round than the root ball. To make moving easier I use a length of wire-mesh netting and work this under the root ball leaving the ends exposed as handles. Quite large trees are made manageable using this method. There is no need to remove the netting after transplanting as the roots just grow through it. Watering, mulching, staking, and cultural care should be carried out as described above.

Hedge Planting

The first consideration, stimulated by an urgent seeking after privacy, is what to plant as a screen or hedge, assuming the budget will not run to a $1\frac{3}{4}$ m (6 feet) wall or paling fence around the whole garden. Specialist hedging plants, well-established in popular esteem, are comparatively few in number, yet almost any shrub which is tolerant of regular cutting back will suffice. There is no practical reason or consideration other than tradition which insists that a hedge should be restricted to one species or variety. Indeed, a tapestry hedge formed from shrubs with differently coloured leaves makes a most attractive feature. For example, a mixture of purple- and green-leaved beech in the ratio of five to three is pleasing to the eye. An alternative scheme with a similar foliage blend and a bonus of pink flowers in season would be the varieties of cherry plum (Prunus cerasifera pissardii which is purple, or rosea which is bronze-tinted), and the plain green type species. Or you could plant a complete cross-blend of the beech with golden- and plain-foliaged yew.

Over forty years of gardening I have had association with a wide variety of hedging plants, and it would be extraordinary if some were not favoured above others. Beech (Fagus sylvatica) is my first choice; it is a deciduous hedge which will grow in almost any soil and situation. Planted at 45 cm (18 inches) apart, beech will make a tolerable barrier over 1 metre ($3\frac{1}{2}$ feet) high in five years. Seed is the best method of propagating the species. Hawthorn (Crataegus) and holly (Ilex) make a useful mixed screen for gardens bordering farm land. Both have prickles which are a menace to those who have the job of weeding near them. Propagate them from seed and plant the hawthorn 30 to 40 cm (12 to 15 inches) apart, and the holly 60 cm (2 feet) apart. Leylandii (Cupressocyparis) has had a very bad press and yet continues to gain in popularity. My garden is exposed, on a hilltop 250 metres (800 feet) above sea-level, and a leylandii hedge has become my best friend. Almost any soil from clay to sand is suitable. Plant 90 cm (3 feet) apart and keep it clipped hard. It may be propagated from heeled cuttings. Yew (Taxus) makes a superb hedge which is the tortoise compared to the leylandii hare in the growth stakes. Plant 45 to 50 cm (18 to 20 inches) apart and treasure it as an heirloom. Propagate it from seed. Laurel, in the two species commonly used, is not suitable for a small garden. Both the cherry laurel (Prunus laurocerasus) and the Portugal laurel (Prunus lusitanica) make handsome, shiny-leaved, evergreen barriers for those with space and time to spare when planted 1 to 2 metres ($3\frac{1}{2}$ to 7 feet) apart. Privet (Ligustrum) in both the gold and green forms are

above, *Mahonia 'Charity' in habit, leaf shape and quality of flower is a medium-sized, evergreen shrub of exceptional value – to the flower arranger almost indispensable*

left, *Senecio greyi contributes foliage interest and an abundance of yellow daisy flowers, coupled with a tolerant good-natured acceptance of most soils*

right, *Contrasting shapes, textures, flower and foliage colours combine to emphasise the beauty and utility of the mixed border*

notable hedge formers, spaced 45 cm (18 inches) apart. They root very easily from cuttings so are rather cheaper to buy than some. Of Lonicera nitida I will say that for those who enjoy hedge clipping this small-leaved evergreen is without equal. The correct planting distance is 45 cm (18 inches) for a hedge 1⅔ metres (5 feet) high, and cuttings will root with flattering alacrity.

Gardeners close to the sea will find in Escallonia macrantha a most acceptable way of achieving privacy. Its dark, evergreen leaves and red flowers provide a festive decoration from May to August. Because propagation of all the escallonias is not difficult I buy just half the number of plants required, space them 2½ metres (8 feet) apart and fill in the gaps with cuttings rooted from them.

For those with an interest in flower arranging, or who prefer a neutral background to the borders, then a hedge formed from the apple-green-leaved New Zealander Griselinia littoralis, which is also available with variegated foliage, would suit very well. I also hold in grateful memory the shelter offered by those equally attractive evergreens Pittosporum crassifolium, and the wavy-leaved Pittosporum tenuifolium. The last named offers several variations in leaf colour as an additional incentive. Griselinia and Pittosporum are not suitable for general planting, thriving only in the milder climate of the west coastal region.

There is such a variety of hedging plants to choose, from dwarf lavender to field maple, Berberis to Weigela, and a myriad permutations thereof that a diligent investigation must reveal a hedging shrub to suit every need, soil and situation. That the majority are capable of being raised from seed or cuttings makes hedge planting economically practical.

Specimen Trees

Not all gardens can accommodate in comfort the bulky presence of an oak or copper beech, yet even a window box landscape can be fashioned around a suitably proportioned 'tree' as a focal point, even if only a modest 45 cm (18 inches) high. I have so often held a forest in my hand as a handful of seeds or a bundle of saplings that it is my conviction that those people who plant a tree serve not just themselves but the community at large.

There are so many trees to choose from, and the consequences of making a wrong selection so obvious to even the non-gardener when walking around most towns, that the venturesome tree planter would be well advised to make haste slowly. Find out by obser-vation which plants grow best in the vicinity of your garden, then decide whether foliage, flowers or berries will contribute most to your enjoyment. Being greedy, I demand all three – with permutations. Then to narrow the field appreciably, measure carefully the amount of space which can be allocated to tree cultivation. Remember how, with the passage of only a few years, a purple-leaved beech can change from an asset to a potentially expensive liability.

I am forced through lack of space to offer a very personal list with the assurance, nay guarantee, that any that are planted will make a worthwhile addition to the favoured garden.

Maples (Acer) in themselves contain enough variation with species and hybrids that selection could begin and end with them. In limited space, try a variety of sycamore (Acer pseudoplatanus 'Brilliantissimum') which is slow-growing with attractive bronze-pink young growths and umbrella outline. I have yet to find a soil unsuitable for the ubiquitous sycamore. No pruning is required except to maintain the characteristic shape. Although not one of my top favourites, it is a popular choice. Acer griseum with cinnamon-red peeling bark is in my opinion of exceptional quality, and is particularly lovely in the autumn when the leaves turn scarlet and gold. Over many years it will eventually reach 9 metres (30 feet). For the rock garden or choice border, a cut-leaved maple makes a densely rounded bush of quite exceptional beauty, which in twenty years may achieve 1½ metres (5 feet) in stature. Of the many forms I have grown, Acer palmatum 'Dissectum' is the most burnished in my memory.

Next to the majestic beech, that lady of the woodland, silver birch is my favourite tree. The native species Betula pendula, white of stem and weepingly graceful in habit, will very quickly grow 12 metres (40 feet) high. A form of the species called 'Youngii' is less ambitious, ultimately forming a 6-metre (20-feet), round, canopied weeping tree, lovely to look at in all seasons. I have a seedling Betula costata with creamy-white bark and leaves that in the autumn colour luminous yellow, and this is dear to my heart. The said seedling shows ambition to become a tree, however, and after ten years has reached 4½ metres (15 feet) in stature.

The Honey Locust looked of such a delicate construction when I first saw it growing in a local nursery that years passed before common sense persuaded me to buy one. In practical terms, gleditsias are a great deal tougher than they look, and grow into very attractive specimen trees. I would recommend the thornless, golden-foliaged 'Sunburst' as it is less tall than the species G. triacanthos. Because they share similar characteristics, mention here must be made of golden false acacia, Robinia pseudoacacia 'Frisia', whose elegant leaves hold their pastel-shaded yellow throughout the summer then deepen to gold before leaf fall in October. Neither Gleditsia nor Robinia require particular care in respect of soil or situation except that very exposed planting places should be avoided as the wood is brittle and prone to wind damage. Pruning of damaged, dead or diseased branches in both cases is best completed in summer rather than the dormant period. The ultimate height is about 6 to 7 metres (20 to 25 feet) in those I have grown.

As gold is the current theme, let me introduce Laburnum×watereri 'Vossii', so aptly described when in bloom by the popular name of 'Golden Rain'. Indeed, as the long, pendulous, yellow flowers flirt with the June breeze the name is singularly apt.

Some years ago I was shown an Embothrium coccineum in full bloom, and immediately the commandment which expressly forbids coveting neighbour's goods was shattered. I was given and sowed seed and now have a 3-metre (10-feet) high specimen growing alongside a Betula pendula 'Youngii'. The seed came from the hardy 'Norquinco Valley' form, and an arrestingly beautiful picture it makes in full bloom in June with its profusion of orange-scarlet flowers. Some shelter, full sun and a free-draining soil are surely a modest imposition on hospitality.

From the list I have drawn up of popular specimen trees, three genera would be classed, in presidential election terms, as front runners. They are crab apples, cherries, and rowan – Malus, Prunus and Sorbus.

Of the Malus I would choose 'Profusion' for the beauty offered by a combination of copper-red foliage and wine-red blooms. In consideration of the pink and white flowers combined with a lax, more pendulous habit, Malus floribunda budded as a standard earns a place. It is modest in stature at 4½ metres (15 feet). But surely, the crab apple which produces no fruit is not to be compared with 'John Downie' whose white blossom is followed in due season by large, orange-scarlet fruits which make superb jelly and a palatable wine. 'Golden Hornet' is a neatly-fashioned, much smaller tree which annually ripens a profusion of small golden apples that persist right into winter.

To turn to cherries, or should the name be 'Legion' for truly they are many, what magnificence the genus Prunus affords. Like the young boy let loose in a chocolate factory I am spoiled for choice. There is, of course, Prunus subhirtella 'Autumnalis' which astonishes the unwary by opening delicate-petalled flowers in midwinter. The twig tracery is so lightly formed that 4½ metres (15 feet) is a tolerable height. Another species not to be overlooked by those with a discerning eye is 'Sargent's Cherry' (Prunus sargentii); this is rather special if a little tall at 5 to 7 metres (20 to 25 feet) for the smaller garden. The bark is a lustrous brown and the flowers single, pink, and open in April. It is in autumn that 'Sargent's Cherry' asserts superiority, as the leaves turn scarlet and gold during October. If 'Sargent's Cherry' favours the gross side of medium, then the Japanese P. 'Amanogawa' is slender to the point of emaciation, forming a 4½ metre (15 feet) column of double pink flowers in May. Taking pride of place, as the most self-assertive of all the Kimono Clan, must be P. 'Kanzan'. The double pink flowers, so aggressively and shockingly pink against the bronze young leaves, could almost be charged with assault on the eyes. A tree 5½ metres (18 feet) high in full bloom against the blue and white of an April sky is, once seen, never forgotten. 'Cheals Weeping Cherry' or, as the Japanese have it, Kiku-Shidare sakura, makes a narrowly weeping tree 3½ or possibly 4½ metres (12 to 15 feet) high, the pendulous branches wreathed with double pink flowers during late April and early May. Because the wrong shade of pink outrages the gentleness of spring, consider the charm of the white blooms of Prunus 'Shirotae' which are also blessed with a pleasing fragrance. My ten-year-old P. 'Shirotae' is now 2¾ metres (9 feet) high with a spread of 4½ metres (15 feet), and is much admired by the bullfinches.

Rowan, or 'Care Tree', is held in great repute among country folk for the curing of ills which arise from supernatural as well as natural causes. I grow them for the bird-busy orange, white, pink or red berries and the brilliant autumn colour of the leaves, while not despising any protection they afford. Sorbus aucuparia 'Fastigiata' makes a narrowly upright tree 4½ metres (15 feet) high with crops of orange berries eagerly sought after by the birds. Sorbus 'Joseph Rock', though not so determinedly upright, makes a narrow-headed tree 7½ metres (25 feet) high, and the berries, being amber yellow, last much longer and are well-orchestrated by the brilliant leaf colour. But there is complete unanimity in that the three of us agree that the choicest of all the rowans must be Sorbus vilmorinii of the fern-like foliage that turns red-purple in October. The white berries are

suffused with rose as they ripen. All the trees I have mentioned show no marked soil preference in my experience of them, and this includes a glacial clay, blow-away sand, and light loam in gardens located both in southern and northern England, so they should be capable of growing in most locations.

Wall Plants and Climbers

Walls perform several important functions to a builder; they are roof supports and keep out the elements, while a gardener appreciates them as support and providers of shelter to plants for which it would otherwise be extremely hard to find a congenial habitat.

There are climbing plants which are so fashioned as to be capable of scaling a wall unaided. 'Boston Ivy' Parthenocissus tricuspidata or 'Ivy' Hedera helix are well-known examples of the self-help principle. The majority of those plants referred to as climbers do, however, need some form of support. My preference is for plastic-covered wire fitted to vine eyes, or eyed bolts, which are in turn attached to galvanised brackets screwed securely on the wall. They are neat, unobtrusive and virtually indestructible. Trellis fashioned from wood or plastic makes an alternative second choice. Whatever the support chosen let it be so adjusted as to stand off from the wall by 5 to 15 cm (2 to 6 inches) to allow air to circulate, a concession not required by self-clinging climbers.

The soil at the foot of a wall or fence is often dust-dry, arid, short of plant food and humus. To make certain conditions are right at the root I excavate the old soil and exchange it with a similar amount of soil from the vegetable garden, adding a liberal dressing

above left, *Syringa vulgaris 'Madame Lemoine'*

above, *Hydrangea paniculata 'Grandiflora'*

below, *Hydrangea paniculata 'Floribunda'*

opposite, *Wisteria floribunda 'Macrobotrys'*

of rotted manure or compost. Even then, when planting I step the roots out 30 to 45 cm (12 to 18 inches) from the wall foundations so they have the immediate benefit of any rain which falls.

Walls offer four-star accommodation and permit me to grow plants which would not survive in the open garden, so I take a great deal of care when assessing a candidate's qualifications before making a final selection. Not all the plants chosen gain a place because of floral beauty. Actinidia kolomikta has insignificant flowers yet, with leaves variously shaded pink, cream and green, it merits attention. A well-grown plant will cover about 3 by 4½ metres (10 feet by 15 feet) of wall space. Being non-clinging, the stems need tying to supporting wires. It is deciduous so offers nothing to relieve the ennui of winter. Pruning is merely a tidying up of stray shoots and dead wood.

Clematis are, surely, the loveliest and most amiably versatile of climbing plants. In my garden, I have them growing in pots trained over any shrub which will tolerate competition, also direct planted and trained over house and garage wall; then because they are so accommodating I permit cuttings taken from the original plants to scramble at will over boundary walls and outhouses. There is a Clematis for every situation except desert or bog, for dryness or excessive wet at the root they will not tolerate. They prefer above all a cool, moist, light loam, well-drained and on the limy side of neutral. On ill-drained clay, I build a box one brick deep to lift the roots above the wetness, and plant into that. Always remember they like to have their roots in shade and head in sun. For a low wall my choice would be C. macropetala, or one of the hybrids from it such as 'Markham's Pink'. For romping over a high wall, sprawling to camouflage an unsightly building, or even scaling a convenient tree a Clematis montana type of hybrid has no competitor. That it also roots readily from semi-ripe or mature hardwood cuttings is further recommendation. Choose from C. montana 'Rubens', or C. 'Tetra Rose' with pink flowers, or my own favourite the dusky-rose-coloured, sweetly-scented Clematis 'Elizabeth'. I also grow a white-blossomed variety which came as a chance seedling and now competes with C. 'Elizabeth' for pride of place. The large-flowered hybrids produced from cross-pollination between various species are deservedly the most popular. They grow up to 4 metres (13 feet) or slightly more in height. In my garden, there are Clematis in bloom from the middle of April until the first frosts of autumn. I grow only ten varieties

and am constantly trying to find room for more.

Clematis 'Nelly Moser' has mauve petals barred with lilac, blooms in May then repeats the display in August. If grown in partial shade, the flowers will hold their delicate colour. I grow C. 'Perle d'Azur' on a north wall, intertwined with a Pyracantha whose orange berries and evergreen foliage show the delicate azure flowers of the Clematis to advantage. On a south-east wall, the large magenta flowers offered by C. 'Ernest Markham' look particularly handsome across the sandstone masonry. Plant associations when successful are cause for comment, and the enormous blue flowers of C. 'Lasurstern' making a patchwork over a flat-topped, golden-foliaged juniper form a feature in June which is repeated again in September.

Even in a company so well-endowed as the Clematis there always has to be a favourite. Mine just happens to be C. jackmanii 'Superba'. The dark-purple flowers which interweave in the tapestry of my gardening experience from early childhood are welcomed each August with a pleasure as keen now as they were in those early years. I prune the large-flowered hybrids back to within two or three buds of the old wood in August. The species are given a general tidy up by removing old and overcrowded wood. As a token of my appreciation they receive a mulch of peat and 70 g per square metre (2 oz per square yard) of bone-meal each spring, plus a dusting of rose fertiliser in June.

Ivy (Hedera) is one of the most useful and amiably dispositioned of all climbing plants. There is such a diversity of leaf shape and variegation that the temptation is to over-plant. There is a certain truth in the assertion that ivy will grow where little else will survive. For an interesting combination plant the variety H. 'Buttercup' which is gold, together with the green H. 'Goldheart', which as the name describes has foliage striped at the middle with gold. Hedera 'Marmorata' is most unusual in having leaves marbled with grey. All will furnish better if clipped once a year. Propagation is by means of cuttings or layers.

Limited space forces a discipline which may be good for my eternal soul yet is a penance in that I am driven to be more selective than would otherwise be the case. Though Jasminum nudiflorum is not by any definition a climbing plant it will flower with greater freedom when pruned and grown against a wall or similar support. The bright-yellow flowers which open during the winter months have a tonic effect on flagging spirits. Pruning the long shoots by two-thirds maintains winter jasmine in peak blooming

condition. Cuttings made from current season's growth in midsummer are an economical way of increasing stock. It is catholic in taste so far as soil is concerned, and equally unconcerned about aspect.

Honeysuckle (Lonicera periclymenum), the 'Woodbine' of the poets, will, when suited by soil and situation carry on burgeoning with cream and pink, intensely fragrant flowers all summer through. A moist, leafy soil, and a place in dappled shade will be much to the liking of this most evocative climber. There are improved forms: the spring-flowering L. 'Belgica' with tubular blooms of purple-red and L. 'Serotina' whose red-purple petals unfurl in autumn. When required, I just remove old and overcrowded stems.

Parthenocissus includes two climbers which, though they need a little help for a couple of years, soon adapt to a self clinging role. P. tricuspidata with three-lobed leaves turning more scarlet than scarlet in October is the best known. For some reason this, the 'Boston Ivy', is always labelled 'Virginia Creeper', a title which properly belongs to P. quinquefolia whose every leaf is as the name suggests composed of five leaflets. Both make an excellent wall-covering, with autumn colours of unsurpassable brilliance. Most soils seem to suit them and, indeed, it appears that the more arid the root run, the more richly coloured the autumn tints.

Wisteria, with its convoluted stems and pendulous fragrant blossom of blue or white, conjures up a picture of the essential English garden, and the timeless quality it represents. Any good loam enriched with rotted manure or compost will suit. Of the species, W. sinensis is so rampantly invasive it needs careful pruning twice a year to keep it in bounds. In August once the allotted space has been filled, cut back the current season's growth to four or five buds (about 15 cm or 6 inches usually). Heavier pruning of surplus growth can be carried out in February. The flowers of W. sinensis are mauve or deep lilac. Variations are offered by W. s. 'Alba' – white; W. s. 'Black Dragon' – dark-purple; or the double-blossomed W. s. 'Plena'.

The other species W. floribunda, or Japanese Wisteria, is less invasive and is available in a dozen varieties, offering variations on the main flowering colour scheme of fragrant violet racemes. Of the varieties I prefer the quite magnificent W. 'Macrobotrys' whose petals are lilac suffused with bluish purple. These then are my crème de la crème of climbing plants. I have omitted others such as Hydrangea petiolaris because in a small space the understudies must make way for the star performers.

Shrubs

Unlike bedding plants or even herbaceous perennials which make a strategic withdrawal at the onset of winter, shrubs remain a permanent framework which even in bleak December offer in twig tracery, foliage and flower a subtle beauty in defiance of the all-pervading chill. When designing a border I consider first the focal points to be planted with those shrubs which in leaf, flower and, above all, reliability can be guaranteed to exert the most positive influence. Then around these centres, by careful selection, I try to build up a pattern of complementary or contrasting shapes combined with a proportionate admixture of colours from the foliage, flower or berry. I am grateful that never yet has the completed picture achieved perfection. The natural quality of the plants themselves ensures that a well-designed border marks the pattern of the seasons with a character that is ever changing and always attractive. One thing I have never hesitated to do is that if the shrub is in the wrong place and would perform a more worthwhile function elsewhere, then I move it.

Consider the ultimate size, characteristic shape, colour of leaf, flower and, most important though often overlooked, fragrance. Then, after making certain so far as is possible that it will suit your soil and situation, buy it. Properly planted and cared for, shrubs, like diamonds, are for ever. The following list includes only shrubs of proven worth, tested in that hardest school of all – my garden.

Though 'Snowy Mespilus', Amelanchier, will grow $3\frac{1}{2}$ metres (12 feet) or more high it is amongst the first shrubs planted when I am starting a new border. Of the species, choose either A. laevis which with admirable timing opens fragrant white flowers and tufts of delicate pink foliage at the same time, or A. lamarckii, bulkier in stature with leaves which are copper-tinted when young, then turn scarlet-gold before shedding in November. The flowers in loose trusses open in May. Both will tolerate the most brutal pruning when necessary. Two years ago I planted a selected form 'Ballerina' which has larger individual flowers combined with an upright growth; its main virtue is it takes up less space. Stefan waxes so lyrical on the charms of Amelanchier that Clay has threatened him with compulsory attendance at an Eisteddfod unless he exercises more self-control!

Spotted laurel or Aucuba japonica has the reputation of growing where little else would survive which is, indeed, true. I grow my male form A. j. 'Crotonifolia' with the yellow-spotted-leaved female

left, *Malus 'Golden Hornet'
makes up for the lack of fruit size
by producing them in an
overflowing abundance. It is one
of the best Crab apples for
general planting.*

right, *Cotoneasters are
essentially notable as handsome
berrying rather than flowering
shrubs. That they are a useful
food source for birds is also a
consideration to be taken into
account.*

below, *Berberis darwinii with
shining, evergreen leaves hidden
under a billowing mass of
flowers in spring and with
blue-black berries in August
ranks in my top twenty shrub list*

variegata in a sheltered corner with partial shade, and am filled with admiration for the combined qualities of foliage they give me. Prune as required and use the pieces as cuttings which root with consummate ease.

For many years I suffered from a plethora of Berberis, an over-indulgence bordering on the excessive. They served a purpose of filling acres of empty border and did it very efficiently. In a small garden, restrained selectivity is essential, as anyone who has weeded or push-hoed amongst Berberis will have discovered. In the vast array of species and hybrids there are Berberis which rank in the shrub world's top twenty. Berberis darwinii with tiny, holly-like, evergreen leaves and rich, orange-yellow flowers is one which grows 2½ metres (8 feet) high. In due season a mass of blue-black berries provide a second season of beauty, and a profitable means of propagation. Berberis candidula, another evergreen in character, with large single primrose flowers, makes a 1-metre (3-feet) high dome which is firm enough for those with an armour-plated posterior to sit on. In my present garden, exposed as it is on a hilltop, Berberis thunbergii in variety possibly gains most acclaim with plantings confined to those with coloured leaves. All the B. thunbergii forms lose their leaves in winter.

For the partially-shaded border B. t. 'Aurea' with leaves coloured deep primrose yellow is excellent, especially when used as a foil to spring-flowering heathers. B. t. 'Atropurpurea Nana' has darkly purple foliage which makes a perfect foil to white-flowered bulbs; or possibly B. t. 'Bagatelle' whose red leaves are copper-tinted should be first choice. Both will grow to about 40 cm (16 inches). B. t. 'Red Pillar' is so determinedly upright it makes a useful 2-metre (6-feet) high hedge, while B. t. 'Rose Glow' with purple leaves splashed with pink and cream looks like a creation by Picasso. Most soils and situations will be suitable, and pruning can be as required. Propagation of hybrids by layering or semi-ripe cuttings is a fair test of green fingers, or the lack of them!

Until making a new garden and neglecting to plant a butterfly bush I did not appreciate just how important a role the Buddleia plays in the garden theatre. Only when during a visit to a local nursery where I saw a B. 'Lochinch' embroidered with peacock and red admiral butterflies did the awareness of my deprivation dawn. Buddleia davidii has grey-green leaves and cone-shaped spikes of lavender flowers with a scent of warmed honey which open in July and August and needs only good drainage and sunshine to thrive. There are numerous hybrids with flowers in red, blue, purple and white. The long stems which carried the previous year's flowers are pruned hard back to two buds in February or March. Recently I bought two Buddleia 'Nanho Blue' which are dwarfer than B. davidii and just one season has cemented our friendship.

To stand in August looking over a heather-covered moor rolling in purple-hazed undulations into the deepening violet distance is an experience to be savoured. The common heather (Calluna vulgaris) of the moors has spawned so many varieties that like Abraham's children they are as numerous as grains of sand. Some will grow up to 75 cm (30 inches) high, others make moss-like mounds no more than 23 cm (9 inches) at the apex. A number have foliage which is variously coloured gold, red, bronze, yellow or silver. The flowers cover almost the entire broad spectrum of purple, reds and pinks with white adding piquancy to good fortune. All have one thing in common, they will not grow in any soil containing lime. A well-drained, peaty loam facing full into the sun, and a clip over with shears in March to remove the previous season's dead flowers will suit the ling admirably. 'H. E. Beale' and 'Peter Sparkes' with long spikes of deep-pink flowers are colourful for several weeks from August onwards, while the double white 'Alba Plena'

will suit the superstitious. Foliage varieties include 'Orange' and 'Silver Queen', 'Gold Haze', 'Golden Feather' and 'Blazeaway'.

Camellias in all except favoured areas are a risk. Frost and cold winds can bring black ruin to the flowers all too frequently. Given shelter and an acid soil laced with peat and water in droughty times, they do make handsome, evergreen, flowering shrubs. Beginners might start with C. japonica 'Adolph Audusson' which is dark red, and C. × williamsii 'Donation' which is pink.

There are not many shrubs with blue flowers in late summer, so Caryopteris deserves special consideration with its grey-green, aromatic leaves and a wealth of powder-blue flowers in September. It is a low-growing, neatly-fashioned bush a metre high, and is a fit companion for Fuchsia and Sedum 'Autumn Joy'. Full sun and a well-drained soil are prime essentials. Pruning consists simply of cutting back all the top growth to soil level in March.

I hesitate to include Ceanothus for they do get severely punished in a very hard winter. But as they include several of the most attractive of blue-flowered shrubs, and do root so easily from cuttings it would, indeed, be churlish not to include the most reliable, particularly so when grown as wall shrubs. Ceanothus 'Autumnal Blue', and C. 'Cascade' are the toughest of the evergreen types, with C. 'Gloire de Versailles' of the slightly paler blue pom-pom flowers most resilient of the deciduous forms. They do need the benefit of shelter and a well-drained soil. Prune out dead and surplus wood as necessary on the evergreens, while C. 'Gloire de Versailles' should have the previous year's flowering shoots cut back to three buds, or 10 cm (4 inches) of the old wood.

Three blue shrubs in succession smacks of favouritism, yet Ceratostigma willmottianum, the hardy 'Plumbago', is not to be overlooked. It is a compact, low-growing shrub which in a well-drained soil will provide a late show of indigo-blue flowers in September. Top growth may be killed back to soil level, but cut this away and cherry-red shoots soon break to show all is well. Propagation may be effected by division or semi-hardwood cuttings.

The ever popular Japanese quince is better trained on a wall so that it can be hard pruned for maximum flowering. Good humoured Chaenomeles japonica certainly is, for it will make shift to grow in most soils. Scarlet flowers in spring are followed by golden quince fruits which are agreeably fragrant. Keep the young growths hard-pruned during the summer to within three buds of the parent branches and flower-

ing will be prodigious. Layers or cuttings serve to increase stock if required. Try a selection from C. 'Brilliant' – bright scarlet flowers; 'Crimson and Gold' – burnished red; C. 'Pink Lady'; or my own favourite C. 'Knap Hill Scarlet'.

Cornus, which can scarcely be flattered by the common name of dogwood, are handsome shrubs too frequently taken for granted. C. alba has attractive red stems yet is a little too robust, so try the less invasive C. alba 'Aurea' with yellow foliage, or the even more compact C. alba 'Sibirica Variegata'. Given a good soil in dappled shade, C. kousa with creamy-white, flower-like bracts makes a pleasing specimen planting. From all the throng, I would choose a variety of the Cornelian cherry, either C. mas 'Variegata' with silvery leaves or C. mas 'Elegantissima' with pink and yellow leaves. Both improve on excellence by opening yellow pom-pom flowers in February. Propagate all dogwoods by semi-ripe or hardwood cuttings.

The 'Venetian Sumach', or Cotinus coggygria, prefers a well-drained soil in full sun, and is worth a choice site. Most attractive are the wine-purple varieties such as C. coggygria 'Foliis purpureis' or C. 'Royal Purple' which can be hard-pruned like the type plant if required, in April. The height will then reach about 1 metre (3 feet).

There are some shrub genera so numerous and so varied in height, shape and quality that stern resolution combined with rigid selectivity is the only recourse. Cotoneaster is one of these so I will choose one representative of each group. I have found any garden soil to be suitable and though full sun brings out their quality, part shade will suffice. C. 'Cornubia' grows 4½ metres (15 feet) tall with larger than average berries while the herring-bone branch arrangement of C. horizontalis, patterned first with pink flowers then with dark-red berries looks splendid fanned over a wall or bank. Then there is C. 'Hybridus Pendulus' which in my garden makes a most handsome, modest-sized weeping tree, and berries profusely. Recourse must be made to budding to propagate C. 'Cornubia', or C. 'Hybridus Pendulus', but the species will, of right, breed true from seed.

Though Cytisus have only one brief season, they produce such a prodigious quantity of brilliant flowers that they more than pay ground rent. They occur in nature on poor, sandy soils, yet in my experience they will make shift to grow in most soils given full exposure to the sun. To prune them trim over the bushes, cutting back spent flowering stems by half. Hybrids of Cytisus scoparius, the common Broom,

will grow to around 1½ metres (5 feet) and offer flowers in various shades of yellow, gold, purple and red. A packet of seed will supply all most gardeners have space for. C. 'Killiney Red'; C. 'Andreanus' – red on yellow; or C. 'Windlesham Ruby'; are all useful named varieties. All brooms are easily increased by way of cuttings taken in summer. C.×praecox is the most widely planted and has a fountain of creamy-yellow, pea-shaped blooms in May.

Scented shrubs are of special merit whether the distillation comes from flower or foliage, which is why the dark-red, early-flowering and sweetly-perfumed Daphne mezereum earns recognition. Though only short-lived in my garden, there are more than sufficient self-sown seedlings for this to be no drawback. A mulch with peat or forest bark each year will keep them content. Other species for the adventurous include D. cneorum, very dwarf at only 30 cm (12 inches) with pink blooms, and D. odora 'Variegata' with purple blossoms and handsome variegated leaves.

Deutzias, though very striking when covered in gaily-coloured flowers, are somewhat nondescript for the remainder of the year. They are fairly compact growing, being on average under 1½ metres (5 feet) tall, and will thrive in almost any soil. Pruning consists of cutting out old wood clean at the base. Also, tip back flowering stems when time permits in June after the petals fall. Deutzia elegantissima 'Rosalind', a deep rose pink; D. 'Perle Rose', of the slightly taller-growing form; and D. scabra 'Plena' are eminently worthwhile.

Foliage, being perennial, is as important as the seasonal flowers, and Elaeagnus make very useful and effective border shrubs. Elaeagnus pungens 'Maculata' is the pick of those available, the glossy leaves splashed with gold at the centre and much coveted by floral artists. Consider also E.×ebbingei 'Gilt Edge' whose large leaves are variously coloured gold on green. Any shoots reverting to plain green should be cut out at the base. Cuttings taken in July or August into a cold frame will root given encouragement by regular damping over.

There are under a dozen hardy species of Erica, yet such is their fecundity they have produced innumerable hybrids. These range in height from a few centimetres to several metres. The Erica carnea varieties are to a degree lime-tolerant, flowering from January through to April. Varieties of Erica erigena (=mediterranea) grow taller at 1 to 1½ metres (3 to 5 feet), and bloom from March to June, which brings in the E. cinerea and E. tetralix varieties. The lovely

121

above, *Magnolia stellata is a slow-growing species with fragrant flowers in early spring*

right, *Photinia fraseri 'Red Robin' is one of a newer breed of foliage plants which are playing an increasingly important role in our gardens by offering a long season of interest*

opposite, *That Pieris forrestii 'Forest Flame' should be so determinedly intolerant of lime is regrettable for there is no other shrub which so effectively complements the beauty of young growth with the demure, modest loveliness of its flowers*

Cornish heath, E. vagans, competes vigorously with the 'Common Ling' for our favour from July to November. Interesting foliage patterns, shades of yellow, bronze, copper, orange or even red make a selection of ericas an asset to any garden. A peaty, well-drained soil and a light trim over after flowering will suit them all. Semi-ripe cuttings or layering provide ready and effective means of increasing stock.

Shrubs which are evergreen and free-flowering are guaranteed universal approval, a fact which explains why escallonias are so widely planted. They are used as hedges in coastal areas, and are also valuable elsewhere in the border. Flowers are white, pink or red, and the height on average is between $1\frac{1}{4}$ to 2 metres (4 to 6 feet). E. macrantha is tall, large-leaved and well-adapted for use as a hedge near the coast. For the borders, choose any of the Donard hybrids. Most soils will suit Escallonias although in the less kind northern gardens a little shelter from easterly winds will be needed.

There are genera which, in their anxiety to please, offer a selection of species, some deciduous and others evergreen. Euonymus (spindle) provide this facility which makes selection something of a lottery. They make no special demands in the matter of soil but show a marked liking for a place in the sun. E. europaeus 'Red Cascade' is a selection from the native spindle which is handsome both in autumn leaf colour and when its curiously lobed, coral-red fruits split to reveal orange seeds. E. fortunei includes several varieties which make useful ground cover, including E. fortunei 'Variegata', and E. f. 'Emerald 'n' Gold', both grown for the quality of the foliage.

Forsythia could well be considered for the title 'Commonest of Spring-flowering Shrubs', for the golden blossoms reflect the spring sunshine over the length and breadth of Britain. They are handsome enough for a place in full sun, and any soil will suit this most amiable of shrubs. Regular pruning out of old wood will restrict growth to around 2 metres (6 feet) and if the prunings are just pushed into the soil they will usually strike roots. F.×intermedia 'Spectabilis' is the most popular, with F. 'Lynwood' and F. 'Beatrix Farrand' offering larger flowers in slightly different shades of yellow. There is a hybrid F.×intermedia 'Minigold' with which I am seeking closer acquaintance as a shrub worth knowing.

I can think of no other shrub except the rose which flowers like the Fuchsia from July to the commencement of November. There are sixteen varieties of hardy fuchsias with flowers of typical bell-like, flared ballerina-skirt shape, in various shades of red, pink and blue growing outdoors all year round in my garden. I protect the crown at soil level with a mound of sharp sand, then prune the previous year's stems back to live wood in early May. Handsome they are, deserving a well-drained soil and a place in the sun. High summer would not be complete without F. magellanica 'Riccartonii' with the scarlet tube and dark purple corolla. Fuchsia 'Mrs Popple' is another in the violet and purple theme, though the individual blooms are larger. F. 'Lena' a semi-double flower in pale flesh-pink and rose magenta would grace any garden, as would the lime-green-foliaged 'Genii'. Cuttings root without difficulty and provide good insurance against winter losses.

Of Garrya I will say little, for it is too funereal for my liking, the darkly evergreen leaves and silvery grey to yellow catkins adding their own melancholy undertone to February. G. elliptica 'James Roof' is the funeral director supreme, with tassels 32 cm (14 inches) long, growing $2\frac{1}{2}$ metres (9 feet) or more high and needing wall shelter in colder areas. Propagate if necessary from cuttings taken in summer. Let me say here that most gardeners are besotted by garrya's charm, while I, like Stefan, refuse it garden room.

Genista hispanica, 'Spanish Gorse', I would describe as a vegetable hedgehog which smothers an armoury of prickles every May under a bevy of golden flowers. It is an excellent dwarf shrub for a hot, sun-baked place. Genista 'Lydia' also grows about 60 cm (24 inches) high, though it spreads out to cover a further $1\frac{1}{4}$ metres (4 feet) with its lax branches wreathed in flowers during May and June. Cuttings or seed will provide a means of increase.

Some shrubs are so prohibitively expensive that the cost must be weighed very carefully against the value of the contribution they make to the garden. 'Witch Hazel' (Hamamelis mollis, and H.×intermedia) are expensive, yet who on seeing for the first time those intensely fragrant, spidery, yellow flowers wreathing the naked branches in midwinter would question the asking price? Full sun, a sheltered corner and a fertile, well-drained acid loam is modest hospitality to offer such a special guest. The only sure method of propagation is by layering. H. mollis 'Pallida' is primrose yellow, and H. intermedia 'Diana' a coppery-red. Both are free-flowering and notable in autumn leaf colour.

Though most hebes are natives of New Zealand, there are those amongst what is a very large group hardy enough to survive outdoors anywhere in the

British Isles. They adapt to our climate better when grown in a well-drained soil, and do prefer a place in the sun. Hebe rakaiensis is a bright-green-foliaged evergreen shrub less than 45 cm (18 inches) high with white flowers. If forced to choose between them, I consider that H. 'Quicksilver' with its silvered, glaucous-hued leaves is even better. H. armstrongii, and H. ochracea are like bronzed whipcord; then there is H. pinguifolia 'Pagei' making small, blue-grey hummocks topped in early May with white flowers. If forced to select one from many, then let it be H. 'Carl Teschner' whose violet and white tipped blossoms topping 20-cm (8-inch) high stems are a feature in midsummer. All hebes root easily from summer-struck cuttings.

Everyone who gardens will have a personal top twenty shrubs and yet I think most lists would include the ever popular Hydrangea. They are all equally valuable, flowering as they mostly do late in the summer when even the best-kept garden takes on a jaded appearance. They need a deep, rich, moisture-retentive soil, and thrive especially in clay soil and a north-facing border. All require copious watering in dry weather. Of the H. macrophylla varieties which have small, fertile flowers surrounded by sterile florets (hence the popular name 'Lacecaps'), H. 'Blue Wave' and 'Lanarth White' are good value. H. 'Bluebird' with blue central and dusky-red outer florets, neater and more upright, is unusual; while H. paniculata 'Grandiflora' is a 2½-metre (8-foot) high shrub opening cone-shaped flowers in August. Most widely planted are, of course, the 'Mopheads' or hortensis types. Some varieties in this section change colour according to soil type – blue in acid conditions, pink to dark red in lime. Choose from H. 'Altona' – rose pink heads, and H. 'Generale Vicomtesse de Vibraye' who blushes in lime and turns vitriolic blue in more acid loams. Cuttings of non-flowering shoots taken during the summer and rooted in sand provide a method of stock increase that I find works well.

Some shrubs are so adaptable in regard to soil and situation that shameful advantage is taken of their good nature. Hypericum, the 'St John's Wort', is a good example of a 'put-upon' plant. The best-known is the 'Rose of Sharon', H. calycinum, which makes a weed-suppressing carpet 38 cm (15 inches) high and produces a succession of golden-yellow tufted flowers throughout the summer. H. moserianum 'Tricolor', as the name implies, has leaves which are splashed with green, cream and pink, while H. 'Hidcote' grows from 60 cm (2 feet) to 2 metres (6 feet) high, depending on how it is pruned. With large, deep-golden

flowers it is a feature in late summer. Any soil it seems will suffice, while cuttings or rooted pull-offs are both easy ways of raising new plants.

There are so many species and varieties of holly (Ilex), the majority of them eventually growing into large trees, that it is no surprise they are planted so often. They will grow in most soils accepting full sun or shade, yet they are such handsome evergreens as to deserve our best hospitality. Nothing surpasses the 'English Holly', Ilex aquifolium, available in plain green or gold and silver variegated forms. In the majority of cases, the male and female flowers are carried on separate plants, a fact which should be kept in mind when planning a shrub border. They will even make a useful hedge. Pruning may be done as required, while propagation is by means of layers or 7½-cm (3-inch) cuttings in August to September.

Jew's Mallow, Kerria japonica, is another of those easy-going shrubs though its shoots are easily damaged by strong winds. The most widely grown is the 1¼-metre (3½–4-feet) K. japonica 'Pleniflora' with large multi-petalled, yellow flowers. Any soil suits them in sun or light shade, and pruning just involves cutting out the shoots which have flowered in July. To propagate, dig up a length of root with a shoot attached. That is all there is to it!

The name lavender is so much a part of garden tradition that my garden would not be complete without a full complement of this fragrant shrub. Grown as a low hedge, edging a path, as a border to a rose bed, or just dotted about the garden, lavender provides a living link to centuries of garden history. Grey-green leaves topped in late summer by spikes of blue, lavender, white or pink blooms are worth the effort of preparing a free-draining soil in full sun. Pruning consists of a trim with the shears in April. Cuttings can be rooted during summer. One variety I always grow is the violet-flowered, 45-cm (18-inch) high, L. spica 'Hidcote'.

It is a sad fact that magnolias should have the reputation of being difficult to please. Provide them with a well-prepared, humus-rich soil, mulch the roots with peat or similar material each March and in spring enjoy the reward for labour. When in doubt, plant M. soulangeana 'Alba Superba' – 3 metres (10 feet) and white-flowered; the purple-tinged M. 'Lennei'; or M. 'Alexandrina', the goblet-shaped blooms in May sunshine are truly magnificent. In limited space, plant M. stellata, with narrow-petalled, creamy-white flowers on naked branches, distilling their perfume in March to April. Prune as required but not to excess. For propagation purposes, it is

left, *Clematis are surely the most beloved of climbing plants. In vigour of growth and flower production, combined with an easy-going good nature C. montana 'Rubens' is unbeatable. It is not practicable for the small garden for it will spread twenty feet without pausing to ask permission.*

above, *Paeonies always carry with them an aura of cottage gardens, and it is in that context they look most at home. Though the flowering season may be short, those great chalices of bloom make full payment of ground rent.*

above right, *The Japonica, as it is popularly known, with naked branches wreathed in flowers is assertive enough to write its own reference. A thought in passing – the fruits make very good jelly.*

right, *'Mrs Popple' was the first Fuchsia I planted in my tiro days. I still grow it for no shrub stays longer in flower, except the Potentilla or rose.*

generally best to buy a plant then layer a branch.

Mahonias are, it seems, all things to all gardens – everyone's favourites, and in consequence there is a danger of this lovely evergreen suffering over-exposure. Forms of the 'Oregon Grape' M. aquifolium make a useful ground cover in sun or shade. The yellow cluster heads of flowers open in spring and are succeeded in due season by blue-black fruits. M. a. 'Apollo' is the variety I grow and which is unsurpassed – it will reach over 1 metre (3 to 4 feet) in height. M. japonica is regarded as one of the best-quality, evergreen shrubs. Certainly, a 2-metre (6-feet) high shrub adorned with drooping racemes of pale yellow fragrant flowers in midwinter is a notable sight. Any reasonable, fertile, well-gardened soil will suffice but some shelter and shade is needed too. You can propagate the 'Oregon Grape' by just digging up rooted suckers; and M. japonica from cuttings in summer rooted in a cold frame.

Only a decade ago, tree paeonies were considered suitable only for cultivation by experts, yet they are such very easy shrubs to grow. The red-flowered Paeonia delavayi, and the yellow P. lutea 'Ludlowii' look most at home amongst shrub roses, thriving in the conditions provided there. Moutan (P. suffruticosa) imports from China, Japan and the United States need shelter and a well-prepared soil to give their best. The hybrids are grafted, and I find that burying the union between stock and scion 5–10 cm (2 or 4 inches) deep in potting compost helps stem rooting to give a stronger growth. Mulch each year with compost, rotted manure or other similar material. The species are best raised from seed whereas hybrids are best raised by layering or grafting.

'Mock Oranges', the Philadelphus of botanists, have distilled their orange scent over all the gardens of my memory. Some are too tall for modern gardens; all are easy to grow in any well-drained, sun-blessed soil. White flowers in summer are offered in abundance so long as some old stems are cut out each year. Propagation is by cuttings rooted in a cold frame. P. 'Virginal' is most fragrant, with full double blooms turning a 3-metre (10-feet) bush into a white canopy. P. 'Belle Etoile' is smaller and the intensely fragrant flowers are touched with maroon. P. 'Bouquet Blanc' grows just 1 metre (3½ feet) high here, also with double white flowers. P. coronarius 'Aureus' with golden-yellow leaves and white flowers is lovely on an east or west exposure.

Photinia × fraseri 'Red Robin' is for those who garden a limy soil and are deprived thereby of a beautiful Pieris which I shall describe in a moment.

Given a well-drained soil and full sun this handsome evergreen will delight with its brilliant scarlet young growths. Providing shelter from late spring frosts is essential.

Pieris are the acid soil counterparts of the Photinia. In April and May the long, arching racemes of white flowers and brilliant scarlet young growths make P. forrestii 'Forest Flame' a spring poem. Both Photinia and Pieris require little pruning, and may be rooted from summer-struck cuttings housed in a frame.

The 'Shrubby Cinquefoils', the hybrids derived from Potentilla fruticosa, are in bloom from late spring to autumn. Classing them as indispensable is no exaggeration. It is no lie either to say that almost any soil will suit them if not given to waterlogging. Yellow-flowered compact varieties up to 1 metre (3 feet) high include P. 'Gold Finger', P. 'Elizabeth' and P. 'Longacre'. Potentilla 'Abbotswood' has white blossom, while P. 'Red Ace', and P. 'Tangerine' offer a vermilion and copper-red theme. Potentilla 'Princess' is a pink-flowered variety if grown in shade; otherwise dirty white would be a fair description of its flower colour. Clay and Stefan, pink-bespectacled Prince Charmings that they are, insist that my dirty white Cinderella really is a Princess – presumably unwashed. To propagate potentillas, use seed if you like to gamble on flower colour; cuttings in summer otherwise. Pruning consists of a general tidy up in spring.

The pyracanthas are grown for the beauty of their berries rather than for the clusters of white flowers or the evergreen foliage. Popularly known as firethorns, they will make bushes or wall shrubs 2½ to 3 metres (8 to 10 feet) high. Almost any soil will grow Pyracantha. The most favoured varieties are P. coccinea 'Lalandei' with orange-red berries, and 'Orange Glow'. Pruning should be done after flowering to shape up the bush. Propagate by seed for the species, and cuttings for the varieties which may be rooted in a cold frame, though this is not as easy as it sounds.

It is a shame, indeed, that rhododendrons so obstinately refuse to grow on an alkaline soil without endless applications of trace elements. These hundreds of delightful species, battalions of magnificently beautiful hybrids are denied to all those who garden a lime-rich soil. The larger growing species and hybrids developed from them are not for the small garden. Fortunately, there are innumerable small-leaved species and varieties delightful in foliage, brilliant in flower, twelve of whom in maturity would need no more space than would be necessary for one of the large-leaved types. Prepare the soil with peat on the north side of the house or boundary until it is of the spongiest texture, then plant any of the rhododendrons on offer in the nearest garden centre which fancy chooses and bank balance permits. I grow R. 'Blue Tit', grey in leaf, lavender of flower, and 1 metre (3 feet) in height. R. 'Elizabeth' is taller, the leaves larger and the flowers vivid red. Species you should certainly have for beauty of leaf, and R. yakushimanum sets an impossibly high standard for the rest to beat. Explore the low-growing R. repens hybrids, or enquire of R. (Azalea) obtusum, and the lovely common yellow, honeysuckle-scented, brilliantly autumn-coloured R. luteum. In a border 3 metres (10 feet) wide by some 18 metres (60 feet) long, I grow around fifty species and varieties, and wish there were room for fifty more. Propagation is by seed or summer cuttings. Pruning is easy – do not dare do more than remove spent flowers or dead, broken branches.

Of Rhus I would say, where space permits grow R. typhina 'Laciniata' for the scarlet and gold autumn colour of the fern-like leaves. In February, prune hard to keep the habit compact. Suckers are available in abundance when extra plants are wanted. Clay and Stefan insist that people misguided enough to grow Rhus are suckers anyway.

Ornamental currants, with pink and red flowers, and their unfortunate distinctive fragrance reminiscent of an amorous tom-cat are easy, quick-growing, colourful garden fillers for any soil or situation except dense shade. Ribes 'Pulborough Scarlet', or the deep-crimson R. 'King Edward VII' are good value. To prune, just cut out old non-productive, worn-out wood. Propagation is by cuttings taken in late summer, using any length of young growth.

Rosemary, of the long, narrow, evergreen leaves, and pale violet-blue flowers is, like lavender, part of garden folklore. The soil must be light, well-drained and in full sun. I grow Rosmarinus 'Jessop's Upright' with deep-blue flowers, and the type species R. officinalis. Cuttings of young shoots will root without difficulty dibbled in a cold frame. To prune, just snip the young shoots to flavour roast lamb.

Though ornamental brambles may be encouraged in the larger garden, the white-stemmed Rubus cockburnianus and others of similar ilk do not rate inclusion in a small, essentially select border. I would possibly include R. tridel 'Benenden' for the mass of large, white 'Dog Rose' flowers each with a central boss of gold stamens. Cuttings taken in summer should root in a frame. Prune out old wood as

required. Most soils will suit it – sun or part shade makes little difference.

The larger growing willows (Salix) I have so often heard roundly cursed root, branch, seed and generation, that diplomacy restricts me to suggesting only Salix lanata with silvery-green leaves and erect catkins which look like plump, white owls, and S. caprea 'Pendula' (Kilmarnock willow) which makes a choice, small, weeping tree 2 metres (6 feet) high. It is much beloved of caterpillars with a liking for the leaves. Given a moist soil, all willows will flourish as the green bay tree. Cuttings? Well, it takes skill to *stop* them from rooting.

Elderberries do not qualify as good garden plants, yet Sambucus racemosa 'Plumosa Aurea' is one I grow and am delighted to share bed and board with. The delicate, fern-like foliage is a bright yellow all summer, and red berries follow the white flowers. Most soils and full sun bring out the best in this sunshine plant. Pruned hard each spring it will make a shrub 2 metres (6 feet) high and is easily propagated by means of hardwood cuttings.

Yellow daisy-like flowers against down-dusted silvery leaves make Senecio greyi (which is frequently found masquerading as S. laxifolius) a most rewarding shrub to grow. Any well-drained soil will do, with a place in the sun and a modicum of shelter. Plants raised from summer cuttings growing in a south-facing border are 1 metre (3 feet) high toadstools of silvery grey leaves in five years.

'Bridal Wreath' (Spiraea arguta) I have grown all my gardening life; the pendulous, arching branches festooned with white flowers are a snowstorm in May. At 2 metres (6 feet) high it is too large for the modest garden, so possibly S. nipponica 'Snowmound' would suit better. S. japonica at 60 cm (2 feet) high with pink flowers, or the far superior S. 'Goldflame', or S. 'Golden Princess' also with pink flowers but with golden foliage as contrast are useful. A good, moisture-retentive soil but not waterlogged, in sun or light shade will meet these shrubs' needs. To raise new plants, take summer cuttings into a cold frame.

Lilacs, of the clan Syringa vulgaris, are synonymous with thatched cottages and gardens of romance. They thrive best in chalk though all will grow in any reasonable soil if the drainage is good. S. 'Marechal Foch' is rose carmine, and S. 'Maud Notcutt' white and single-flowered. For full double blooms search out S. 'Madame Lemoine' which is my favourite, or S. 'Charles Joly', a purple red. All grow to 3 metres (10 feet) or thereabouts. For the small garden try S. velutina of the oval leaves and pink flowers on a rounded

above, *Winter-flowering heathers brighten the garden*

left, *Conifers and heathers skilfully arranged will make a garden for all seasons which needs only minimal maintenance*

below, *A well-grown hedge of purple- and green-leaved beech offers a beautiful tapestry of colour*

bush 1 metre (3 feet) high. To prune, remove dead flowers and weak or ill-placed branches. Mulch and feed with compost as well as bone-meal. Propagation of varieties is usually performed by grafting. I try cuttings taken in late summer – some you win, some you lose – but on the whole it is worthwhile.

Viburnums, like heathers, by careful selection can be used to give year-round colour. For winter V. × bodnantense opens a succession of pink, sweetly-scented flowers on a 2½-metre (8-feet) high bush from October to April. Viburnum tinus 'Eve Price' a pleasant evergreen at 2 metres (6 feet) high, has pink buds opening to white flowers in midwinter. V. carlesii makes a large, rounded bush 2 metres (6 feet) high, covered in ball-shaped, very fragrant blooms during May. I grow V. c. 'Diana' which is more compact and has pink flowers. Of the V. plicatum varieties, I can only express an opinion that if space permits V. p. 'Tomentosum is like a table spread with white flowers; unfortunately, a very large table, so for the small garden I would choose V. p. 'Watanabe' which has a rounded habit and increases in height very slowly. I also grow the evergreen, 1 metre (3 feet) high V. davidii, both male and female in order to enjoy the turquoise-blue berries in winter. All viburnums like a well-gardened soil and, with the exception of V. davidii, a place in the sun. To propagate them you can layer branches, or remove suckers, or

plant cuttings into a cold frame during the summer.

The ubiquitous periwinkle (Vinca) has served me well over the years as flowering ground cover, so it deserves a mention. I prefer the low-growing V. minor, available with plain or variegated leaves which flowers all summer, varying according to variety from white through shades of blue and purple to near-violet. Any reasonable soil, except a dripping bog, will suit it. To propagate, just lift a selected stock plant and divide up the rootlets. V. m. 'Gertrude Jekyll' (white); V. 'E. A. Bowles' (leaves variegated cream and green and the flowers azure); and V. 'Multiplex' with flowers plum purple are all choice forms.

Weigelas are such stalwarts I class them with lilac, Forsythia and Ribes as essential. Grown in a rich soil and regularly pruned to remove old worn-out wood they make well-shaped bushes of 2 metres (6 feet) in height. W. florida 'Variegata' with creamy white and green leaves, complemented by tubular pink flowers in June, and W. 'Bristol Ruby' with deep-red flowers on plain green foliage would be my choices. I have a new hybrid, W. 'Evita' with bright-red blooms which is much slower growing, reaching only ½ metre (18 inches) in two years. Most soils, even pure chalk, will grow Weigela. Propagation is carried out by hardwood cuttings set outdoors in October.

Conifers

I was once informed, in answer to my enquiry how conifers could be distinguished from other shrubs, that they bear cones, which at that stage in my career was no help at all. So the next request had to be to show me a cone! A selection of conifers introduced into a landscape will add very quickly an air of maturity and, by virtue of their being evergreen, year-round interest. Some of them do not thrive in limy soils – swamp cypress (Taxodium) is one, though there are exceptions. The majority will grow in any reasonable garden soil. There is not sufficient space in this book to deal with more than a few select conifers from the hundreds of varieties I have grown during the last forty years. Those with acres to plant will consult monographs on the subject.

Abies koreana is almost painfully slow-growing – the five-year-old seedlings in my garden are only 30 cm (12 inches) high. Yet past experience shows that they will produce their violet-purple cones when they reach 45 cm (18 inches).

Monkey puzzles (Araucaria) and most cedars are just too large for the average garden, lovely though they are. Cedrus deodara 'Aurea' with a golden foliage in spring is smaller and could be used as a boundary planting. C. libani 'Brevifolia' is also possible, or C. libani 'Sargentii', a weeping form. My plants are only 2 metres (6 feet) high at fifteen years old and much admired. A ten-acre plot could be filled with that most popular of all evergreen trees, Chamaecyparis and its numerous offspring. Varieties which will not soon outgrow their welcome include the blue-green C. lawsoniana 'Allumii', or the determinedly upright C. l. 'Columnaris'. As a golden-leaved contrast choose from C. l. 'Stewartii', or the primrose yellow of C. l. 'Lutea'.

I must not ignore Abies procera 'Glauca Prostrata', or the various Picea pungens varieties which spread silver-foliaged foils to the golds and greens. Picea pungens 'Koster' is useful as ground cover, a character I maintain by pruning off any shoots which grow up instead of out. Picea pungens 'Globosa' is superb planted amongst winter-flowering heaths.

My own garden is over-planted with junipers, and I make no apology for they are, in an exposed garden, the most reliable conifers. J. media 'Old Gold' is quite lovely when draped with blue alpine Clematis. J. media 'Pfitzerana' with horizontal branches may not grow tall but covers yards of garden. A twelve-year-old specimen here is 2 metres (6 feet) high by some 3¾ metres (12 feet) across and worth every inch of the space. J. communis 'Depressa Aurea' is the golden-leaved form of the Canadian juniper. Its foliage turns bronze in winter and makes a perfect foil for the purple Crocus. My oldest specimen is 60cm (2 feet) high by 1¼ metres (4 feet) across after eighteen years.

I have a great liking for native plants, so yews (Taxus) are dotted at regular intervals all about the borders. T. baccata 'Fastigiata Aureomarginata' makes a neat golden column only 1½ metres (5 feet) high and 60 cm (2 feet) wide in fifteen years. Conversely, T. baccata 'Repens Aurea' makes a totally prostrate gold carpet and is much quicker growing and almost as ground-hugging. T. baccata 'Summer Gold' is also very handsome.

Of the thujas I grow, undoubtedly the most attractive is Thuja orientalis 'Aurea Nana' with the curiously flattened, golden, upright fans of foliage. Growth is neat, compact and very slow. T. occidentalis 'Rheingold' is a very popular conifer with feathery foliage, tinted the old gold colour which looks beautiful when planted round with spring bulbs. Growth is very slow and the habit rounded in outline.

This has been just a brief flirtation with some of the moderate-sized conifers. I will mention several more which are suitable for rock gardens in the chapter on alpines.

OF ROCKS & WATER

Geoffrey Smith

Alpine plants, whether growing wild on a boulder-strewn mountainside or under cultivation in the garden, offer to me an inexhaustible source of pleasure and interest. For years I laboured under the popular illusion that to grow alpines really well entailed first constructing a miniature Snowdon or even a replica of the Matterhorn in the front garden. Experience has taught me that this piece of garden mythology has only become established through over-frequent repetition on the part of alpine experts who have never actually had to build a rock garden. To date, I have constructed eleven, three of them holding several hundred tons of stone each, and I am convinced that 'dogs' graves', 'devil's lapfuls', 'almond puddings' (to quote from the most famous of rock gardeners), or even copies of limestone rock outcrops indistinguishable from the real thing, are no more essential for the successful cultivation of most mountain plants than a thick covering of snow all winter.

In support of this contention I offer you some hard practical facts. Good stone for rock garden construction for most would-be alpinists is virtually unobtainable, and when it is offered the cost is prohibitive. In most cases, loads of water-worn limestone are acquired at the expense of our already impoverished countryside. More important, even the well-designed and well-constructed rock garden looks totally out of character in the context of a town garden. A warning also: anyone who is not used to hard labour runs a risk of serious injury moving heavy stones into position.

I will now go a stage further and suggest that alpines growing in a properly made scree or table bed are more likely to succeed than in most so-called rock gardens. A table bed is a box-like structure built with stones from a demolition site, or even raked up from the garden. The height can be anything from $\frac{1}{2}$ to 1 metre (18 to 36 inches) above soil level, and the most convenient size for ease of maintenance is $1\frac{1}{4}$ metres wide by 2 metres long (4×6 feet). The four walls offer a north aspect for Ramonda, Haberlea and other shade-loving plants and a full southerly prospect for Saxifraga of the Kabschia group and others which demand a combination of sunlight and perfect drainage. Then there are the west and east exposures for those plants liking all things in moderation. Use soil instead of mortar to bed the walling stones, leaving larger crevices for plants which are best installed during construction. The box can be filled with a compost made up of four parts of garden loam, two parts of peat, two parts of sand, and one or two parts of $\frac{1}{2}$-cm ($\frac{1}{4}$-inch) stone chips. A few weathered stones on top, carefully placed, make a proper finish and give a change of level.

Screes and moraines are formed in nature by the weathering of rock. The broken fragments roll down the slope to form, eventually, stable heaps of stone in varying sizes. A home-made scree is an easily maintained method of growing alpines which will not look out of place in a town garden. Admittedly, a scree is easiest to construct if the site has a slight slope, although, on a totally flat site it is possible to have perfect drainage at one end and a miniature bog garden suitable for

In a garden, as in the broader, wilder, natural landscape, water exercises its own unique influence. Cloud shadowed or sunlight patterned, the mirror surface of the pool induces a mood of tranquillity, calling for a pause in the busy round of gardening.

moisture-loving plants at the other by allowing a fall of about 15 cm (6 inches) from top to bottom.

Construction is hard work, though nothing like the labour involved in building a rock garden. Excavate the soil to a depth of 60 cm (24 inches) sloping at the bottom, if the site is level, to around 75 cm (30 inches) at the lower end. I put the fertile topsoil to one side and lose the rest by working it into the vegetable garden, shrub borders, or a site for a new lawn. I then place 30 cm (12 inches) of broken stone in the hole to form the base of the scree. This makes sure that drainage is unimpeded. I then cover the stone with reversed turf, leaves or even several layers of newspaper; this stops the fine top-mix from washing down to block the drainage. The planting mixture can be made with three parts of the excavated soil (which must be absolutely free of all perennial weeds), three parts of peat, one part of sand, and five parts of $\frac{1}{2}$-cm ($\frac{1}{4}$-inch) down gravel or stone chips. Richer pockets are provided at planting time by adding extra loam if required. A valuable refinement would be to lay an underground watering system before putting down the mixture. This would simulate exactly the natural conditions where screes in the mountains are constantly supplied with nutrient-enriched moisture from the melting snow.

Pools

The picture is improved further by adding a pool to the design, and here again in hard practical terms, experience has taught me important lessons. After constructing pools of concrete, installing two preformed from fibreglass, and two using specially manufactured PVC or rubber liner guaranteed to give fifteen years' service, I am now a confirmed liner man. Making a cement pool is, admittedly, a once and for all operation, providing it is done correctly and it remains watertight. Pre-formed fibreglass pools are available in all shapes, although there is an upper size limit, and they require nothing like so much hard work to install as one made from concrete. Easiest of all is the liner, and my present pool, which is 5½ by 2¾ metres (18 by 9 feet), took just three days to lay from removing the first turf to the finished, water-filled end-product.

I first marked out what seemed to me the right shape by skimming the turf. I then removed the soil to a depth of 60 cm (24 inches) in the centre (this is essential if fish are to be safe from injury in cold weather), but left a flat platform 37½ cm (15 inches) wide all round the edge to be covered in just 15 cm (6

inches) of water. Varying the depth offers more scope for planting, be the pool formal or informal, for some aquatics will need deep water to grow in, whilst others just like wet feet. After digging out all loose soil and making certain there were no stones or roots protruding to punch holes in the liner, I covered the excavated area in a 10-cm (4-inch) layer of soft, pebble-free builder's sand. I then stretched out the liner over the hole and placed stones around the edges to hold it taut. Simply running water on to the stretched liner and gradually moving the stones pulled the liner gently down into the sand without leaving wrinkles and, more important, gave no risk of tearing the material. The sand provides a soft base for the liner. Do make sure that the pool edges are flat, so the water fills the pool to rim level all the way around to catch, then reflect for your pleasure, the sky, or mirror images of the garden. And finally, remember to trim the surplus liner overlapping the edges. Now, with aquatics established in the water and alpines growing all round, it really is a major garden feature.

Before planting the scree, furnish the pool so the two mature together, for pot-grown alpines can be installed at any season when the weather is suitable. May is the safest time for transplanting aquatics such as water lilies, Water hawthorn, and bogbean as the water warms up. Water lilies do make a great deal of growth in a season so I used meadow loam, sieved to remove stones and other debris, for bedding their roots. For actually holding the loam I used the purpose-built baskets made from a wickerwork of plastic lined with hessian so the compost could not wash out to foul the pool. Under each root I placed a sachet of slow-release fertiliser, and covered the soil-filled container with a layer of aquarium gravel to hold everything in place – and to provide a spawning place for the fish. Do not plunge the containers straight into deep water but start them in the shallows then gradually work them to whichever depth best suits the plant being installed. Arrange the planting so that in maturity no more than one-third of the pool surface is hidden by vegetation.

There are so many lovely varieties of Nymphaea or water lily to select but whenever possible, see the plants in flower first. N. Albatross is white, spreading to 75 cm (30 inches); N. odorata 'Minor' has white, star-shaped blooms with a pleasing fragrance; and N. 'Ellisiana' has lovely, wine-red flowers. N. 'Froebeli' is another very popular water lily with blood-red, sweetly-scented flowers while N. 'Sunrise' is the best yellow I have grown, its green leaves blotched with

*Varying depths of a pool afford different plant
habitats as can be seen in this diagram*

brown. I would not now be without the rose-pink,
sweetly-scented N. 'Rose Arey' despite getting a wet
foot through once trying to enjoy the closer acquaintance of its aniseed-like perfume.

Iris laevigata, 60 cm (2 feet) high with finely-
pencilled blooms, will grow quite well on a ledge with
the container top just under water, as will the water
forget-me-not, Myosotis scorpioides, which is 15 cm
(6 inches) high with dainty blue flowers. Pickerel
weed, Pontederia cordata, with heart-shaped leaves
is valuable because the light-blue flowers open in late
summer. Some submerged oxygenators and a collection of hardy fish, plus a handful of scavenger snails,
will bring coloured movement to tempt even the most
dedicated gardener to lean hand on hoe and take up
day-dreaming.

Blending a pool into the surroundings needs care
and thought. In a formal setting the task is easier for
paving flags can be set around it to mask the edge and
give access. A pool situated in a lawn may be given
similar treatment but the water feature forming part
of a scree or rock garden needs marrying into the
landscape by carefully contrived planting. In one
place you can let the gravel run down into the water
and possibly plant in it the 15-cm (6-inch) high white
marsh trefoil, Menyanthes trifoliata. Stimulated by
memories of flower-fringed mountain tarns, I planted
the double-flowered marsh marigold Caltha palustris
'Plena'. This has golden yellow globes in May and will
settle happily in a moist corner. Two mat-forming
saxifrages I have found to be most content with a
moist soil are Saxifraga oppositifolia 'Splendens'
with purple-red flowers carried on 5-cm (2-inch)
stems, and S. retusa, which forms a carpet of rich red
flowers in April.

Proportion must be the key word for all gardening
design. Nowhere is this more vital than in a rock
garden or scree where coarseness of growth in just

one plant can completely destroy the illusion. To give
a change in height, low-growing conifers are excellent, and in giving shade to plants which need it they
have an additional advantage. A suitable juniper
would be J. communis 'Compressa', a genuine dwarf,
slow-growing column of a tree. Chamaecyparis pisi-
fera 'Nana Aureovariegata' grows almost impercept-
ibly into a rounded green mushroom of tightly packed
leaves. Pinus mugo 'Gnom' with several shoots com-
peting for dominance is in itself a forest of dark-green
mini-pines. Little bun-shaped, grey-green foliaged
Picea mariana 'Nana' will never outgrow its welcome, so is always included in the guest list.

If a plant is common to many gardens, this either
means it is a weed or very good value. Aubrieta, at
least in dwarf-growing varieties such as A. 'Red Carpet', and A. 'Olympica' with purple flowers is useful
around the scree edges. The stems should be cut right
back to the base after flowering. In the free draining
yet moisture-retentive conditions created by a well-
constructed scree the Kabschia group of Saxifraga
make hard cushions of grey-green spiky leaves 8 cm
(3 inches) high which are hidden in spring under
packed masses of flowers. S. burseriana hybrids are
typical examples, all of them good value. S. × 'Cran-
bourne', and S. × 'Irvingii' with pink flowers are
similar to S. burseriana, though earlier blooming.

One or two selected pieces of naturally weathered
and sculptured rock can be planted with vertical face
denizens. The silver-grey encrusted rosettes of S.
cochlearis growing like lichen over a piece of limestone are particularly handsome when covered in
plume-like sprays of white flowers in May. Self-
seeding is a natural habit of this little beauty from
the Maritime Alps.

137

The immense variety of plants suitable for scree cultivation makes selection difficult but here are a few favourites: above, the Maiden Pink, Dianthus deltoides; top right, Erinus alpinus, native of the West European mountains; middle right, Helichrysum milfordae, originally from South Africa; right, Gentiana verna will flourish if divided regularly

138

above, *A well-contrived and planted scree which has become part of the overall garden design. A scree needs less work to keep it in order than any other part of the garden.*

left, *Under natural conditions in the Swiss Alps the plants grow in fierce competition with each other to produce an exuberant display of colour*

There are Primula species also which, though difficult to grow in the open beds, thrive in a scree. Primula marginata 'Linda Pope' with pale-blue flowers over yellow-dusted grey leaves is one. I pull my plants to pieces every third year and root the long-stemmed leaf tufts in the frame to increase stock. P. rubra of the pink, white-eyed flowers on 5-cm (2-inch) stems will potter along happily in a scree given the shady side of a stone or conifer as protection. Indeed, some of the European and several Asiatic primulas make first-class shade scree plants in the moistest soil around the pool edge.

Foliage plants are equal in importance to flowers, for their contribution extends over several seasons. Artemisia schmidtii 'Nana' makes a 25-cm (10-inch) mound of fern-like, silver-grey foliage, and is easily propagated by means of cuttings made in summer. I have noticed that in lime-rich soil the foliage is more silvery-grey.

Campanula, the ever popular bellflowers, are indispensable summer-flowering plants in borders, rock, or scree. In a group so large there are numerous gems and some whose cultivation requires all our skill and ingenuity. Equally, there are others so rampantly invasive they should not be allowed through the front gate. But C. cochlearifolia 'Cambridge Blue', allowed to wander amongst the stones, will open a succession of fairy-thimble blue flowers on 8-cm (3-inch) stems while the tuft-forming C. 'G. F. Wilson' has dark-blue flowers that sit tightly on the foliage. Slugs share my affection for Campanula but, unfortunately, their concern is gastronomic, and often the only way of foiling them is to grow the choice species and varieties in a scree. In my experience, C. allionii will only thrive in a scree, pushing out hairy tufts of leaves which in June erupt with large purple-blue flowers. But try also those natives of the Caucasus, C. aucheri, C. saxifraga, and others loosely grouped under the collective name C. tridentata. All push a long, parsnip-like root down into the scree and are topped by a tuft of leaves with a prodigious mass of flowers in summer. C. zoysii is a gem of gems to test the skilful: it has a tuft of glossy leaves 10 cm (4 inches) high and short erect stems which carry clear blue bells whose edges are fluted and puckered like a disapproving grandmother's lips. Only by division each year can this remarkable alpine be stopped from flowering itself to death.

Dianthus were plants that I never thought of putting into a scree until I found them growing wild in the Cheddar Gorge where D. gratianopolitanus spreads pink curtains of flowers over the stones.

Choose wisely from the divergent forms available, for this rare native makes a close mat of silver-grey leaves which form a foil to the deep rose-pink, delicately perfumed flowers poised above them on 10-cm (4-inch) stems. Like a vegetable hedgehog, D. erinaceus makes a prickly ball-like cushion of stems, and has fringed petals of deep pink. A native of Asia Minor, it revels in the hottest part of the scree. The 'Maiden Pink' D. deltoides may be sown where it is to flower, and there the dark-green foliage, combined with the lustrous red flowers, is most effective.

Geraniums feature in all my schemes for greenhouse, mixed borders, rock and scree gardens. I choose those for scree planting very carefully. Certainly, the silver-leaved G. argenteum 'Roseum' is meritorious enough, and its finely-divided foliage and rose-coloured blooms held aloft on 10-cm (4-inch) high stems are sufficient recommendation. G. farreri, too, with cup-shaped, flesh-pink flowers will never betray a confidence by straying out of bounds, or grow taller than 8 cm (3 inches).

Two carpet-forming 'everlastings' are Helichrysum bellidioides with grey leaves and rustling, paper-textured, white flowers which grows to a height of only 15 cm (6 inches) in a scree and the even more desirable H. milfordae from South Africa with silver rosettes and flowers of crimson in bud, opening to pure white. I grow them with a Greek broom Cytisus demissus, a shrub-like grey, hairy, wire-netting plant covered in yellow flowers.

Alpine Phlox are not so vigorous when grown in slightly enriched scree, but manufacture even more flowers, if that were indeed possible, than when grown in soil only. Choose from any of the Phlox douglasii or P. subulata hybrids; all are worth growing.

Houseleeks, the effulgent sempervivums, are much at home in the scree. Select those with as many different leaf shapes and colours as you can; plant them and watch the congested rosettes of succulent leaves make a tapestry over the pebbles. Although they do flower, they do so in a variety of colours and these should be removed as a rebuke to vulgar ostentation. Make sure you include the cobwebbed S. arachnoideum and, of course, S. tectorum as essential representatives.

Though most gentians prefer the richer soil of a peat garden or shade border, there are two which grow well when planted in a lightly shaded corner of the scree in a pocket of compost. G. verna 'Angulosa' opens vivid blue, white-edged flowers in May, and looks beautiful when in association with bird's-eye primroses, Primula farinosa; an idea I copied for my garden after seeing them happily cohabiting in Teesdale. Both require regular division or they languish and die. G. macaulayi 'Wells variety' grows at the scree edge in a rich pocket of soil with a stone supplying root shade. There it sprawls luxuriantly to open ice-blue flowers in August. Division every three years is essential, and watering must be resorted to in times of drought.

After watching Lithospermum 'Grace Ward' and 'Heavenly Blue' die when grown in rich soil, I tried planting them in lime-free scree. There they grow slowly to make hummocks of dark green, and give a succession of blue flowers from June to October. Cuttings taken in midsummer are not difficult to root in a frame. I also find the wandering, grey-leaved, light-blue L. oleifolium well-suited in a scree. Both need regular top dressings of compost to keep them in prime condition.

I have noticed both in Europe and elsewhere that alpines in their natural habitat grow in close-packed yet harmonious competition, but in the garden I had always spaced them well apart with a carefully cultivated ring of bare soil around each one. Now I encourage, amongst certain select species, a spirit of healthy competition.

Polygala chamaebuxus, with hard, evergreen, box-like leaves, is a yellow-flowered milkwort reputed to prefer peaty soil, yet it grows and flowers superbly in rich scree. P. chamaebuxus 'Grandiflora' with carmine and yellow flowers is even more spectacular – it grows only 10 cm (4 inches) high and will flower for months. I let it fraternise with Frankenia thymaefolia, a mat-forming, grey-leaved Spaniard which displays masses of tiny, rose-pink flowers.

Potentilla nitida is a singularly lovely, high mountain plant which will only survive with me when grown in a specially prepared sunny corner of the scree. There, with roots bedded in leaf-mould the stemless, pink, strawberry flowers sit close on a bed of silvered leaves. As with other mat-formers, I cover selected stems with sandy soil to make them root, then pot them up to grow on.

The moister, lower end of the scree, or a place close to the pool edge would suit Salix reticulata, a tiny native willow which forms a twisted mat of prostrate stems clothed in deeply veined leaves. The erect catkins sit like little grey gophers on the stems as the leaves open. It is not a spectacular plant, but one which pleases me enough to spare it garden space. One day I shall plant alongside a Lady's Slipper orchid, Cypripedium calceolus with its chocolate and yellow pouched flowers to keep it company; but I must first find the orchid before that can be achieved.

Thymes are in general either too invasive (albeit beautiful as in the case of Thymus serpyllum hybrids) or not worthy of a place. Exceptions are the hybrid T. × 'Porlock' which is like a moss-green, aromatic toadstool covered in season with pink flowers, and T. herba-barona which smells like caraway seeds and is an interesting Spanish species that spreads its stems over the stones.

Silene acaulis will only flower really well on a spartan diet so the scree is the best place to grow this beautiful rock plant. In poor soil it will make a ground-hugging carpet of small, vivid green leaves which disappear under a pink colour wash of near stemless flowers.

Try also Androsace primuloides varieties which spread grey rosettes of leaves over the stones, each one carrying 10-cm (4-inch) high stems crowned with many-headed umbels of red flowers. This is a plant intolerant of winter wet, so the scree is its only possible habitat. Zauschneria californica 'Glasnevin', a 20-cm (8-inch) high bush topped with tubular scarlet flowers, has the same aversion to winter and water so I grow it in the scree where it too revels in hot, dry conditions and blooms late in the summer.

Several alpines can be sown direct into the scree much as they grow naturally on the open mountain. The alpine poppy, Papaver alpinum, is just such a dainty species making tufts of leaves amongst the stones. Its solitary flowers in pink, white or soft yellow nod to every passing breeze in May and June, and self-sown seedlings perpetuate the colonies. Another useful, early coloniser of newly-stabilised screes under natural conditions is the Alpine toadflax, Linaria alpina, which has blue-grey leaves on trailing stems and opens a succession of orange and violet blooms throughout the summer. Self-sown seedlings are satisfyingly abundant.

Aquilegia scopulorum, a dwarf American columbine with blue leaves and bluer flowers, grows only 8 cm (3 inches) high on the weightwatchers' diet offered by a scree. Erinus alpinus, a pretty tufted-leaved plant sown in a scree will open 8-cm (3-inch) corymbs of lavender, pink, white or red flowers, week in and week out during the summer.

I have given just a tongue-tingling, eye-tantalising glimpse of the alpine world in which I have immersed myself, with a keen appreciation of the beauty these flowers afford. For the gardener with limited space they give more interest per square metre than anything else I grow and almost every form of growing

Alpines are capable of adapting to cultivation in sinks, trough gardens and pots. Whether easy to grow or difficult, they are all expressively beautiful.

condition can be artificially contrived in a well-constructed scree, from arid dry to moist, yet well-drained wet land.

Maintaining a scree or table bed in good order requires less work than would be necessary to look after a rock garden. Yet weeds do seed in to establish themselves and so must be removed. Some of the plants do spread beyond their alloted space but are then banished. At least, in a scree, this will not mean demolishing carefully contrived rockwork to remove roots which, if left, will recolonise all the empty space. Because the scree mixture is more crushed stone than soil, recourse must be made to regular mulching – at least once a year – as a means of ensuring that plant nutrients removed by the growing plants are replaced. A mixture made up with sterilised loam and bone-meal, or powdered seaweed, spread as a top dressing around the plants in February will be sufficient. In practice, I buy bags of John Innes Seed, or No. 1 potting compost, mix in the

bone-meal or seaweed fertiliser and thus save the trouble of sterilising the loam myself. A top dressing of stone chippings will also much improve the whole appearance and show the flowers to better advantage. Indeed, elderly plants which are beginning to die back can often be rejuvenated by working a handful or two of John Innes Seed Compost in amongst the stems.

Plants will die even in the best-ordered alpine garden. These should be removed with all the root possible, together with the scree mix in which they were growing. The hole, refilled with fresh compost, should offer a better start to whatever is planted in it than the original, worn-out, impoverished scree mix.

Skill, which comes only from experience, will suggest ways of adjusting the growing conditions so that some of the really difficult yet particularly beautiful alpines can be persuaded to establish, and even more importantly, to flower as they do in their native homes. Carpets of Geum reptans, lawns of Ranunculus glacialis, or rock faces blue with Eritrichium nanum present a stern challenge to my skill that at present is impossible to resolve. It is enough that I keep trying in spite of repeated failures.

142

II

BULBOUS & BEAUTIFUL

Geoffrey Smith

Bulbs are the embroidery of coloured threads weaving seasonal patterns through the multi-hued tapestry of our gardens. Compulsive bulb-buyers appreciate the wealth and diversity offered by what in a wide interpretation are termed bulbs. For the purpose of this breviate, my definition will include also corms and tubers which are not in the strictest sense true bulbs.

Though the majority of bulbs will grow in any reasonable garden soil there are those which need specialist understanding to give of their best. Equally, there are those which need brutal expulsion to prevent them, weed-like, from invading the whole garden. From when the snowdrop offers spring's challenge to the dominance of winter, to the sight of frost-blasted petals on the kaffir lily, Schizostylis coccinea, announcing that another gardening year has passed, bulbs are an essential part of my annual gardening cycle.

The time to plant depends in some cases on the season of flowering. For autumn bloomers, July to August is to be preferred, although September to October both for pot culture and for those grown outdoors is the more usual time for bulb setting. Consider the pleasure a bowl of bulbs in full bloom on a windowsill during mid-winter can bring – enough to make anyone reach for compost and pots. Bulbs to be grown in pots, whether for indoors or as patio decoration, should be of top quality. Why waste time and effort on second-rate bulbs which, no matter how well they are grown, will only produce inferior flowers?

The compost I prefer for pot-grown bulbs, for forcing or patio decoration, is either peat- or loam-based, with added charcoal. For early flowering, select those bulbs which have been specially treated to induce premature blooming. Where possible, use growing containers with proper drainage, indeed, these are essential for bulbs to be grown outdoors. Tubs and troughs for patio decoration require no special treatment, just plant them up at the normal time – August to September for all except tulips which go in during October or November.

All bulbs need eight weeks of cool, moist darkness after being potted and this is vital with those which are being flowered indoors. Bury them by the north side of the house and cover them in sand, or put them in a cellar ideally: this enables them to develop a strong root system before starting into top growth. Never stand them in the airing cupboard, or bring the bowls straight from a cool into a high temperature but make the adjustment through easy stages.

Bulb-planted containers do make handsome decoration for a patio, terrace or balcony. I have two tubs which are filled with Narcissus each year. The bulbs are grown in soil-based compost, for after doing duty on the terrace they will then be planted out in the garden to naturalise. To get the best possible display of bloom the bulbs are planted in two layers. First, I prepare an 8-cm (3-inch) bed of John Innes No. 2 compost into which a number of daffodils are bedded. I cover these with another thick layer of compost, then plant the rest of the bulbs which are in turn covered with more compost to fill up the tub to within 2½ cm (1 inch) of the rim.

Though the depth of planting varies so markedly, all the flowers open together.

Planting bulbs in the garden should be an unhurried, well-considered, seasonally vocational part of the gardening year. I find a trowel the most efficient tool for the job, in preference to a dibber or purpose-designed bulb planter. When planting bulbs in grass for naturalising, the trowel is set aside in favour of a spade. Rules in gardening are always general rather than precise, but a good rule of thumb guide for depth of planting is that bulbs should be covered with twice their own depth of soil. A large bulb like a tulip therefore should be buried 10 cm (4 inches) deep whereas the very much smaller Crocus corm needs to be covered by about 5 to 8 cm (2 or 3 inches) of soil. There are exceptions to any rule and the madonna lily (Lilium candidum) and Nerine bowdenii must be planted almost on the surface. A sound policy then, is to enquire into the cultural requirements of any bulb, corm or tuber before attempting to grow it in the garden.

When planting bulbs, particularly Narcissus, to naturalise in grassland, make certain they go down in groups of a single colour as the ultimate effect is more pleasing than that achieved by mixing several hues. By varying the size and shape of each colony the composition becomes more natural; as if the parent colony had seeded around about like Wordsworth's daffodils beside Ullswater. Use a sharp spade to remove the turf carefully with the least amount of damage. Insert the bulbs to a suitable depth and replace the grass sod. There is no need for alarm if it stands a little above the general level for as the disturbed soil sinks so will the turf. Above all, do not plant bulbs which are being left to naturalise too close together; leave plenty of space or they will quickly become overcrowded.

What then to plant? As with every other aspect of gardening there are what could be termed the 'must have' and 'the nice to have', so first, the essentials without which a certain quality of excellence would be lost to the garden. All spring-flowering bulbs are planted in early autumn with a few noted exceptions. Ornamental onions make an odd beginning, yet Allium moly with deep-yellow flowers on 25-cm (10-inch) stems in June is useful for naturalising under tall-growing shrubs. I also grow the round-headed leek, Allium sphaerocephalum, with large egg-shaped clusters of deep-purple flowers in late summer because of the butterflies which cluster to feed on them. They grow to around 60 cm (24 inches). I grow them all mixed up with the deep-blue Agapan-

thus 'Slieve Donard' which is of similar height, and obligingly blooms at the same time.

Alstroemeria I hesitate to recommend, for when suited by soil and situation they can become philistines and take up too much space. Plant the white tubers of A. 'Ligtu' hybrids, 10 cm (4 inches) deep, on a bed of sand. Your reward will be a succession of flowers in shades of orange, flame, yellow and pink on 1-metre (3-foot) stems in midsummer.

Anemones are so coquettishly modest they persuade rather than command attention. A. apennina is best planted in grass or in a border where it can be allowed to grow undisturbed. The large, daisy-like, blue flowers appear above the divided foliage in April. The height is an unambitious 15 cm (6 inches). A. blanda is even smaller and the flowers range from deep red, through pink, violet, blue and white, and also appear in April. A quiet corner of the garden where it can seed gently is most suitable. 'Glory of the Snow', Chionodoxa luciliae, with arching 20-cm (8-inch) high stems of blue, white-eyed flowers in spring is also best left to naturalise in the shrub border.

'Naked ladies', 'meadow saffron', the Colchicums of botanists, are not, and never will be, 'Autumn Crocus' for unlike true Crocus they have six stamens. Botanical niceties apart, they do produce magnificent goblets of flowers out of bare earth in September. The leaves appear in spring and are best disguised by sowing annuals such as Godetia to grow up and hide them. Both C. speciosum (lilac) and particularly its white form C.s. 'Album', also C. autumnale growing between 15 and 23 cm (6 and 9 inches) tall are very desirable. They look magnificent when grown under autumn-colouring cherries or azaleas. Plant the bulbs in July to August, 15 cm (6 inches) deep, and in two years' time they will have worked to the surface and need division, followed by replanting.

Crocus I plant in quantity every year, the fat-flowered Dutch varieties to naturalise in grass and species such as C. chrysanthus, C. susianus, C. angustifolius, C. tomasinianus and their hybrids and varieties all about the garden to gladden my heart with their flowers, and to rejoice the bees by providing brood food pollen. Consider also the autumn-flowering species for naturalising amongst dwarf shrubs. Two which are excellent are C. laevigatus with lilac flowers, and the deeper violet-petalled, orange-stamened C. speciosus. Those flowering in spring are put down in September, whereas those flowering in autumn are better planted in July or August. I shall list no particular varieties here, but urge you to choose any or all for there has never been an ugly Crocus, or ever will be.

For those who have not yet discovered hardy Cyclamen, let me now introduce just two species of such rare quality that I shall, God willing, always grow them. Cyclamen coum has glossy leaves and chubby, deep-carmine to pale-pink flowers which open in my alpine scree garden from January to April on 5-cm (2-inch) stems. C. hederifolium offers white to carmine flowers in autumn, followed by silver- and green-patterned leaves as winter decoration. Both adapt well to most soils and are easily raised from seed if this is sown freshly harvested. Otherwise, plant pot-grown corms in spring.

Why dog's tooth violets do not enjoy the popularity that the lovely lily-like flowers warrant is difficult to discover. My own plants grow happily in amongst dwarf rhododendrons. Erythronium dens-canis offers lavender and pink flowers during April, while the golden-yellow E. tuolumnense which, together with hybrids such as the white-petalled E. 'White Beauty', or the yellow E. 'Pagoda', show colour a fortnight later. They are best planted while in growth from pots during March.

Snowdrops, Galanthus, are never happier than when allowed the freedom of centuries to spread in drifts through open woodland, or down grassy hillsides. They are easier to establish if the bulbs are planted just as the flowers open. Varieties? Well, forced to select just one, then let it be G. nivalis 'Sam Arnott'. Fortunately, I am not so restricted and plant any that come my way. Grow them with winter aconite, Eranthus hyemalis of the yellow buttercup flowers, which are also best planted in bloom.

Bulbous irises, I plant every year, for they cannot, except in specially favoured soils, be considered true perennials. Iris histrioides 'Major' flowers first, usually in March, followed by Iris reticulata and hybrids from it, also with blue or violet blooms. Iris danfordiae offers an alternative in yellow. A well-drained soil is essential, and life expectancy is improved by feeding with John Innes base fertiliser, as used in composts of the same name, each year in late winter.

Just a brief mention of a selection from the species and varieties of lilies at present available will, I hope, excite a desire on the part of readers to grow more of them. The most important single factor governing the successful cultivation of any lily is good drainage. Depth of planting varies, but on average a 10 to 15-cm (4 to 6-inch) covering of soil will suit most species, Lilium candidum with ivory-white blooms being the exception. The bulbs in this species are overlayed by only 2½ to 5 cm (1 or 2 inches) of sandy soil. When buying bulbs, make certain they are plump, firm and have live roots, not the shrivelled, dehydrated, rootless objects so often seen on cheap offer. I grow species from seed where possible, although it is a long-term business. Failing this, I buy a bulb, take scales from it and grow them on to flowering.

Lilium regale is my first choice, with ivory-coloured trumpets feathered yellow inside, stained dark-red or purple on the rib outside, and with a fragrance that is purely delightful. Easily grown in a sunny corner, Lilium bulbiferum, 'Orange' or 'Cottage Lily', is a strong-stemmed species with bright-orange, upright trumpets. The purplish bulbils at the base of the florets can be used to propagate fresh stock. Of the hybrids, L. 'Enchantment' is of similar colour and vigour. L. 'Tiger Babies' is a new, strong-growing hybrid of a curious fawn shade. I can only suggest that you try those which come to hand, the rewards are manifestly obvious when the flowers appear.

Some flowers are beloved by young and old alike. The primrose is one, the daffodil another. Even the most inhospitable chill day gains warmth from the dancing legions of gold which usher spring into our gardens. A deep, moisture-retentive though not waterlogged soil suits daffodils best, for in nature many of them grow in what I can only describe as weeping bog conditions. Plant the bulbs immediately they are available in August. The choice of hybrids is entirely a matter of personal taste.

Of the species, Narcissus asturiensis, 5 to 7 cm (2 to 3 inches) high, flowers in February. N. cyclamineus 'Peeping Tom' and its hybrids bloom in April, the height varies up to 25 cm (10 inches) for the tallest. Grow also the native N. pseudo-narcissus, and the intensely fragrant 'Pheasant's Eye', N. poeticus. Golden-yellow N. 'King Alfred' naturalises well, as does the paler N. 'W. P. Milner'.

Nerine bowdenii will grow and flower even in the north if planted at the foot of a south-facing wall in well-drained soil. Set the bulbs in position during the summer with the top of the bulb poking above soil level. The branched heads of pink, wavy-petalled flowers will display themselves on 30-cm (12-inch) high stems in early autumn.

Kaffir lily, Schizostylis coccinea, has neither bulb nor corm, but root-like underground stems similar to certain irises, yet in appearance it is allied to a mini-Gladiolus. I am bending the rules therefore to include this most attractive native of South Africa. It

adding to a list already so extensive that long ago I decided enough was enough and concentrated on the species which, like the seasons, do not change. The hybrids are classified into groups according to parentage and time of flowering, beginning with single, early tulips in April and ending with the late doubles in June. Search then amongst the catalogue lists for the colour and time of flowering you require from Mendels, Triumph, Cottage, Darwins, and Lily-flowered. Before making a final decision, consider some of the species which if planted into a well-drained soil on a south-facing aspect will prove themselves stalwart perennials. I first saw the native Tulipa sylvestris growing wild as a colony of fragrant yellow flowers amongst boulders of limestone under a centuries-old hedge. The slender stems grow up to 25 cm (10 inches) tall and look their best naturalised in a grassed-down orchard.

Tulipa batalinii is my favourite, with wavy-edged, grey leaves and lovely peach-yellow flowers. T. 'Bronze Charm' is a useful offspring with bronze and apricot blooms – both grow 15 cm (6 inches) high. Even easier to grow and the earliest to flower, T. turkestanica will spread colonies of white, yellow-centred flowers carried several to a 20-cm (8-inch) high stem. T. griegii has broad leaves beautifully mottled with dark purple which are topped with brilliant scarlet flowers. There are, as one would expect, numerous hybrids all growing to a sturdy 20 to 25 cm (8 to 10 inches) height. T. kaufmanniana, water lily tulip, is a dwarf species of 10 to 20 cm (4 to 8 inches), with enormous flowers cream-tinged yellow and pink. Again, there are numerous hybrids between this and other species, some with flowers so outrageously coloured they assault the eye. With several red flowers to a 25-cm (10-inch) stem, T. praestans is an easy to please species suitable for rock garden planting, and T. tarda is another frequently used for furnishing a sunny pocket in the scree; up to five white-with-yellow-centre flowers are carried on stalks 15 cm (6 inches) tall. Also dwarf and suitable for the scree garden is T. urumiensis, in which the yellow-pointed buds are shaded bronze on the outside.

So much for the 'must have' bulbs. If there is space available for more then the following are 'nice to haves'. Fritillaria, the majestically imperious 'crown imperials', require planting 15 cm (6 inches) deep on a bed of sand in good, fertile loam. Pendant orange or yellow heads nod approval of the May garden from the top of 1-metre (3-foot) high stems. F. meleagris, the 'native snakeshead' is smaller and altogether daintier at 23 cm (9 inches) and has nodding pink, white or purple blooms chequered with brown squares. Plant the bulbs 10 cm (4 inches) deep amongst dwarf rhododendrons where the soil will be agreeably moist.

Among Gladiolus species I will make especial mention of G. byzantinus which displays magenta flowers on 60-cm (2-foot) high stems during July. Another is the lovely 'Painted Lady' of South Africa, G. debilis, whose elegantly curved stems offer creamy-white flowers, patterned with vivid scarlet fleurs-de-lis. Planted 10 cm (4 inches) deep, both survive without lifting in northern gardens.

Leucojum, summer snowflakes, deserve more than casual dismissal as out of season snowdrops. First to flower is L. vernum which in my own garden pushes up 30-cm (12-inch) high stems amongst winter-flowering heathers. The flowers are white and bell-shaped with a green tip to each petal. L. aestivum 'Gravetye Giant' produces larger flowers on slightly taller stems a month later than L. vernum. Both grow best in a moist soil. L. autumnale is a dainty, autumn-flowering species 10 to 15 cm (4 to 6 inches) high with slender, rush-like leaves and four or five pink and white bells opening per flower stem. An alpine scree is an excellent place to grow them, and I find 'Snowflakes' establish best when planted actually in growth.

Muscaris or grape hyacinths naturalise easily. M. armeniacum is the most widely planted, growing 15 to 20 cm (6 to 8 inches) high with azure-blue, scented flowers. M. botryoides is dwarfer and carries bright, china-blue flowers on a stubby spike. Both flower in spring.

Scilla, popularly known as squills, are a very large group indeed. I grow both the brilliant blue, early-spring-blooming S. sibirica 'Spring Beauty' and the most common species S. bifolia naturalised as ground planting under deciduous azaleas where soil conditions seem to suit them. S. bifolia is diverse enough in flower to offer deep blue, pink and pure white forms.

For those who can offer a well-drained soil at the foot of a sun-baked, south-facing wall, Sternbergia lutea with vivid yellow flowers carried Crocus-like on 10-cm (4-inch) high stems is most agreeable company. Sternbergia should be planted 15 cm (6 inches) deep during August, unlike the Nerine which prefers surface planting. Both require the same soil conditions and situation. Propagation of bulbs is generally by division. The species will, of course, reproduce themselves by means of seed and this method, though it may mean waiting several years for the resulting bulbs to flower, is one to which I often resort.

12

THE GRASS IS ALWAYS GREENER

Stefan Buczacki

Did you realise that 80 per cent of British gardens boast a lawn? Boast may not in reality be the most appropriate verb to use in connection with some of the green areas that I have seen masquerading under the name. None the less, the cultivation of grass for mowing falls within most gardeners' activities and it is in the hope that you would prefer to view your results with at least a measure of pride that I pen these lines. British gardeners as a group certainly have a very special relationship with their lawns and, indeed, to quote to you a few more statistics, over £100 million is spent on lawn-mowers and £12 million on lawn chemicals each year. Clearly, the spirit, and even the pocket, is willing, if the flesh and the end-product are sometimes rather weak.

Why a lawn?

There are several reasons for gracing your garden with a lawn. It enables you to maintain an area of plants in a reasonably attractive state much more simply than is possible with almost any other form of vegetation; it provides a pleasing and attractive contrast to the predominantly upright form of other plants that you may have elsewhere in the garden; and it provides an amenity in itself – somewhere to walk, sit, play, even to eat and sleep, if that is your wont. There are, however, alternatives to almost all of these functions. For carpeting a large area, the alternatives to a lawn are paving, in its various forms, and gravel. Even at its cheapest, using the dullest of concrete slabs, paving represents a considerably higher capital outlay than grass. At its dearest, using the best of natural stones, it is an option for millionaires alone. Good-quality stone, or the best of the modern artificial versions, can none the less create a very attractive and certainly a highly durable surface requiring the minimal maintenance of weed control. It has its place in most gardens but there is a size above which it takes on an air of monotony. The gaps within a paved area provide interesting and valuable habitats for growing some of the thymes and other carpeting plants. But I like gravel; it has the great advantages of relative cheapness, ease of laying and the ability to fill the most irregular of shapes. Plants may be allowed to grow through it to very appealing effect, but constant attention is needed to limit such appearances to those types that you find attractive; weed control among gravel is a chore, although greatly alleviated by modern weedkillers.

When I talk of a lawn, I use the word as my dictionary defines it; a space of ground covered with grass, but we are asked so often about alternatives that a comment on them seems called for. For a small area, such plants as thymes and some species of Dianthus might be used, provided you selected those tolerant of being walked on, but they would be impracticable and almost prohibitively expensive over a large area. The alternative to grass that is offered most frequently is the herb, chamomile, in its non-flowering form called 'Treneague'. Chamomile lawns certainly exist and they have some of the attributes of grass in being green (for at least part of the year), fairly tolerant of being walked on and, to a certain extent, amenable to light mowing. But they are highly intolerant of wet, poorly drained sites, even more intolerant of shade than is grass, and look unutterably dismal in winter, especially after a period of hard frosts. And weed control in a non-grass lawn is a nightmare. I much prefer to go with my dictionary, therefore and have my lawns of grass.

Siting of and Preparation for the Lawn

Although the same basic preparation is applicable to both seeded and turfed lawns, the choice is one that is best made early in your planning; if for no other reason than that the optimum times for starting with each are not identical. The major advantage of turf over seed is speed of establishment; its major disadvantage is the higher cost, appreciably higher if you buy the best-quality turf. When choosing and ordering turf, take great care, especially with the type offered most commonly, meadow-turf. My idea of a meadow is rather different from my idea of a lawn and turf offered thus is very likely to include a blend of grasses that is ideal for grazing cattle but not to grace your garden. It will also almost certainly contain a high weed population – the designation 'weed-treated' means nothing and is certainly no guarantee that any weeds have actually been killed. If you are able to inspect the turf beforehand and satisfy yourself of its quality and uniformity, you may be lucky. None the less, my advice is always grit your teeth, pay more and buy downland turf, although even this will not be totally free from weeds. But forget about the legendary Cumberland turf, which is for bowling greens, not gardens.

With seed, you are much more likely to achieve good-quality grass, provided you buy a reputable brand and avoid loose, unnamed seed from unnamed sacks. Most seed companies offer choices between blends that contain modern dwarf rye grasses, which are ideal for lawns subject to a fair degree of wear and tear, and mixtures without rye grass which produce a fine lawn but one intolerant of heavy traffic. Most modern lawn seed mixtures are dressed with a chemical bird-repellent; these are by no means entirely effective but they do help.

Grass will grow in most situations but thrives very much better in some than in others. The types of grass used for lawns are those most tolerant of being

There is nothing magical about creating a good lawn but it takes time and it costs money

mown, capable of forming a closely knitted turf, not prone to flowering and robust enough to enable certain activities to take place on them. Unfortunately, the types of grass falling into such categories are generally intolerant of shade and of very wet or very dry sites. It is futile to try to establish a lawn beneath deep shade therefore, although a modern shade-tolerant seed mixture will enable you to have a modest sward under light shade. There are very much better ways of making use of more deeply shaded parts of the garden with truly shade-tolerant plants.

When a lawn is to be established on a dry site, thorough incorporation of organic matter beforehand will repay dividends many times over in the long, hot summers of years to come; but beforehand is very much the operative word, for adding organic matter to the soil beneath established turf is a task more suited to the conjuror than the gardener. On a very heavy, wet site, installing a drainage system as I illustrated in Chapter 1 makes a great deal of sense.

Prepare the site for the lawn as far as possible in advance of seeding or turfing and always remember that it is the care and thoroughness adopted at this stage that will very largely dictate the standard of the lawn subsequently. The best months for seeding a lawn are September and April, although these times are not sacrosanct and the main criteria are a warm and moist soil and freedom from frost, cold and drying winds or very hot, drying sunshine. Turf is also best laid in similar conditions, and although a new lawn can be turfed at almost any time of year provided the ground is not frozen and it can be watered when dry, early autumn is certainly the best time. In general, therefore, mid-autumn or mid-spring make good calendar points towards which to plan your preparations.

If the site is weedy, make full use of the potential offered by modern weedkillers to remove both annu-als and perennials. A large population of annual weed seeds in the soil will give rise to serious problems in the early stages of establishing a lawn from seed (especially as there is no longer available a reliable weedkiller for use among seedling grasses), but will be less important later, or with lawns established from turf. A residual population of deep-seated perennial weeds such as couch or bindweed is likely, however, to give problems throughout the life of any lawn. Remember that most weedkillers work best in the summer; an autumn start in preparation for a spring sowing on a weedy site is really two or three months too late. Whatever you do, moreover, don't make the mistake of applying a pre-emergence weedkiller before you sow grass seed!

After the weedkillers have achieved their objective, you can begin the first site preparation which, if you are fortunate, will comprise thorough digging and the incorporating of organic matter. Those less fortunate may need to grade the area first, as shown in the diagrams, in order to obtain a level surface. On a garden with fairly shallow topsoil, it may be necessary to buy more to assist the grading if you are to avoid bringing subsoil to the surface. It is a mistake, however, to imagine that grading carries the implication that a lawn must, of necessity, be dead flat; a gentle slope is perfectly acceptable but it should be uniform.

After grading, soil preparation and weed removal, levelling and firming the site should next exercise your attention and your muscles. The rake is the most useful tool for rendering the surface level, and the wider the rake, the better. The narrowness of the conventional garden rake simply encourages you to produce a surface more reminiscent of a railway marshalling yard than a potential lawn. Once major irregularities have been removed, I find the spring-tine lawn rake very satisfactory but some gardeners

To level the site, hammer in a grid of wooden pegs 2 metres apart and use a plank and spirit level to ensure the tops are in the same plane, as shown. Then attach string between the pegs at the level you wish the lawn surface to lie. Remove and/or add topsoil to bring the whole area level with the string. Firm the surface and then check the level once more before you remove the pegs.

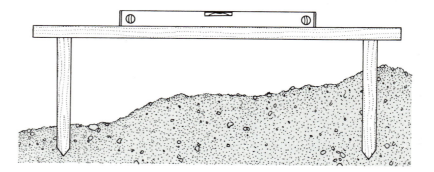

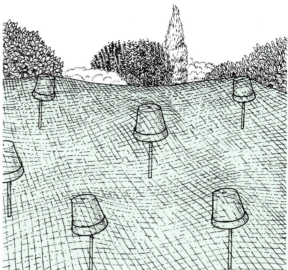

swear by a wide, wooden hay rake for the preliminary work and follow this with the closer teeth of a lawn rake or so-called lawn comb in the final stages before seeding or as soon as the area has received its final digging. About one month before you plan to add the grass, should come a very thorough coarse raking when as many as possible of the pebbles should be taken off, together with any remaining clods of soil. Having done this, however, it is a mistake to begin too soon the finer raking needed to produce a seed-bed tilth, for heavy rain on such a surface very quickly causes a cap or crust to form that will impair the establishment of the grass roots.

Once the rake has rendered the surface fairly smooth, the soil must be firmed and there is no better tool for this than a pair of feet shod in wellington boots. This is a laborious and time-consuming operation but there are no easy shortcuts; an average garden roller is likely to undo all your hard work and replace the humps and hollows that you have so religiously removed. On a very large area, of course, advice to tread in is academic and if you can borrow or hire (and transport to your garden!) a very wide, but lightweight, roller this will give good results, used carefully. About one week before sowing or turfing, begin the final preparation and gently rake the top couple of centimetres, taking care to rake each time at 90 degrees to your last direction of draw in order to maintain the level surface. As you make this final raking, apply a base fertiliser. To my mind, this is quite essential to obtain the best plant establish-

left, A wheeled fertiliser spreader more than repays its modest cost in the accuracy of its coverage

above, Simple but effective protection from birds – some canes, plastic pots and fruit cage netting

ment, but as specially formulated pre-sowing lawn fertilisers are not easily obtained, much the simplest plan is to use an autumn and winter lawn fertiliser with a low nitrogen content at the rate of 70g per square metre (about 2 oz per square yard).

At last, you are ready to add the final ingredient, the grass. For sowing, choose a warm, damp and still day if possible and divide up your area with canes and string into conveniently sized zones in order to assist in obtaining uniform seeding. Some seed companies supply a small measure with the seed and suggest that you use the contents of this to sow a defined area. In the absence of such a measure, I prefer to weigh out the seed into batches of 170 g (about 6 oz) and use each to seed four square metres or yards. (Remember, however, that the seed may have been treated chemically, so wash the scale pan thoroughly afterwards.) After sowing, rake very lightly over the seed-bed so the seeds are barely covered. Although you will often see a recommendation not to cover the seed at all, I have always obtained the best results by scattering finely sieved damp peat over the whole. Certainly the seeds should not be buried but, unless you are very fortunate with the weather, they will dry out if left on the surface. If rain doesn't fall soon after sowing, you

must water the seed-bed but this should be done very gently if the seeds are not to be washed away. Easily the best way to achieve a soft and gentle watering is with a perforated 'sprinkler' hosepipe.

Even when seed has been treated with bird-repellent, problems can arise through birds scratching for worms or even through using the seed-bed as a dust bath. But please don't stretch black cotton over your new lawn; it can be a death trap for birds. I always use very lightweight fruit cage netting supported on upturned plastic plant pots on the tops of split canes. Such netting is relatively inexpensive and can be used over and over again whenever protection from birds is needed in the garden.

Grass seed should germinate in from one to three weeks and once it has reached a height of 5 to 8 cm (about 2 to 3 inches), it may be lightly topped with the

opposite, *Simply by alternating the mowing direction, an otherwise monotonous lawn can come to life – this example is at Sandwich, Kent*

left, *An alternative to grass is a chamomile lawn but although charming in theory, it represents a great deal of hard work in practice*

below, *The remarkable properties of modern selective weedkillers are seen in the contrast between the treated and untreated areas of a lawn*

mower set very high. A wheeled rotary is ideal for this. Any lawn grown from seed should not be subjected to what may be described as normal activity for at least a year.

Laying turf is hard work, so unless you are well experienced, don't overestimate the area that you can lay in one go. When delivered (and do try to arrange for it to be stacked as close to the new lawn as possible), it will almost certainly be rolled up. Left in this state for more than about five days, the grass will begin to turn yellow so if it is not to be laid promptly you will need to allocate an area where it can be opened and spread out; but remember that this area will need to be at least as large as the lawn itself! It really is very much better to plan your time to allow you to begin laying as soon as the turf arrives.

It is important to be systematic when laying turf; the diagrams on this page show the operation step-by-step but remember always to use a plank when walking over newly laid turves and always to treat them with some respect. Firm them down with the wooden tamper but please don't beat them into submission with the back of your spade! It is absolutely essential to take your time and ensure that each turf is laid flat by adding small handfuls of topsoil beneath if necessary; this is immeasurably easier than trying to correct matters later.

Caring for your Lawn

Once established, a lawn needs careful and regular attention to give of its best but I see no merit at all in the quite obsessive lengths to which some gardeners will go in order to try to emulate the local bowling green. A lawn is not a bowling green and never will be; it contains different types of grass for different purposes. Moreover, whilst my lawn is, I hope, more or less weed-free, it is certainly not moss-free and I know of no other lawn that is. I counsel, not perfection, but common sense, therefore in offering you a plan for lawn care divided into feeding, watering, mechanical care and weed control.

I have always advocated lawn feeding twice a year; once in the spring and once in the autumn. Summer feeding with high nitrogen 'booster' or 'green-up' fertilisers generally does no harm but is merely a short-lived, cosmetic exercise. There are many excellent proprietary lawn fertilisers now available, the spring

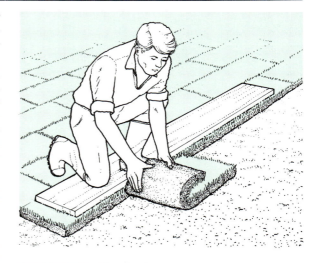

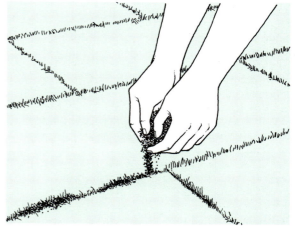

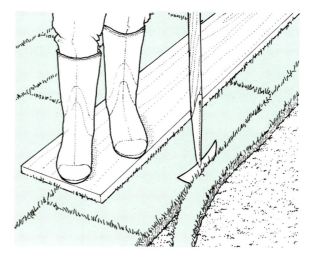

Lay turves offset from each other, rather like bricks in a wall, and fill in gaps with soil. Always stand on a plank, not directly on the turf and trim edges with a half-moon lawn edger.

feeds being relatively high and the autumn feeds relatively low in nitrogen. It is essential not to use any leftover feed at the wrong time of year as you run a high risk of encouraging disease and other problems in the turf. For any other than a very small lawn, an inexpensive wheeled fertiliser spreader is not only time-saving but also highly beneficial in ensuring uniform application.

Many spring feeds include a selective weedkiller but I find that I always need an additional treatment later; the fertiliser is generally used too early in the season for its weedkiller component to work optimally. Many autumn feeds contain a wormkiller but this is far from necessary and I fall into the fraternity that believes that worms do more good than harm in a lawn. Although I am aware of the unsightly appearance of worm-casts and their role in bringing weed seeds to the surface and blunting the blades of cylinder mowers, it has always seemed to me somewhat illogical to spend time and money to apply a wormkiller and also time and money on artificial lawn-aeration.

Lawn grasses, like other plants, need water in order to grow. They are also shallow-rooted and suffer appreciably during periods of drought. However, no sooner do the signs of thirst begin to appear than a ban on hosepipes and lawn sprinklers is imposed. There is no answer to this, but when watering is permitted, do choose a device commensurate with the area over which the water must be applied. And never underestimate the recovery powers of a lawn; after the summer of 1976, my lawn, like almost everyone else's, had much in common with the Gobi Desert but within a few days of rain returning, it reassured me of its continuing vitality.

Mechanical care of the lawn may be divided into mowing, edging, raking and spiking. All lawns need mowing; certainly once, and preferably twice each week, especially during vigorous summer growth. Choosing a lawn-mower is, for most gardeners, ultimately a financial decision but I have been forced recently to revise some of my views on the relative merits of rotary and cylinder mowers. There are modern, petrol-engined cylinder mowers with power drive that seem to cope with most of the grass that a rotary can; and to give it a better finish. On an uneven surface, though, a cylinder machine will still scrape the surface. Among the very popular, small, electric rotary machines, those with nylon cutters are efficient and much safer than those with a conventional, whirling metal blade.

The height of cut to which your lawn-mower should be set is important; most are set too low and many very much too low. Three cm (1¼ inches) at the beginning and end of the season and 2½ cm (1 inch) in summer are adequate for most lawns but both of these values could be reduced by about one-third for a fine lawn. And should you leave on the grass-box? For most lawns, the answer is yes; apart from other considerations, the cuttings make valuable additions to the compost heap. Conversely, the lawn itself may benefit in respect of the added nutrition and improved moisture retentiveness if the cuttings are returned during the summer; but only if the grass is cut at least twice each week and only if a very thorough raking or scarifying can be performed in the autumn to remove the thatch of dead grass.

As far as aesthetic appeal is concerned, much of the time and effort spent on mowing is rather wasted because of the general neglect given to lawn edging. I am quite aware that it is a chore but I do believe it is a chore worth doing. Use a half-moon lawn edger after the first mowing in the spring to define the edge for the season – slope the cut slightly away from the lawn to prevent the edge from collapsing, and use right-angled, long-handled edging shears subsequently. Long-handled shears for cutting the horizontal edge are only necessary if your mower will not mow right to the edge itself or if you have a large lawn; normal shears and a bent back are perfectly satisfactory for a small area. Although modern technology has produced an electric mower with a removable edge-trimming device that can do a pretty passable job, it can't give you the slope to the edge that I much prefer.

Lawn raking is the masochist's task; I cannot think of many more laborious ways of whiling away the hours. It does pay handsome rewards, however, in the improvement of the lawn through permitting better penetration of water and fertiliser. The same ends can now be achieved with much greater facility with electric appliances that may be adjusted to give a fairly deep scarifying, a lighter raking or a simple leaf-sweeping action. Light raking should be carried out in spring and in autumn (when it is especially important to remove the leaves that so rapidly block the surface), but deeper scarifying should be restricted to the autumn when it will have the additional benefit of stimulating the development of new side-shoots and thus encouraging the thickening of the sward. If I tried really hard and was pressed to name one task worse than vigorous lawn raking, it would be lawn spiking! Spiking, or making holes in your lawn, is no game for the faint-hearted so do be sure that your lawn will benefit from it. The purpose

A foot-powered hollow-tine spiker represents hard work but benefits the lawn greatly

is to break through compacted soil and so permit water, air and fertiliser to penetrate. This compaction will be greatest on lawns subject to a great deal of traffic and those with a heavy clayey soil. The simplest method (and I use the term in a relative sense), is by repeatedly driving in the tines of a fork to about 10 cm (4 inches), with about 15 cm (6 inches) between thrusts. It doesn't take a mathematician to work out the time that this will take and superficially quicker, wheeled devices are available but I have never found them very easy to manipulate. Spiked shoes are available too and the idea of simply walking over the lawn is appealing although the length of spike is not really long enough and I feel that shoes with an adequate length of spike would be more likely to replace your horticultural problems with medical ones. All of these methods, moreover, work by actually compacting the soil to produce the hole. The ideal technique is hollow-tine spiking which, carried out every three or four years, will be highly beneficial; the hollow tines actually remove small plugs of soil. Manual, fork-like, hollow-tine tools are available but much the best plan is to hire a powered device and do the job properly.

Every lawn, no matter how good the turf or seed with which you started, will sooner or later develop weed growth. As lawn weed control is a specialised branch of the art, I shall discuss it here although I have left the general principles of weed control to Chapter 15. Annual weeds can be problematic on lawns if they produce large quantities of seed, have

an efficient means of dispersing them (your lawn-mower, for instance) and especially if the seeds can germinate without needing a period of dormancy. Perennial weeds may also spread by seeding but are more important because they have the type of growth (a sunken rosette or creeping rhizomes, for example) that tucks their growing point neatly out of harm's way. The choice of lawn weedkillers is now fairly restricted but they can be loosely divided into those sold for 'general' use and those recommended for 'problem' weeds, although the recent withdrawal of the chemical ioxynil from sale to gardeners has severely restricted the number of the latter. With persistence (by which I mean several applications during periods of warm, damp weather in the summer), most lawn weeds can be controlled. Usually, complaints of failure are the result of the chemical not having been applied during optimum weather conditions. A few lawn weeds, including creeping speedwell, remain very difficult to control satisfactorily and, for these, I can only suggest ringing the changes with weedkillers and using lawn sand. Lawn sand has been with us for a long time. It is a mixture of ferrous sulphate, ammonium sulphate and fine sand and is sold ready-mixed. Its greatest value is as a moss-killer (when it is at least as good as some modern products) but it will certainly check many weeds too. It is best applied in late spring; after its application, do not walk on the lawn for two to three days and, if rain hasn't fallen by then, water liberally. The effect is dramatic; weeds and moss are blackened (and even grass may temporarily darken) and should be raked up after two or three weeks. (There is little merit in raking up live moss without treatment for you will merely spread it further.)

Weed grasses create special problems in lawns for they are, of course, not affected by selective weed-killers. Slashing the crowns is sometimes suggested but is only really effective with the creeping species. Try digging out the patches and returfing or, alternatively, if your lawn is only of moderate quality, carefully spray the weed grass patches with the systemic, total weedkiller, glyphosate and re-seed directly into the dead patch.

Finally, for a small lawn, a few weeds and a gardener unwilling to use chemicals, don't forget that it is still possible to buy the small 'V'-shaped forks or grubbers once used extensively to dig out daisies, dandelions and similar weeds from turf.

13

CONCRETE & CONTAINERS

Clay Jones

I must begin by recounting a period of some three to four years in my life that were significant for their frustration. It occurred just after the war, when I was an ex-service student at Aberystwyth and my wife and I lived in a third-storey flat in the town centre. The house had no garden and I was initially deprived of the unbounded joy of growing things, a situation I could not tolerate. Fortunately, that flat had five large windows blessed with five wide windowsills and I decided that here I would have my garden. A local greengrocer provided me with an appropriate number of tomato boxes which were just wide enough to sit comfortably on the sills. I painted them sky-blue, not because I particularly liked the colour, but because it happened to be the only tin of paint in my possession. I then borrowed a large potato sack from a wholesale fruit and vegetable merchant, leapt on my bike and rode out into the country, with a coal shovel in the saddle-bag. I found a field strewn with molehills, filled the sack with the crumbly, clean earth, pedalled, pushed and puffed my way back to the flat, heaved the sack upstairs and filled the tomato boxes, and the plants that I grew in them were a source of constant joy to us as a family and to countless passers-by below, with the exception of a few who were dripped upon!

I relate the experience as an illustration of how someone with sap in his veins in place of blood will always find ways and means of growing things. This is the prime purpose of a patio, as a place where man, woman and plants can cohabit in a confined space, especially in urban areas where gardens as such are either tiny or non-existent. If I ever doubted that there might be places where gardening was not possible, those doubts were dispelled when, on a 'Gardeners' World' programme, I visited a balcony garden 60 metres (200 feet) up in the skies at the top of a high-rise block of flats in the Tower Hamlets area of London. In that unlikely situation, a determined lady grows vegetables, shrubs, climbers, annuals, in fact a bit of everything, in an area that measures a mere 6 by $1\frac{1}{4}$ m (20 by 4 feet). She has to contend with constant wind (100 mph gales are commonplace) and driving rain. In addition, everything has to be grown in containers which in turn need to be filled with compost and the lifts are often out of order. Her little garden is a mass of colour in summer and there is something to look at and admire all the year round. It is her Eden in a concrete jungle.

However, lack of space is not the only reason for a patio, balcony or windowsill garden. Patios in particular have their place even in large gardens. From the one-time window boxes we have advanced, over the years, to our present plot that is just under an acre in area. When we came, the back door opened on to a barrow-wide path that led straight up the garden. Now some years later, the door opens on to a large paved patio where in summer we can sit out, dine 'alfresco' or just relax and enjoy the fruits of our labours. It also has a rotary clothes line where my wife can hang out the 'smalls' without getting her footwear wet and muddy. When not in use the drier is lifted out of its hole and stored in the garage out of sight.

Our patio is bounded on one side by the house and on the other three sides by dry stone walls that look attractive and also serve as retaining boundaries between the patio and the higher ground of the garden beyond. Building stone walls without the bother of mixing concrete is a job I thoroughly enjoy. All that's needed is a supply of stones, a few barrowloads of soil, a good eye, some suitable plants and patience. Begin by taking out a shallow trench about 15 cm (6 inches) deep and about 45 to 60 cm (1½ to 2 feet) wide into which goes a foundation layer of the largest, heaviest stones. From there on it is simply a matter of covering each succeeding course of stones with about 2½ cm (1 inch) of soil before placing another course on top, the soil acting as a binding substitute for concrete. Shovel in more soil behind the stones and firm it well, and remember to alternate the stones layer upon layer, as is the normal practice in brickwork. To achieve stability it is advisable to slope the wall backwards slightly by about 2½ cm (1 inch) for every 30 cm (12 inches) rise in height.

Now, dry stone walls are pleasing in their own right but they look even more pleasing when pretty plants put forth their flowers from the crevices. So, before building starts obtain a collection of pot-grown wall lovers and put them in as building progresses – it is much easier to do this than trying to plant them into a completed wall, although that is by no means impossible. The plants that are enjoying life in my walls are a variety of sedums and saxifrages, some dwarf campanulas, aubrietas of all colours, and the very lovely lewisias. The latter detest getting their rosettes of leaves soaking wet and the only way I can grow these beauties is to have them on the vertical. In summer, they reward me with spikes of starry flowers in all shades of red, pink and mauve. There is more. Walls have tops where the soil is permanently well-drained and they can be home to a host of low-growing plants, some of which can be allowed to cascade in a torrent of colour down over the wall. Among my choices are the gravitating Cotoneaster dammeri bedecked with fiery red berries in winter; catmint, a cascading mist of blue in summer; an almost prostrate, golden-flowered Potentilla; a dwarf, variegated Euonymus; Hebe pinguifolia 'Pagei'; a Lithospermum; a group of heucheras; and drifts of brightly coloured rock roses. It is a wall of living colour.

However, dry stone walls can only be built on to banks and for areas on level ground there are other alternatives. Wooden fencing panels are an obvious but not ideal choice for providing privacy and shelter. They need regular, preservative treatment and I regard them as impenetrable barriers that are apt to collapse in the face of the irresistible force of strong winds. Living barriers are much better and elsewhere in this book Geoffrey has hedged his bets with a selection of shrubs that are just the thing to protect you from prying eyes and penetrating winds. Another alternative in a strictly formal setting is to use open-work blocks of pre-cast concrete. They are easy to erect, provide a good degree of shelter without being claustrophobic and make ideal supports for climbing plants.

When the 'surrounds' are up and not before, you will have to decide on the best paving material for your purpose. In the last few years I have constructed two patios in different gardens in different places. In North Wales I had the good fortune to be about to build a patio when the local Council was demolishing some old slate-stone cottages. I hired a tractor and trailer, spoke nicely to a few people and acquired several loads of excellent stone for next to nothing. The great thing about slate-stone is its grain. It can be split to almost any thickness in seconds with a hammer and cold chisel, leaving nice, flat surfaces on both sides of each slab. As the patio area was rock hard, I covered it with a layer of sand 2.5 cm (1 inch) deep and set the stones on it at an easily attained level. They were left to settle for a few weeks and I then poured a viscous concrete mix between them which anchored them for good and all. I should add that I left quite a number of hand-span width spaces here and there into which I put a few plants to relieve the monotony of an otherwise flat surface. In some I sowed seeds of sweet Alyssum. They seeded themselves in subsequent years, and their cloying perfume filled our senses every summer. The other spaces were occupied by either Sedum acre, the yellow rock cress, or the carpeting blue bells of Campanula portenschlagiana, a name that Stefan only attempts when he is stone-cold sober!

The second and more recent patio I made is the one bounded by the aforementioned dry stone walls and this I paved with concrete slabs set on a concrete mix of cement and a coarse chippings aggregate. The slabs cost a few pounds but if you are lucky you may find that your Local Authority is tearing up pavements somewhere in the vicinity. If they are, and if they want to dispose of the broken slabs, ask for a load or two, they make superb crazy paving. A point to bear in mind when paving a patio is that if you intend to plant climbers to clothe the house walls, or the boundary walls or fences, leave a 60-cm (2-feet) wide border of soil unpaved. It is possible to grow climbing plants in containers but their life is restricted to about five to ten years, whereas planted out in a soil border they will live out their allotted span.

Patio gardening is largely a matter of growing plants in containers and they come in a variety of shapes, sizes and materials. The choice lies between concrete, terracotta, wood, plastic and growing bags. Concrete containers and concrete paving are obviously well-matched and they are comparatively inexpensive but I sound a warning. I once bought a concrete urn at a garden centre, filled it with good, sieved soil, planted a Fuchsia as a centrepiece and ringed it with trailing Lobelia and ivy-leaved pelargoniums and put a few 'Non-stop' begonias in between. It was a complete failure. The Fuchsia turned a sickly yellow, the pelargoniums and Lobelia died and the 'Non-stop' begonias came to a grinding halt. I was mystified, where had I gone wrong? Nowhere it seemed, as I later discovered that a chemical used in the manufacture of at least some concrete containers is toxic to plants until it has been weathered to neutrality by the elements. The urn I bought was under cover at the garden centre, so ever since I have always purchased ones standing in the open with a weatherbeaten look about them, and they have been trouble-free.

Terracotta containers look good in any setting and they too are variable in shape and design, but don't forget to put them under cover at the first suggestion of frost. Before I knew better, I once left a beautifully made large pot outside and forgot about it. Eventually I found it with most of the outer skin flaked and when I lifted it the bottom stayed on the ground and I was left with a totally useless pot open at both ends.

Plastic containers are virtually unbreakable but somehow I just cannot accept that they look as good, or are as good, as ones made of concrete or clay. Maybe I'm prejudiced or old-fashioned but they are not for me. The only point I find in their favour is their price, which is lower than any others of their kind.

Wooden containers look as natural as the material of their construction and they set off plants to perfection. If they have a drawback it is simply the necessity to protect the wood from wet soil and the weather. Lining them with polythene helps to preserve the wood and nowadays there is a wide choice of wood preservatives to paint the external surfaces to prevent rot.

Finally, there are growing bags which are purely utilitarian. They are certainly not decorative but, for all that, they are ideal for growing plants such as vegetables, especially in unobtrusive places.

Growing bags, of course, are compost-filled and need only plants and water to convert them into production units. All other containers need to be filled with a good growing medium and the cheapest is sieved, fertile soil from the garden. Any nutritional deficiencies it may have are easily rectified by liquid feeding during the growing season. If the garden soil is poor and worked out, or unobtainable, then the best container filler is John Innes Potting Compost No. 2. Before filling, place a few small stones over the drainage holes at the bottom of the container and then fill to within 2½ cm (1 inch) or so of the rim to allow for watering. Should you happen to buy a container without drainage holes either return it or drill them yourself using a 1-cm (½-inch) masonry 'bit'.

A word of advice – before filling, position the containers where you want them as they are a considerable weight when filled with soil or compost. Arrange them to their best advantage so that they may be seen and admired from all possible vantage points but bear in mind that most of the plants you put in them like nothing better than a place in the sun. I recognise that some patios may perforce be in shade, surrounded on all sides by high walls. Such situations can be lightened to a degree, by painting the walls white to catch every gleam of reflected light. Even so, plants for cultivation in shade should be selected from the retiring kinds that shun the limelight, among them hostas, ferns, the Primula family, columbines, Lady's mantle, Bergenia, ivies, Solomon's seal, Thalictrum, periwinkle and others.

After planting, regular attention is essential. All too often I am saddened by the sight of containers holding nothing more than wisps of desiccated, dead plants, victims of ignorance and neglect. On sunny patios, plants lose moisture rapidly and will require a good soak at least every morning and possibly in late afternoon as well. They will also need liquid feeding, once-weekly within five or six weeks of planting. For containers to look really colourful, don't be afraid to cram the plants in as close as you can but remember that their intensive cultivation makes constant feeding an absolute necessity. Always water the plants before feeding, so that the dilution of the feed is at the correct concentration. Plant roots don't have nostrils but nevertheless they do breathe; and do so more freely in a soil that is not hard and compact, a condition that easily affects the contents of containers being frequently watered. When my wife isn't looking I borrow a kitchen fork and poke it about between the plants to loosen the surface soil. The containers that require watering more often than any others are

hanging baskets and the only way of ensuring they get enough water is to take them down and immerse them in a tub until the water has permeated the moss lining and penetrated through to the surface. Baskets lined with polythene have to be watered from above, which is a very good reason for not lining them with polythene, or any other impermeable material. Window boxes and containers attached to walls also tend to dry out quickly in direct and reflected heat and they too need copious watering.

We now come to the prime purpose of the containers, namely getting the very best from our investment and labour throughout the year. First to flower are the spring containers planted with suitable subjects the previous autumn. Here we are spoilt for choice between a range of daffodils and narcissi, dwarf tulips, Polyanthus, wallflowers in window boxes, hyacinths, forget-me-nots, crocuses, grape hyacinths and Chionodoxa. Almost any combination of these brings a spring to my step and to the patio. When they are over, the summer sirens take their place. Empty the container, sprinkle some Fish,

above, *The face at the window smiles and small wonder – it's a grand show*

above right, *Well-planted, colourful containers will always bring a patio to life*

right, *A brimming basketful of colour*

far right, *Little pom-pom daisies fill an attractive clay container and make a pretty display*

Blood and Bone fertiliser on the surface and give it a good forking over. If the soil is dry water it and then, well, where do I begin? From the vast range of summer-flowering plants that enjoy container life I can do no more than list a few of those that never fail to please me. Fuchsias are fantastic, there is no other word for it. Some people call them Mary's tears but mine don't weep, they smile all summer long and make an ideal centrepiece for any container. Pelargoniums actually like dry, arid conditions and I will have at least one tub with a zonal pelargonium in the

centre and at her feet an array of the ivy-leaved trailing sorts in all colours. Of the annuals, I have high regard for Busy Lizzies, tuberous and fibrous-rooted begonias, Tagetes, Lobelia, petunias, Phlox drummondii, salvias, verbenas and the little 'Thumbelina' zinnias. They will be a riot of colours from June to frost, then out they come and the exciting cycle begins all over again.

I am often asked how long the same soil in containers can be used. My experience tells me two years, then it should be replaced with new. During the two years it should be rejuvenated with a dressing of general fertiliser between plantings.

So far, I have devoted my attention to containerised colour, without thought for the gastronomic delights a patio can produce. Practically any vegetable you care to mention can be grown in growing bags with the exception of the long, tapering varieties of carrots and parsnips and I have never had much success with the cabbage family. Otherwise, salad crops grow wonderfully well as do marrows, melons, shallots, onions, dwarf peas, dwarf broad beans, tomatoes, peppers, all the common herbs and runner beans. Yes, runner beans, although they will obviously need supports and you will need a ladder to reach the beans at the top of the vines. Come to think of it, you could gather some of them from the bedroom windows, unless you live in a bungalow, of course!

Have I covered everything? Not by a long chalk, for a patio garden will literally bear fruit. Strawberries crop well in growing bags and there are also purpose-built strawberry barrels with holes in their sides. The strawberries are planted one to each hole with another half-dozen or so planted in the open top. There is only one snag. Someone I know who lives in a gardenless London house with a small but sunny patio at the rear was given a strawberry barrel as a present. What a lovely thought, he thought, but it cost him a week's beer money in compost and plants to fill it. He has gone right off strawberries!

It goes without saying that stone fruits such as apples, pears, plums, peaches, nectarines and cherries will yield good crops planted in the soil at the foot of patio walls. Stefan has been his usual fruity self in Chapter 5 so I need not elaborate. What is not so readily realised is that within certain limits, all these fruits will also yield good crops from containers. In the first place, a large container must be used, the bigger the better to provide the tree with a reasonable root run. Second, the best growing medium is John Innes Potting Compost No. 3. Third, and vitally, the tree must be on a dwarfing rootstock that natur-

ally limits its top growth. When visiting a nursery to buy dwarf fruit trees for patios these are the rootstocks to ask for: apples – M27; pears – Quince A; plum – Pixie; peaches and nectarines – St Julien A; cherries – Colt. Bearing in mind that space on patios is limited it is worth considering buying a family tree where apples are concerned. They usually carry three varieties, a cooker and two eaters, grafted on the one tree and they have the added advantage that cross-pollination is assured. If you fancy a bowlful of red-ripe cherries, grow the variety 'Stella'. It is self-fertile and bears a heavy crop of delicious fruit with commendable regularity. Fruit trees in containers must be adequately watered and fed and the top few centimetres of soil should be scraped away and replaced with fresh in early spring every year. Try them, if only for the sheer pleasure of picking a juicy fruit and eating it off the tree at its peak of perfection while sitting in the shade of its branches.

Fruits are not the only trees that may be grown on patios. Large, flat areas need a measure of visual relief and, providing it is of a suitable shape and size and is judiciously sited, a tree brings a new dimension to the patio. It may be planted in a large container or, better still, a few paving stones may be omitted when laying the patio to leave an area of bare soil for planting. The ideal choice would be a tree of columnar growth that would not cast much shade. My pick of the bunch is Prunus 'Amanogawa', a stirring sight in May with its upright branches decked with cherry blossom. I once saw one underplanted with hyacinths– a sight and scent I shall never forget.

Having built and planted a patio, we surely merit a well-earned rest. We need something to sit or lie on in the sun. There are chairs, seats, tables and loungers in all kinds of different materials of varying durability. For sitting on, I prefer wood. I like to park my posterior on a natural material that feels warm and inviting, rather than on cold, unyielding metal. For sunbathing, I prefer the soft, padded surface of an adjustable lounger. Whatever material you choose remember that most kinds will last longer if placed under cover in winter. Wooden garden furniture will also give longer service if it is treated with a preservative at the beginning of each year.

In conclusion, I suggest that patios and balconies are for people who prefer to live outdoors in the fresh, scented air of a warm summer's day and who have an appreciation for the beauty of living plants. I further suggest that if you have a patio you will not be satisfied until it is a complete garden in miniature with a pool and a barbecue to add the final touches.

14

POTTED PLEASURE

Clay Jones

For many people in our modern, high-rise society, gardening is confined to the windowsill. Not for them the simple, satisfying pleasure of caring for and cultivating a plot of ground however large or small. Deprived of soil, they must indulge their urge to garden by growing plants in pots. Gardeners with outdoor opportunities may also feel the need to bring a little of their gardens indoors, especially in winter when dormancy and inclement weather compel them to forsake their plots for the warmth of the greenhouse or living room.

Sadly, the death rate among houseplants is high. Many are doomed and destined for an early grave from the moment they are acquired. Indeed I have met people who regard pot plants as disposable, inanimate objects which they cheerfully discard once their useful life is over. To me, a pot plant is a living thing, a friend who shares my home and gives me infinite pleasure. The least I can do in return is to tend it with care and affection and give it the good life.

Giving it the good life is not as easy as it sounds. Some pot plants will tolerate conditions that are little short of total neglect. Aspidistras are virtually indestructible. Many spend their lives on 'grin and bear it' windowsills, their leaves shrouded in dust, and their diet an occasional drink of cold tea or flat beer provided only when someone remembers. They look so much better for having their leaves wiped with a damp cloth, and when given a feed now and again they have been known to flower. Many other pot plants are very fussy, resenting the slightest deprivation of their exacting needs. In fact plants are like people; they respond only when they are properly treated. My co-writers are prime examples. Stefan visibly wilts unless he is fed and watered at regular intervals and Geoffrey only really flourishes under the harsh conditions of the highest windswept crags of his native Yorkshire!

The first essential, therefore, is to know your pot plants, bearing in mind that the vast majority are living in an alien environment in our homes. In the same room you may well have plants from widely varying geographical regions and climatic conditions. Cacti, for example, hail from arid, desert regions where the temperature is over 35°C (100°F) in the shade, except that there isn't any, and where the rainfall is minimal and occurs very infrequently. They have ingeniously adapted to these conditions, absorbing the precious water when it comes and storing it for future use. In fact, cacti are nothing more than rather strange and often beautiful water reservoirs. In complete contrast are plants such as the maidenhair fern, a native of the damp, tropical forests of South America. To be happy it must have a good deal of warmth, high humidity, shade and be completely protected from cold draughts. It stands to reason that such widely different plants can never co-exist on the same windowsill or even possibly in the same room. I say possibly because there are ways of creating a micro-climate for each individual plant. Those that require high humidity can be given the moist atmosphere they need either by standing the pots on a base of wet sand or gravel, or by employing the 'pot-in-pot' method. The only way I can keep a maidenhair fern reasonably happy is to house it in the

left, *It looks like a bird and is called the 'Bird of Paradise' flower – Strelitzia regina needs a hot-house to bring it into bloom*

below, *Dieffenbachia picta or 'Dumb Cane' – spotty and spectacular*

right, *Fill your window with plants and you won't want to look outside*

subdued light of the bathroom in a pot within a pot. The fern is planted in a 13-cm (5-inch) clay pot that is itself housed in an 18-cm (7-inch) pot with the space between the sides and bottoms of the pots packed with peat which is kept consistently moist. It is a system that suits a great number of pot plants that detest the very dry atmosphere consistent with central heating.

Whether pot plants are hardy, half-hardy or just plain delicate they almost all have one thing in common. They need some kind of growing medium of which, basically, there are three sorts. My colleagues have dealt with composts in other chapters and I will add only that they are all good (the composts that is) but nowadays I use John Innes only for large, tall plants that tend to be top-heavy and topple over in a lightweight, peat-based compost. Should garden soil be used for potting? I don't see why not provided it is of a good, friable quality and has been sieved before

use. It will, of course, be riddled with weed seeds which will germinate, but the seedlings can easily be weeded out before they begin to compete with the potted plants for food and water. The major risk in using soil lies in its unknown inhabitants. It may contain any number of diseases and insect pests which is why I mix a little insecticide in with the soil before potting. However, for most things I use the peat-based composts. They are light and clean and the performance of most plants in them is generally better.

All plants need water and pot plants are no exception. In the garden, plants derive their water from the soil with little or no help from the gardener. Indoors, they rely entirely on us and it is imperative that we get the balance right. I am convinced that more pot plants succumb either to an excess of, or a lack of, life's essential ingredient – water – than from any other cause. Too much water saturates the compost to the point of stagnation. It becomes airless, the plant's leaves show signs of yellowing or tip-browning and eventually it dies of drowning. The first sign of acute thirst is wilt which occurs in two stages. Stage one is incipient wilt from which the plant will recover after a good drink. Stage two is permanent wilt – the point of no return that no amount of water will put right.

The volume of water plants need is variable and depends on several inherent, environmental and seasonal factors. As I have mentioned, desert plants need comparatively little, as do other plants that have leaves modified or adapted to an uncertain water supply in nature. For example, thick, fleshy leaves carry reserves of water and plants with hairy leaves, such as saintpaulias, have a comparatively low transpiration rate because the myriad, tiny hairs reduce water loss from the leaves, and therefore the volume absorbed through the roots is correspondingly less. The rate of growth also has a direct bearing on water requirements and this applies particularly to pot plants with large, thin-textured, hairless foliage. As a general rule, most pot plants rest in winter and accelerate their growth rate from spring onwards, reaching a peak in summer. Logically, therefore, they need regular watering in summer and a spare-the-can policy in the dormant winter period, when they need no more than just enough to prevent incipient wilt.

Nowadays, science has provided us with a variety of gadgets that are designed to indicate when a pot

In a dry indoor room, provide humidity for plants by the pot-in-pot method of planting

plant needs water. You stick them in the compost and they emit signals. Some change colour when the moisture level is low whilst others give voice with a series of urgent-sounding bleeps and yelps. I suppose they are of value to the casual, or inexperienced pot planter but I can tell when a plant needs water simply by looking at the compost and lifting the pot. If the compost looks dry on the surface it does not necessarily mean that it is dry at the bottom but if the pot also feels light in weight then water is needed and plenty of it. I don't subscribe to the little and often school of watering. I prefer to let the plant dry out almost completely and then give it a thorough soaking, either by standing the pot up to its rim in a bowl of water until the surface of the compost feels moist to the touch, or by watering from the top, letting it stand for a few minutes and then discarding any surplus water in the drainage dish. But if you have only a few pot plants the immersion method is the safest and best, although some pot plants detest getting too wet around the collar. Cyclamens, for instance, tend to rot when watered from above and if a few drops of water accidentally fall on the leaves of saintpaulias they, too, will rot and the whole plant may die.

Then there are clay pots, plastic pots, and crackpots who will argue vehemently and endlessly on their relative merits! When I was a lad and Stefan merely an ambition, there were no plastic pots. We used clay pots for everything. The breakage rate was high but at least we used the broken bits of crock as drainage in other pots. The major difference between the pots is that the clay ones are porous whereas the

plastic ones are not. Clay pots are said to 'breathe'. Air and water can seep through them with the result that the compost dries out more quickly than in plastic pots and they need more frequent watering. On the credit side, a plant in a clay pot is less likely to drown from careless overwatering. I have no particular preference for either except in instances when I am potting, or repotting, tall plants. Then the heavy, clay pots are an advantage. Their sheer weight renders them less likely to topple over, even when the potting compost is peat-based.

Room temperatures have a tremendous influence on the growth and well-being of pot plants. Whilst generalisation is dangerous, it is fairly safe to assume that those that are indigenous to tropical and subtropical countries are more likely to flourish and flower in a summer temperature of 20°C (68°F) or over and a winter warmth of no less than 10°C (50°F). Nevertheless, their tolerance of lower temperatures is quite remarkable providing they are kept very dry. Many years ago we moved house in late September. At the time I possessed a collection of some fifty cacti lovingly raised from seed. The new garden had no greenhouse so those plants spent the winter months in a cold frame covered with sacks in very cold weather. The compost became so dry it shrank from the sides of the pots but when the new greenhouse went up in March, I moved forty-nine living cacti into it and sadly bade farewell to a single casualty that just didn't survive.

Temperature will also affect flowering. Strelitzia reginae, the bird of paradise plant, will not put forth its gorgeous flowers in summer if the winter temperature falls below 12°C (55°F) for any length of time. In contrast, the popular, winter-flowering cyclamen is a sad and sorry sight in rooms where the warmth is much over 10°C (50°F). At higher temperatures its leaves turn yellow and flowering is inhibited. Please

To repot a plant first knock the pot sharply to release the root ball. Then replant in a pot one to two sizes larger and fill in with fresh compost, firming gently with your fingers. Water well to settle the soil.

don't let the technicalities put you off growing pot plants. If you love them and wish to fill your house with their beauty, buy a good book on the subject and study each plant's individual requirements. The book will cost a few pounds, but better a few pounds wisely spent than many more pounds spent on plants that are doomed to premature death owing to your ignorance.

To give of their best, pot plants need feeding, even more so than plants with a free root run in beds and borders. In pots their roots are confined within a predetermined volume of compost. They can't get out in search of additional nutrients so it is up to us to provide them. All potting composts contain a quantity of balanced plant foods sufficient to last the first six weeks or so of the plant's life before it is exhausted. Thenceforth regular feeding is a must and there is a wide selection of suitable fertilisers. When you think about it, life is so much easier for present-day gardeners than it was for our predecessors. There were no handy pre-packs of plant foods in their day. They roamed the fields gathering cow and sheep dung which they put in sacks and steeped in barrels of water to produce an odorous fertiliser. Greenhouses and sitting rooms in those days sometimes smelt like diluted farmyards. Even the liquid in the flowery pot under the bed had its uses! All we need do today is visit a shop or garden centre and choose whichever particular concentrate takes our fancy. There are bottles of liquid feed that need diluting to the recommended strength, and rather more economical soluble powders claiming that a teaspoonful in two gallons of water works wonders – and so it does.

169

above, *A collection of cacti and succulents can be grown from seeds quite easily*

left, *Aphelandra squarrosa, the 'Zebra Plant', comes from Brazil and enjoys life in a warm, light room*

right, *Another beauty of Brazil, the 'Urn Plant' – Aechmea fulgens – also needs warmth and light*

One of the problems of feeding pot plants is remembering when the next feed is due or, to put it another way, when the last feed was given. How frequently should they be fed? During their winter rest period not at all, but as soon as growth starts in spring I like to feed them about once every two or three weeks. It really depends on how well they are doing and how big they are. For the forgetful, there are ways and means of ensuring that their house-plants never go hungry. 'Fertiliser sticks' are small, solid cylinders that are pushed into the compost around the rim of the pot. They release their goodness gradually over a period of weeks and then need replacing. There are two kinds. One has a high pot-ash content to induce flowering and the other, with a higher nitrogen content, is intended to induce leaf growth in foliage plants. Then there are 'fertiliser mats'. These are circular, felt pads impregnated with fertiliser granules and they are placed in the drain-age dish under the pot. Watering into the dish pro-

duces a nutrient solution which is absorbed into the compost and the roots. They are comparatively expensive but on the other hand each 'mat' lasts a whole season and gives very good results. There are also fertiliser granules, like small airgun pellets, that have a year-long life too. They are sprinkled on the surface of the compost and a little liquid fertiliser is released each time the pot is watered. With all these modern aids at hand there is really no excuse for pot plant starvation, yet it happens. Slow growth and stunted and discoloured leaves are sure signs of deprivation that can immediately be put right by simply *feeding*. But finally on feeding, I confess I seldom buy a flowering pot plant fertiliser. I grow tomatoes in the greenhouse and feed them with a specific, high-potash tomato fertiliser and when the 'toms' have a feed so do the pot plants. Why not; it works.

At this point a few tips on potting and repotting might prove useful. The first and golden rule is – never over-pot. It is often a temptation to plant a seedling into a large pot to save repotting later on. It may be time-saving but it can also be disastrous. Imagine if you will a tiny seedling in a 15-cm (6-inch) pot. Its roots occupy a fraction of the total compost volume, yet the entire potful has to be watered if the seedling is not to go thirsty. The greater part of the water is superfluous and all it does is make most of the compost rank and stagnant and as a result the seedling stunts and perishes. When growing pot plants from seed, the first transplant should be into an 8-cm (3-inch) pot, or less if it is a very slow starter. I first pot cacti seedlings into 3-cm (1-inch) 'thumb' pots for this very reason. Repotting, or potting-on, becomes necessary when root tips start poking through the drainage hole, an indication that the pot is full of roots. From the 8-cm (3-inch) pot, transplant to a pot a size or two larger, say a 13-cm (5-inch) and so on up the size scale until the plant is in a final pot commensurate with its growth. For most pot plants a 13-cm (5-inch) or 15-cm (6-inch) final pot is big enough, but tall-growing, large plants should finish up in big 25 to 30-cm (10 to 12-inch) containers. After potting, firm the compost gently and water the plant in; not too much, make the roots seek the precious fluid but at the same time don't let them go short.

As always, there are departures from the norm. Some pot plants actually like being pot-bound and the Hippeastrum (amaryllis) is one of them. I let the large bulb grow until it nearly fills the pot before moving it on. In lieu of an annual repotting and when the bulb is about to regenerate growth in spring, I scrape away a few centimetres of the surface compost, replace it with new and push in a few fertiliser sticks for feeding. Some other pot plants are shallow rooters, so shallow that their roots seldom reach the depths of the pots, even at maturity. They do better in half-pots, otherwise called 'pans', where their roots never have to contend with a soggy compost at the base. Two such are Saintpaulia – the African violet, and Achimenes – the hot-water plant.

Having decided that you can and will grow superb pot plants, the last question is where to put them? Very few enjoy sunbathing. In summer, the majority, and this applies especially to foliage plants, prefer the comparative obscurity of subdued light, a few feet back from a brightly-lit window. In winter, when the light intensity is low, they can be moved on to the windowsill. At this point I enter a plea on behalf of all pot plants on windowsills. When you draw the curtains on a cold and frosty winter's night, don't leave the poor things in the 'refrigerator' between the curtains and the glass. Take them into the warmth of the room and replace them when you've drawn the curtains back in the morning. All green plants need light to photosynthesise and produce food, but their light-intensity requirements vary according to their natural habitat. Plants that naturally frequent the forests are in low light, shaded by the great canopies of the trees overhead. Their leaves tend to be large so that they can capture every shaft and shimmer of sunlight that filters through. Plants with small leaves are just the opposite. They naturally grow fully exposed to the sun's rays and can manage very well with a minimum of leaf area. These are ways in which plants tell us of their origins and of their preferences in our homes. They may not utter but they can be read by the observant gardener. Take Monstera, the Swiss cheese plant, for instance. Have you ever wondered why the mature leaves are full of holes? I used to until the day on the island of Bermuda when I met the curator of the botanic gardens. He showed me massive monsteras growing in the shade of enormous trees and growing up through them. Their leaves were huge and, in order to prevent being stripped to shreds by hurricane-force winds, they have developed holes through which the great gusts can pass, leaving the leaves unharmed. Now isn't that clever!

Of course, pot plants don't have to be grown in pots arranged in straight lines on the windowsill, or as individuals strategically placed around the room. I believe they look their best in an indoor garden that is changed and varied by whim or season. All that is

BEAUTIFUL AND NO BOTHER

Botanical Name	Common Name	Temperature minimum		Light Requirement	Propagation	Significant Features
		Winter	Summer			
Exacum affine	Persian Violet	—	—	East or north-east	Seeds	Fragrant purple flowers with a yellow centre.
Primula obconica	—	14°C (58°F)	—	Semi-shade	Seeds	Shades of blue, red and white. May cause a rash in some people.
Sansevieria trifasciata	Mother-in-law's tongue	14°C (58°F)	—	Not fussy	Cuttings and offsets	Leaves edged with golden-yellow.
Pelargonium zonale	Geranium	—	—	Full sun	Seeds and cuttings	All colours. Does well outdoors in summer.
Sinningia hybrids	Gloxinia	—	—	Indirect sunlight	Seeds and tubers	Reds, blues and whites.
Monstera deliciosa	Swiss cheese plant	16°C (60°F)	—	Shade	Cuttings and division	Foliage plant with very large, split leaves.
Crassula argentea	Money plant	8°C (48°F)	—	Indirect sunlight	Cuttings	Lovely silvery foliage, white flowers.
Cactus species	—	10°C (50°F)	—	Full sun	Seeds and cuttings	Keep dry from October to March. Exotic flowers in many colours.
Hedera canariensis	Variegated ivy	—	—	Shade	Cuttings	Climbing plant, tolerant of low temperatures.
Solanum capsicastrum	Winter cherry	10°C (50°F)	—	Full sun	Seeds	Grown for its red berries in winter. Put outdoors in summer to pollinate.
Hippeastrum hybrids	Amaryllis	20°C (68°F)	—	Good light	Seeds or bulbs	Needs high temperature to start bulbs in January. Large colourful trumpets.
Aspidistra elatior	Cast-iron plant	—	—	Cool shade	Division	Very tolerant of neglect and deep shade.
Coleus blumei	Flame nettle	16°C (60°F)	16°C (60°F)	Full sun	Seeds and cuttings	Gorgeous leaf colours. Pinch out flowering tips to prolong growth.
Thunbergia alata	Black-eyed Susan	—	—	Full sun	Seeds	Climbing and trailing plant – orange flowers with a black eye.
Tradescantia fluminensis	Wandering Jew	—	—	Good light	Cuttings	Foliage plant with varying variegation.
Beloperone guttata	Shrimp plant	18°C (65°F)	—	Good light	Cuttings	Drooping, yellow-pink, shrimp-like flowers.
Cyclamen persicum	—	10°C (50°F)	—	Indirect sunlight	Seeds and tubers	Winter-flowering, some with pretty marbled leaves.
Impatiens sultanii	Busy Lizzie	—	—	Not fussy	Seeds and cuttings	The varieties 'Accent' and 'Blitz' make superb pot plants.

Note: Where no minimum temperature is specified the plants will be content with normal room or greenhouse temperature.

needed is a large, waterproof container with no drainage holes in the bottom. It can be of any shape and of any colour although I find that plants look their best against a dark-brown background. Place the container outside and three-quarters fill it with moist peat. After filling, carry the container indoors and site it in good light and away from cold draughts. Now take a long, hard look at your pot plants, decide which are compatible and arrange them on the peat according to height and colour and to your personal satisfaction. When you've got them just right sink the pots right up to their rims in the peat, and water if necessary. You will now have an indoor garden that in spring could be a colourful array of hyacinths, a few saintpaulias, a Cyclamen or two, and a tall Begonia rex for height and leaf colour. As the hyacinths and Cyclamen dim and fade take them out and in their stead put pots of cinerarias and calceolarias. In summer, the entire scene will change. The centrepiece may be a magnificent half-standard Fuchsia, some regal pelargoniums, a climbing and trailing black-eyed Susan and around the rim a few dainty, little, blue exacums interspersed with a Pilea or a Coleus for its pretty leaves. The permutations are endless, the only qualification being that all the plants must like roughly the same growing conditions. In any event, if a plant objects to its neighbours

above, *Adiantum capillus-veneris, the 'Maidenhair Fern', is dainty and lovely yet prefers the privacy of shade*

left, *Trumpeting their colourful presence, the Amaryllis or hippeastrums flower year after year*

above, *Regal pelargoniums are bright and beautiful and will give years of pleasure. They are easily propagated.*

right, *Achimenes longiflora like warmth and shade to give of their best. They are well-suited to our living rooms.*

HANDSOME BUT HAZARDOUS

Botanical Name	Common Name	Temperature minimum		Light Requirement	Propagation	Significant Features
		Winter	Summer			
Achimenes hybrids	Hot-water plant	—	16°C (60°F)	Good light	Tubercles	Needs high temperature to initiate growth 23°C (70°F). Shade at midday.
Ficus elastica	Rubber plant	16°C (60°F)	—	Indirect sunlight	Cuttings	Detests draughts. Water sparingly and keep the leaves clean.
Euphorbia pulcherrima	Poinsettia	16°C (60°F)	—	Filtered light	Tip cuttings	Grown for the winter colour of the bracts.
Saintpaulia hybrids	African violet	23°C (70°F)	—	Indirect sunlight	Seeds and leaf cuttings	Leaves must be kept dry. Grows best in pans and half-pots.
Begonia rex	King begonia	16°C (60°F)	Cool	Filtered light	Seeds and leaf cuttings	Needs high humidity and much water in summer.
Aphelandra squarrosa	Zebra plant	10°C (50°F)	18°C (65°F)	Good light	Tip cuttings	Needs high humidity. Yellow flowers over white-striped leaves.
Aechmea fasciata	Urn plant	16°C (60°F)	16°C (60°F)	Full sun	Offsets	Parent plant dies after flowering, leaving a young offshoot to repot.
Cordyline terminalis	Good-luck plant	10°C (50°F)	—	Full sun	Seeds and cuttings	Direct sun will scorch the leaves. Hates dry air. A foliage plant.
Dieffenbachia picta	Dumb cane	16°C (60°F)	—	Filtered light	Tip cuttings	Beautifully-marked leaves. Wash hands after handling to avoid temporary paralysis of vocal chords.
Gardenia jasminoides	—		18°C (65°F)	Good light	Tip cuttings	Will drop its flower buds if temperature falls below 16°C (62°F) or goes above 18°C (65°F).
Cymbidium hybrids	Orchid	16°C (60°F)	18°C (65°F)	Good light	Division	Water moderately. One of the easiest for living room cultivation.
Calceolaria × herbeo-hybrida	Fisherman's basket	10°C (50°F)	—	Good light	Seeds	Flowers in early spring and prefers a cool room.

Note: Good light means that the plants will appreciate two or three hours of direct sunlight every morning, or late afternoon, but no more. Filtered light implies semi-shade, while in indirect sunlight the plants enjoy a good light level without having the sun directly on their leaves. Where no temperature is specified, normal room temperature will suffice.

have no hesitation in taking it out and replacing it with a more amenable species. The great asset of indoor gardens is that plants do so well in them. They seem to enjoy communal living and the moist peat provides the level of humidity they like.

I have included in this chapter two lists of a few plants that I am sure you would like to grow and admire, together with some tips on their cultivation.

15

BUGS & OTHER BOTHERS

Stefan Buczacki

The garden free from pests, diseases and weeds is the garden of an unattainable Utopia. No one should feel that the presence of some mildew, greenfly, bugs, blights and bindweed is a reflection of, or a commentary on, his or her gardening ability. All of our gardens are host to such afflictions and you will not need to walk far through any of our garden gates to find them; (although I must dispel the notion, promulgated by Clay and Geoffrey, that I set about their cultivation as a matter of deliberate policy!). What distinguishes the good gardener from the not so good, however, is an ability to know just how much pest, disease and weed presence is tolerable, to know which types of affliction are serious and which less so, and which of the innumerable available methods should be chosen to combat them. Whole books have been written cataloguing the many types of garden pest, disease and weed; indeed, I have written some of them myself. To give sufficient information for you to be able to identify an unknown problem with certainty, to understand the way that it causes damage and to select an appropriate control measure is beyond the scope of the space that I have available. None the less, from the plethora of problems I shall abstract a relative few that most gardeners, in most years, are likely to encounter and also, and more importantly, outline the general principles of pest, disease and weed biology and control.

Pests and Diseases

Almost all groups of the animal kingdom include at least some pest species and those likely to be present in gardens range from moles and rabbits at one end of the spectrum to microscopic eelworms at the other. Most, by far, belong to the insects and although they are an extremely varied bunch, I find that insect pests can be conveniently divided into the sap suckers, such as aphids (greenfly and blackfly), whiteflies, scale insects and mealy bugs, and the chewers, such as caterpillars, flies and their larvae, beetles and bugs. A significant practical distinction between them is that the suckers usually succeed through force of numbers – one greenfly is unlikely to cause much harm although, conversely, they do possess very efficient methods of reproduction and the one can very soon become one hundred or one thousand. The chewers, however, generally give you less time still to react, for one caterpillar can make short work of a choice pelargonium while your back is turned.

Plant diseases are caused by fungi (mostly microscopic), by bacteria or by viruses. The latter are the most difficult to identify and to control. They permeate the entire tissues of affected plants, are uncontrollable by spraying or other chemical application and are avoided primarily by controlling the insects or other pests that carry them from one plant to another. They are also avoided by the regular replacement of those types of plant that are propagated vegetatively (potatoes, dahlias, chrysanthemums and soft fruit, for example) with high-quality, virus-free stock, such as Scottish seed potatoes or certified fruit bushes.

Bacterial diseases are of relatively minor importance in gardens and are virtu-

Pests and diseases fall into several distinct categories.

Clockwise from top left, the illustrations show common examples of some of the most important types – a mildew (rose powdery mildew); a leaf spot (rose black spot); a rust (hollyhock rust); a canker (apple canker); soil pests (the wireworm larva of the click beetle and the cutworm moth caterpillar) – by contrast, at bottom right is a *much maligned but beneficial soil creature, a centipede; a scab (apple scab); a root fly (the surface scarring on a swede root caused by the cabbage root fly larva); a wilt (the effects on tomatoes of the wilt that arises so frequently if they are grown in a greenhouse in garden soil); Botrytis grey mould, perhaps the commonest of all garden diseases, seen here on a broad bean pod; a soft rot (bacterial soft rot on Brussels sprouts)*

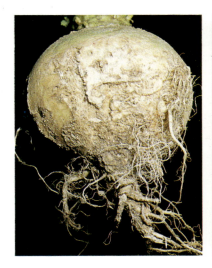

ally unaffected by any chemical sprays. The foul-smelling symptoms of soft rot on vegetables will be many gardeners' only encounter with harmful bacteria.

We are left, therefore, with fungi, of which many thousands of species exist, some extremely harmful parasites, some innocuous or even beneficial decomposers of organic matter and some, like Botrytis grey mould, falling between the two, able on the one hand to live on dead organic matter but also able to turn its attention to living tissues should the opportunity arise. Such opportunity is often afforded by plants being placed under some stress – shortage of or too much water, an incorrect greenhouse temperature or being planted too early into cold soil, for example. Thus, I give you the first rule for a healthy garden; grow your plants in the best possible conditions and pay careful attention to the optimum cultural requirements of each.

My second rule can be summed up in the expression garden hygiene, or, as I often paraphrase it, a tidy garden is a healthy garden. The principle behind this notion is that plant-disease fungi and, indeed, garden pests, do not materialise from thin air. Many, perhaps most, originate from elsewhere in your garden, from hedgerows, from weeds, from piles of rotting vegetation, old prunings, half-forgotten seed boxes and similar habitats. Far be it from me to suggest that you remove your hedgerows, but the remainder are all avoidable hiding places and pests such as woodlice and snails can often be very effectively contained simply by discovering from whence they come and eliminating them at source. Botrytis in greenhouses is perhaps the classic instance of a plant disease that can be kept in check by careful and regular removal of the dead leaves and moribund plant remains on which it survives. This particular problem highlights also my third rule; the importance of understanding your enemy if you wish to have the better of him, for Botrytis is favoured by cool, moist conditions and improvement of the greenhouse ventilation, therefore, avoids the air stagnation that is so commonly the prelude to an attack.

I must now describe in a little more detail the weapons available in your armoury when all your best endeavours of husbandry and hygiene have let you down. I think of the various options as falling into four groups. First, the homespun remedies such as soapy water, salt and beer, the stick of rhubarb, pepper dust and garlic (but not all at once!). Second, the more 'natural' (although I am never quite sure what that means) among chemical pesticides; sulphur, derris and pyrethrum, for example. Third, the hardcore chemicals which we all use and recommend only when we are quite sure that there is no better alternative. Such chemicals include benomyl and thiophanate-methyl (even if we can't always pronounce it) among fungicides, and permethrin, malathion and fenitrothion among insecticides. They can be divided into contact chemicals, which are only effective where they strike and are thus dependent on the accuracy of your spraying, and systemic products, taken up by the plant and moved within its sap to control the problems that contact chemicals can't reach. Finally, there are the so-called biological controls; the 'set a thief to catch a thief' philosophy. These work best in the confined space of a greenhouse where it is possible, for example, to introduce a culture of a parasitic wasp-like insect to control whiteflies. None the less, such techniques work very much better in the monoculture of the commercial greenhouse than with the mixed crops present in yours and mine.

And so to the main groups of pests and diseases that you are likely to encounter, starting at the bottom with the soil and the roots. Soil-inhabiting pests such as wireworms, leatherjackets, millepedes and cutworms are joined, in and around plant roots, by the larvae of flies such as carrot fly and cabbage root fly, underground species of slug and even some subterranean aphids. In general, thorough and regular cultivation will go a long way to help contain these pests, for this brings many of them to the surface and gives the local bird population a treat. Where this fails, a dusting of chemical around the roots at planting time may be the answer. Some gardeners swear by soot or small quantities of ash but among the more conventional insecticides, my choice lies with bromophos. It may be possible to dissuade the adult pests from visiting your plants to lay their eggs; carpeting your brassica bed against cabbage root fly attack is the most effective of these measures. Wall to wall Wilton may be a little extreme, so restrict yourself to 15-cm (6-inch) discs of carpet underlay, laid around the stem base of each plant. The adult carrot fly can sometimes be kept at bay by a 'fence' of plastic sheet about 30 cm (1 foot) high around the plot.

Although living on, rather than in the soil, slugs are the number one pests for many gardeners and there seem to be as many attempted methods to control them as there are sufferers. Slug pellets or liquid controls contain metaldehyde or methiocarb. They are often effective and the small 'dishes' now available enable the chemical to be placed out of reach of pets and birds. Yet, the saucer of beer, sunk to its rim close to the succulent lettuces or other plants so beloved of slugs, will work very well and, as Geoffrey tells me, at least they die happy (even, I am assured, when the beer is brewed in Yorkshire). Clay's more temperate Welsh remedy of installing barriers of soot, ash or gorse twigs around the plants is also effective, if less dramatic.

Disease-causing fungi in the soil present the greatest threat to tender young seedlings and provide the best possible reason for the use of fresh compost in seed boxes. Over-wet soil or compost is the commonest reason for root-rot fungi attacking plants outdoors in the garden and the general maxim not to plant soft or fleshy-rooted plants (bulbs, for example) in waterlogged conditions is one that I follow invariably. Even in my light soil, I always give extra-fleshy bulbs such as lilies the benefit of a bed of sand on which to lay their heads. Peas and beans are very prone to root-rotting diseases and adopting the principle of crop rotation that Clay discussed in Chapter 4 and I referred to in Chapter 1 will help prevent a recurrence. Greenhouse soil, used repeatedly for growing tomatoes, will almost inevitably become contaminated with wilt disease and this is the justification for using growing bags, pots or ring culture. A few soil-inhabiting diseases require special mention. For club root on brassicas, white rot on onions and honey fungus on trees and shrubs, there is no total answer and it is no use my pretending that there is. The best protection I have found against club root, and even against white rot, is to raise and plant out each brassica or onion individually in a peat pot of fresh compost. Honey fungus can sometimes be contained by burying a vertical barrier of heavy-duty plastic sheet about 60 cm (2 feet) deep around an infected tree or stump but if the stump and root fragments can be dug out entire, so much the better. Never replant an area affected by honey fungus with trees or shrubs for at least two years.

Pests on leaves fall into the chewing or sucking categories I have mentioned already. The larger chewers, such as cabbage caterpillars, are best dealt with by the sophisticated equipment called finger and thumb, although if they are present in large numbers, a resort to a chemical spray may be necessary. Many gardeners find soapy water highly effective. (Geoffrey, in particular, advocates this technique but I have never thought it prudent to enquire why he should have available, or indeed need, so much more soap and water than the rest of us.) If you prefer more modern technology, try derris or one of the modern synthetic pyrethroid insecticides such as resmethrin. Similar sprays will work well with many sucking pests although the insecticide pirimicarb is especially valuable as it controls aphids but does not affect other types of insect. Really persistent beasts, such as whiteflies, scale insects and mealy bugs, call for persistent measures. A systemic insecticide (and my choice here lies with dimethoate) may be the best answer for scale insects and mealy bugs, especially on non-edible plants, but a paintbrush dipped in meths will often remove them from house plants. Whiteflies in greenhouses can be controlled with contact insecticides, but the secret lies with regular applications to kill each generation of adults as they hatch out – the immature forms are relatively unaffected.

Fungal diseases on leaves and shoots are many and varied. Those that merely cause isolated spots and blotches can often be combated by picking off the affected leaves. Indeed, in my garden, black spot on roses is the only leaf-spotting problem against which I need to take any regular action and using one of the products that combines both fungicide and insecticide enables me to deal with aphids at the same time. I have old apple trees on which the symptoms of scab appear quite regularly, but the trees are far too large to spray and my regular winter pruning takes out scabby twigs, where much of the disease originates. If I had young apple trees, I would be more assiduous and use the treatment that I apply to an immature crab: a spray with benomyl, thiophanate-methyl or carbendazim every two weeks from the time of bud burst until petal fall. Mildew on apples falls into the same category; my trees are just too large to spray although one of them is 'Stirling Castle', a martyr to mildew if ever there was one. Yet, careful winter pruning goes a long way towards keeping the trees in good condition. None the less, with young trees, I would use the same fortnightly fungicide spray as for scab, but beginning as the buds first turn pink. On other garden plants traditionally affected by mildew, such as lupins or doronicums, the disease is often scarcely apparent until late in the season, when it looks very unsightly but may do little harm. On others, such as Michaelmas daisies, its effects can be avoided by choosing resistant varieties. But if an attack does arise early, as it may do in a hot, dry summer, one of the systemic fungicides mentioned should combat it effectively.

Superficially rather like mildew, potato blight is an infamous disease that every gardener has heard of but one that I have never found it necessary or

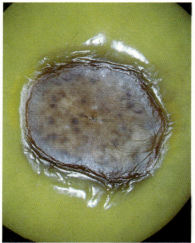

worthwhile to spray against in gardens; at least, in my part of the country. It is a problem of damp summers (admittedly, we see a fair number of these) and more humid areas (Clay tells me that he sees a good deal of it in his subtropical corner of the realm) but very rarely causes significant losses in British gardens.

Rust diseases are characterised by tiny, usually yellow, brown or black powdery pimples on the leaves. Rust occurs quite commonly on some rose varieties, on leeks, mint and on antirrhinums and hollyhocks. On all ornamental plants, the fungicide propiconazole will deal very effectively with rust but there is little that can be done with edible crops. Affected mint beds are best replaced with new plants, some distance away.

And so to the twigs and branches, and to cankers, those disfiguring blisters on old apple and other trees. There is no preventative measure but the disease really can be a killer and the removal of cankered branches is yet one more reason for paying attention to the winter pruning of fruit trees. It is now generally reckoned, even by me, that the painting of pruning cuts probably does little good and may actually be harmful.

I have said nothing about pests and diseases that affect fruit. Partly this is because they are many and varied and generalisations can be misleading. Partly it is because I believe a modest amount of damage is perfectly acceptable and partly because, as with the diseases of large fruit trees, spraying against codling moth, sawfly and similar problems is largely futile. I would, however, propound one notion very strongly; always examine very carefully any vegetables or

top row, left to right,
*Magnesium deficiency – often
causes a leaf marbling.
Magnesian limestone may
correct it.*

*Calcium deficiency – blossom
end rot on tomatoes is best
avoided by not allowing the roots
to dry out*

*Nitrogen deficiency – always
apply nitrogen fertiliser before
planting or sowing, especially to
leafy vegetables*

*Phosphorus deficiency – the
typical leaf bronzing is best
avoided with routine use of
balanced fertilisers*

*Iron deficiency – avoid this leaf
yellowing on chalky soils by
using sequestrene each year*

*Potassium deficiency – use of
balanced fertilisers should avoid
this but liquid tomato feed will
correct a shortage*

Honey fungus (opposite page,
middle), *seen beneath the bark of
an affected tree, onion white rot*
(opposite page bottom) *and
clubroot* (left) *are three garden
diseases of especial importance,
needing specific treatment as
explained in the text*

183

fruit that you intend to store and reject all those with lesions or other signs of damage.

Weeds

A weed, according to the popular definition, is a plant growing in the wrong place. More precisely, it is a native plant growing in a garden intended for the cultivation of largely alien species with which it competes very effectively for light, air, nutrients and water. If you allow weeds to flourish, your garden plants can never give of their best. Weed control is an aspect of gardening very often much easier said than done although direct, physical control of weeds is a much more realistic option than it is with most pests and diseases.

Weeds can be conveniently divided into the annual, such as shepherd's purse, groundsel and chickweed, and the perennial, such as bindweed, stinging nettle and ground elder. With the former, the killing or removal of one individual weed plant may be relatively easy, although if this is delayed until after it has flowered and seeded, its progeny will return in force to plague you in the following year; remember the old adage 'one year's seeding, seven years' weeding'. The perennial weed depends much less on seed production and dispersal for long-term survival as each individual generally possesses a deep or far-reaching root or rhizome system that may fragment easily and be well nigh impossible to dig out. I have yet to encounter a garden weed species that is uncontrollable by either physical or chemical means; my two closest candidates are creeping speedwell in a lawn and horsetail but my present garden is living testimony to man's ability to combat bindweed and ground elder.

First, the physical approach. Actual removal of all annual and some perennial weeds by fork is perfectly possible. Indeed, it is in my fondness for hand-weeding that I come closest to fulfilling my colleagues' image of me as the archetypal mad scientist. For those less inclined to join me in this particular communing with nature, the Dutch hoe, kept sharp, is invaluable; but I stress, kept sharp to ensure that weeds are actually severed, not merely jostled. And do restrict hoeing to warm, dry conditions if your purpose isn't simply weed transplanting. If you can't remove them, smother them, is much of the philosophy behind the weed-suppressing mulch which serves, of course, the additional benefit of aiding moisture retention. Between 5 and 8 cm (about 2 to 3 inches) thickness of mulch will suppress much annual weed growth although the more vigorous weeds will still force their way upwards; and remember that the mulch will need reapplying yearly.

Like insecticides and fungicides, different weedkillers work in different ways and it is essential that you understand their properties before applying them. I now use only a handful of different weedkillers and find they serve my needs admirably. On my list are three total weedkillers: first, the mixture of paraquat and diquat sometimes called the chemical hoe, which is especially valuable early in the season for killing seedling weeds when the ground is too wet to hoe conventionally. Second, one of the blends sold for weed control on paths (although I don't believe claims that only one application is needed each year), and, third, the remarkable weedkiller, glyphosate. This is a systemic weedkiller and has been the means for the clearing of ground elder and bindweed from my garden. The main drawback to glyphosate is the need, lacking in most gardeners, for the virtue of patience, as it takes several weeks after application before you will see any effect. But do remember these are all total weedkillers; they will kill all plants and must be used with care.

To balance the total weedkillers is one selective weedkiller mixture that I use to kill broad-leaved weeds on the lawns and which, together with lawn sand for the moss (and some weeds also), completes the list. I must add a word, however, for one more selective weedkiller that I used when clearing my garden. Alloxydim sodium is a specific killer of couch grass and can be used to eradicate this problem plant when it is growing in and among other vegetation. I am impressed with it, although for optimum effect care is needed to apply the chemical when the couch has reached a certain critical stage of growth.

Nutrient Deficiencies

After all bugs and beasties have been identified and dealt with, there remains a short list of garden problems that have no fungal, bacterial, viral or animal cause. In gardening books, when they are mentioned at all, they are almost invariably grouped with pests and diseases and this book will be no exception. The problems to which I refer are nutrient deficiencies, or, as they are sometimes called, disorders. They can be superficially very similar to the effects of some diseases, especially virus diseases. Nutrient deficiency symptoms are not easily described but the photographs in this chapter show typical effects of the most common deficiencies on the most frequently affected plants, and in the captions I have suggested remedies for these problems.

INDEX

PICTURE CREDITS

Barnaby's Picture Library pages 70 *top*, 80 & 163 *top*; B. & B. Photographs pages 38, 55 *bottom*, 66, 99 *bottom left*, 146 *top right*, 178–9 *all* & 182–3 *all*; Biofotos pages 10 *top* & 11 *top*; Linda Burgess pages 130, 142, 150–1, 167 & 170 *top*; Bruce Coleman pages 51 *top* (Fennell), 51 *bottom* (Burton), 99 *top left*, 135 *top*, 139 *bottom*, 147 *top* & 155 *top* (Freeman); Gardena (UK) Ltd page 22; ICI page 155 *bottom*; John Glover page 47; S. & O. Mathews Photography pages 10 *bottom*, 11 *bottom* & 154; Tania Midgley page 94 *bottom left*; National Fruit Trials/Crown Copyright: Brogdale EHS pages 54, 55 *left* & *top right*, 63 *top* & 67; Photos Horticultural pages 19 *top*, 39, 43 *bottom*, 62 *left*, 63 *bottom*, 72, 73, 74 *top*, 77–9 *all*, 82 *all*, 86–7 *all*, 90–1 *all*, 94 *top* & *bottom right*, 95 *top* & *bottom right*, 98, 99 *both right*, 102 *both*, 105 *left*, 106 *top* & *centre*, 111, 114–5 *all*, 118, 119 *bottom*, 122–3 *all*, 126–7 *all*, 131 *both*, 134, 135 *bottom*, 138 *left*, *centre right* & *bottom right*, 146 *both left*, 147 *bottom right*, 166 *both*, 171 & 174–5 *all*; Smith Collection pages 18 *bottom*, 19 *bottom*, 31 *all*, 34, 42 *bottom*, 43 *top*, 62 *right*, 74 *bottom*, 75 *both*, 81, 95 *bottom left* & *centre*, 103, 105 *right*, 106 *bottom*, 110 *both*, 138 *top right*, 139 *top*, 146 *bottom right*, 147 *bottom left*, 162 & 170 *bottom*; Spectrum Colour Library pages 18 *top*, 30, 70 *bottom*, 71, 119 *top* & 163 *both bottom*; Suttons Seeds Ltd pages 42 *top* & 46.

Line illustrations by Will Giles